"This book adds to our understanding of the role of informal learning as a critical contributor to the future of schooling in a wired global context. The authors show how informal learning deepens and broadens what is learned formally and also contributes to student growth and development while helping solve local and global challenges."

–Karen E. Watkins, Professor and Associate Department Head,
Department of Lifelong Education, Administration, and Policy
(Adult Education, Learning and Organization),
The University of Georgia, USA

Schools and Informal Learning in a Knowledge-Based World

This book has two purposes: To open up the debate on the role of informal education in schooling systems and to suggest the kind of school organizational environment that can best facilitate the recognition of informal learning. Successive chapters explore what is often seen as a duality between informal and formal learning. This duality is particularly so because education systems expend so much time and effort in certifying formal knowledge often expressed in school subjects reflecting academic disciplines. Recognizing the contribution informal learning can make to young people's understanding and development does not negate the importance of valued social knowledge: That complements it. Students come to school with knowledge learnt from their families, peers, the community and both traditional and social media. They should not have to "unlearn" this in order to enter the world of formal learning. Rather, students' different learning "worlds" should be integrated so that each informs the other. In a knowledge-based society, all learning needs to be valued.

Some contributors to this book reflect on how new educational systems could be created in a move away from top-down authoritarian and bureaucratic management. Such open systems are seen to be more welcoming in acknowledging the importance of informal learning. Others provide practical examples of how informal learning is currently recognized. Some attention is also paid to the evaluation of informal learning. A key objective of the work presented here is to stimulate debate about the role of informal learning in knowledge-based societies and to stimulate thinking about the kind of reforms needed to create more open and more democratic school learning environments.

Javier Calvo de Mora is a Professor of School Organisation at the University of Granada, Spain. His main research interest is in policy, institutional collaboration and leadership studies. He is currently coordinator of the European Network on Research on Citizenship Education.

Kerry J. Kennedy is Professor Emeritus, Advisor (Academic Development) and Senior Research Fellow in the Centre for Governance and Citizenship at The Education University of Hong Kong. He is also a Distinguished Visiting Professor at the University of Johannesburg.

Asia-Europe Education Dialogue
Series Editor: Kerry J. Kennedy

This Routledge book series provides a forum for dialogue on key educational issues and challenges faced by Asian and European societies. Its distinctiveness is its broad focus on Education in Asia and Europe. In essence, it will address major issues in education reform, student learning, leadership, curriculum, higher education, multicultural education and other major educational issues affecting Asia and Europe.

Published books:

Class Size
Eastern and Western Perspectives
Edited by Peter Blatchford, Kam Wing Chan, Maurice Galton, Kwok-Chan Lai and John Chi-Kin Lee

Higher Education in the Asian Century
The European Legacy and the Future of Transnational Education in the ASEAN Region
Edited by Christopher Hill and Rozilini M. Fernandez-Chung

Theorizing Teaching and Learning in Asia and Europe
A Conversation between Chinese Curriculum and European Didactics
Edited by John Chi-Kin Lee and Kerry J. Kennedy

Young People and Active Citizenship in Post-Soviet Times
A Challenge for Citizenship Education
Edited by Beata Krzywosz-Rynkiewicz, Anna M. Zalewska and Kerry J. Kennedy

Schools and Informal Learning in a Knowledge-Based World
Edited by Javier Calvo de Mora and Kerry J. Kennedy

URL: https://www.routledge.com/Asia-Europe-Education-Dialogue/book-series/AEED

Schools and Informal Learning in a Knowledge-Based World

Edited by Javier Calvo de Mora
and Kerry J. Kennedy

LONDON AND NEW YORK

First published 2020
by Routledge
2 Park Square, Milton Park, Abingdon, Oxon OX14 4RN

and by Routledge
52 Vanderbilt Avenue, New York, NY 10017

Routledge is an imprint of the Taylor & Francis Group,
an informa business

© 2020 selection and editorial matter, Javier Calvo de Mora and Kerry
J. Kennedy; individual chapters, the contributors

The right of Javier Calvo de Mora and Kerry J. Kennedy to be
identified as the authors of the editorial material, and of the authors
for their individual chapters, has been asserted in accordance with
sections 77 and 78 of the Copyright, Designs and Patents Act 1988.

All rights reserved. No part of this book may be reprinted or
reproduced or utilised in any form or by any electronic, mechanical,
or other means, now known or hereafter invented, including
photocopying and recording, or in any information storage or
retrieval system, without permission in writing from the publishers.

Trademark notice: Product or corporate names may be trademarks
or registered trademarks, and are used only for identification and
explanation without intent to infringe.

British Library Cataloguing in Publication Data
A catalogue record for this book is available from the British Library

Library of Congress Cataloging in Publication Data
A catalog record for this book has been requested

ISBN: 978-0-367-07756-3 (hbk)
ISBN: 978-0-429-02261-6 (ebk)

Typeset in Galliard
by Cenveo® Publisher Services

Javier would like to dedicate this book to his sons, Willian and Eduard, and his grandson, Hiryu; and Kerry would like to dedicate it to his grandchildren, Zoe, Jamie, Oliver, Henry, Annabele, Rose, Fletcher and Sam

Contents

List of figures	xi
List of tables	xii
Series editor's note	xiii
List of contributors	xv

1	**Towards a new educational contract** JAVIER CALVO DE MORA	1

PART I
Schools and informal learning: Shaping the future   13

2	**What we really learn in school?** ROGER C. SCHANK	15
3	**Exploring the foundations of informal learning** JUDITH LLOYD YERO	25
4	**Inventing a public education system for the 21st century** JOHN H. FALK	46
5	**The relationship between formal and informal learning** DANIEL A. TILLMAN, SONG A. AN, AND WILLIAM H. ROBERTSON	62

PART II
Case studies of informal learning's potential   81

6	**Asian students' informal civic learning: Can it enhance civic knowledge and values?** KERRY J. KENNEDY AND XIAOXUE KUANG	83

x *Contents*

7 The Shanghai model for global geography education 99
OSVALDO MUÑIZ SOLARI AND LIANFEI JIANG

8 Academic family and educational *Compadrazgo:*
Implementing cultural values to create educational
relationships for informal learning and persistence for
Latinx undergraduates 119
ALBERTA M. GLORIA, JEANETT CASTELLANOS, MARY DUEÑAS,
AND VERONICA FRANCO

9 Formal–informal, exclusion–inclusion: An empirical
investigation of Swedish music education 136
CECILIA WALLERSTEDT

PART III
Informal learning as lifelong learning and its evaluation 153

10 Governance of informal learning as a pathway for the
development of young adults' agency for sustainability 155
VALĒRIJS MAKEREVIČS AND DZINTRA ILIŚKO

11 Integrating formal and informal learning to develop
self-management skills: Challenges and opportunities for
higher education in the university-to-work transition 168
AMELIA MANUTI

12 Informal learning assessment 179
JAVIER CALVO DE MORA

13 Is an "avant-garde" assessment? The certification of
competencies in the Italian higher education system 189
SERAFINA PASTORE

14 Conclusion: Open schools and shared responsibilities:
Integrating informal and formal learning in
21st-century schools 203
JAVIER CALVO DE MORA AND KERRY J. KENNEDY

Index 216

Figures

1.1	Structure of meaning and pattern of communication.	4
3.1	The jagged profile of one individual.	39
6.1	Proposed model for assessing influences on students' civic knowledge: Demographics, informal learning and social engagement.	89
7.1	Cybernetwork and the expansion of IL.	102
7.2	Reaching global university networking.	104
7.3	Integral geography education with GST in a geo-enabling world.	107
7.4	The Shanghai model for learning and collaboration.	109
7.5	Formal setting towards IL environment.	111
7.6	The Shanghai Model (a two-stage strategy for online IL).	113
10.1	The significance of informal learning.	160
10.2	Rationality and availability of choice for informal education.	161
10.3	Motivation and opportunities for informal learning.	161
10.4	Responses of respondents towards the offered forms of informal learning.	162
10.5	Expectation of participant of informal education.	162
12.1	Organizational culture and assessment tools.	185
12.2	Pyramid of school levels of knowledge.	187

Tables

6.1	Reliability coefficients and CFA fit indices for each scale	90
6.2	Results of structural equation model (SEM) for measurement model shown in Figure 6.1	91
6.3	Mediation effects in the measurement model shown in Figure 6.1	93
7.1	Structure of formal setting (a 3-day workshop)	110
8.1	How academic family promotes informal learning for Latinx students	128
13.1	Validity aspects	195
13.2	Practices of validation and certification of competencies in Italy	197

Series editor's note

Asia and Europe together represent the largest landmass, the largest population and the largest concentration of economic resources as well as a diversity of cultural traditions. The 21st century is characterized as "the Asian century" and therefore its interactions with Europe are fundamental. In this new century, the Asia-Europe connection is of utmost importance. This is indicated by the existence of the Asia-Europe Foundation (supported by the European Union (EU) and housed in Singapore), the Asia Europe Meeting (ASEM), that is the regular platform for dialogue between EU member states and the Association for Southeast Asian Nations (ASEAN) plus other Asian societies, by the flow of students from Asia to Europe and vice versa, and by the growing academic literature that highlights the benefits of two way cross cultural communication. Education is a fundamental policy tool in both regions as each seeks to move to take advantage of the knowledge economy. The EU has recognized this with its policies in support of Asia-Europe mobility programmes and different countries in Asia constantly look to Europe not so much for support, as in the past, but as a source of investment. The success of Asian students in international large scale assessments is a constant reminder to European countries that there is much to learn from Asia.

This Series provides a forum for dialogue on key educational issues and challenges faced by Asian and European societies. Education is a key social practice on both continents and the means by which innovation, creativity and critical thinking can be encouraged and developed. Major issues such school education reform, student learning, leadership, curriculum, higher education, multicultural and intercultural education and other major educational issues are addressed. Most often a comparative perspective is provided to provide insights into these issues but there are also opportunities for focusing on distinctive issues in one or other of the regions.

In the current volume, the focus is on informal learning and its role in an increasingly globalized world where learning holds the key to success both for nations as well as individuals. The argument throughout is that informal xiv *Series editor's note*

learning can no longer be disregarded. It must be recognized along with formal learning and non-formal learning as a source of knowledge production that can assist in understanding and influencing an increasingly complex and unpredictable world.

Kerry J. Kennedy
Series Editor
Asia Europe Education Dialogue Series

Contributors

Dr. Song A. An is an Associate Professor in Mathematics Education for the Teacher Education Department of The University of Texas at El Paso. Dr. An received his doctoral degree in Mathematics Education at the Texas A&M University in 2012. Before his doctoral study, Dr. An received a bachelor's degree in musicology from Nanjing Arts Institution, China, with a specialization in instrument design technologies and acoustical engineering. Dr. Song An's distinctive academic background has led him to develop a unique research focus, which focuses on the study of music-themed mathematics curriculum and mathematics centred interdisciplinary instruction. Dr. An is one of the first educational researchers nationwide to study systematically and empirically the impact of mathematics education that focuses on project-based activities involving music composition and choreography-themed learning for K-12 education and teacher preparation.

Jeanett Castellanos, PhD, is an Associate Dean of Undergraduate Studies and Professor of Teaching at the University of California, Irvine, in the School of Social Sciences. Dr. Castellanos has published in numerous national journals including the *Journal of College Counseling, Journal of Counseling and Development, Journal of Hispanic Higher Education, and Cultural Diversity and Ethnic Minority Psychology.* She also has two edited volumes addressing Latina/o student experiences in higher education. Nationally, Dr. Castellanos is the recipient of the APA Division 12 (Clinical Psychology) Samuel M. Turner Mentorship Award, the 2012 NLPA Star Vega Community Service Award and 2012 AAHEE Outstanding Support of Hispanics in Higher Education. At University of California, Irvine, she has also been recognized with the Chancellor's Research Excellence Award, Lecturer of the Year Award, the Distinguished Faculty Award for Mentorship, and the Chancellor's Living Our Values Award. Castellanos received her Master's in Counseling and PhD in Higher Education from Washington State University.

Javier Calvo de Mora is a Professor of School Organisation at the University of Granada, Spain. His main research interest is in policy, institutional collaboration and leadership studies. He is currently coordinator of the European Network on Research on Citizenship Education. He is author of a number of books and papers which explore how to create a seamless learning process between xvi *Contributors*

schools and their contexts. He has edited books about citizenship culture applied to social relations through school structure.

Mary Dueñas is a doctoral student in the Department of Educational Leadership and Policy Analysis at the University of Wisconsin-Madison. Mary's research explores the educational, cultural and personal experiences of Latinx college students at 4-year institutions. She has published in the *Journal of College Student Development* and is currently the co-director for an educational research programme. She has also worked in multiple student development capacities as a student liaison, student ambassador, teacher and academic coach. Mary has presented her research at multiple national conferences and a member of the National Latin@ Psychological Association, American Association of Hispanics in Higher Education and Association for the Study of Higher Education.

Dr. John H. Falk is the Executive Director, Institute for Learning Innovation and Sea Grant Professor Emeritus of Free-Choice Learning at Oregon State University. He is a leading expert on free-choice learning; the learning that occurs when people have choice and control over when, where and why they learn. Falk has authored over 200 articles and two-dozen books; his most recent book is *Born to Choose: Evolution, Self & Well-Being* (2017, Routledge). His awards include the NARST Distinguished Career Award (2016); Oregon State University, Excellence, Innovation-Partnerships Award (2016); Council of Scientific Society Presidents Award for Educational Research (2013) and American Alliance of Museums John Cotton Dana Award for Leadership (2010). In 2006, the American Association of Museums included Falk in their list of the 100 most influential museum professionals of the past 100 years. Falk earned a joint doctorate in Ecology and Science Education from the University of California, Berkeley.

Veronica Franco, MS, is a doctoral student in the Department of Counseling, Clinical, and School Psychology at the University of California, Santa Barbara. Her research interest focuses on students of colour persistence and resilience patterns specifically, examining Latinx resilience in how they persevere through personal and institutional barriers. Veronica is a graduate student affiliate of the American Psychological Association and the National Latina/o Psychological Association.

Alberta M. Gloria is a Professor in the Department of Counseling Psychology at the University of Wisconsin-Madison. She is an affiliate faculty member with both the Chican@ Latin@ Studies Program and the Asian American Studies Program at University of Wisconsin-Madison. Her research focuses on the educational processes and influencing factors of academic adjustment, wellness and persistence for historically underrepresented and underserved students in higher education. She has held executive boards positions in Divisions 17 (Society for Counseling Psychology), 35 (Psychology of Women) and 45 (Society for the Psychological Study of Racial and Ethnic Issues) of the American Psychological Association. She is a Fellow of Divisions 17 and 45. She has also been recognized with national and university-based mentoring awards.

Dzintra Iliško is a Professor at Institute of Humanities and Societal Sciences, Center of Sustainable Education, Latvia. She is the author of more than forty publications. Her field of interest is gender studies, sustainable education. She is a member of international networks such as BBCC (Baltic and Black Sea Consortium in Educational Research) and ISREV (International Seminar of Religious Education and values). She is a chief editor of the *Journal of Teacher Education for Sustainability* and *Discourse and Communication for Sustainable Development*. She is a national coordinator of NORDPLUS programme "Innovative and Sustainable Aesthetic Methods for Citizenship Education: Nordic and Baltic perspectives" (ISAMCE).

Dr. Lianfei Jiang is a young geography educator. He obtained his doctoral degree from East China Normal University (ECNU), Shanghai, in 2018, and a M.S. from Zhejiang Normal University in 2013. He is a post-doctoral researcher in geography education in the School of Geographic Science at ECNU, besides being a research fellow of Shanghai Geography Education and Teaching Research Base. His experiences overseas as volunteer, conference participant, or research visitor have been in Cameroon, Republic of Korea, Switzerland, England, and the United States of America. The latter in the form of an official visit to the National Center for Research in Geography Education at Texas State University for one year, which helped to connect geography education between China and the United States. He received the Excellent Paper Award in the 9th Korea-China-Japan Joint Conference on Geography.

Professor Kerry J. Kennedy is Professor Emeritus, Advisor (Academic Development) and Senior Research Fellow in the Centre for Governance and Citizenship at The Education University of Hong Kong. He is also a Distinguished Visiting Professor at the University of Johannesburg. He is the Editor of *Routledge's Schools and Schooling in Asia Series*, the *Asia Europe Education Dialogue Series*, the *Perspectives on Education in Africa Series* and Springer's *Civic and Citizenship Education in the 21st Century Series*. His work was internationally recognized in 2012 when he was a co-winner of the Richard Wolf Memorial Award for Educational Research awarded by the International Association for the Evaluation of Educational Achievement (IEA).

Xiaoxue Kuang is a lecturer in Dongguan University of Technology in the People's Republic of China and was a Post-doctoral Fellow at The Education University of Hong Kong. She holds a PhD in Education from The Education University of Hong Kong, and an MEd with emphasis on Applied Psychology, and a BEd in Education both from Shenzhen University, China. She has published internationally refereed journal articles and her major areas of research interest are civic education, international large-scale assessments (such as PISA, TIMSS, ICCS etc.), research methods (such as structural equation modelling, item response theory, multilevel modelling etc.) and educational and psychological measurement.

xviii *Contributors*

Valērijs Makerevičs is a docent at the Faculty of Education and Management, Daugavpils University, Latvia. He is the author of many international publications. His fields of interest are educational psychology, tolerance and ethical identity. He is the author of educational books in psychology and developmental psychology. He was a guest lecturer in the Czech Republic, Lithuania and Bulgaria and other European Congresses in Oslo in 2009 and Istanbul in 2011, international congress in Belgrade and Serbia in 2016. He is the Doctor of Psychological Sciences in developmental and pedagogical psychology. He is a member of the Municipality's commission in licensing of the educational programs for children, youth and adults of Daugavpils, a city in the Eastern part of Latvia.

Amelia Manuti is an Assistant Professor in Work and Organizational Psychology. She teaches training and organizational development and Organizational Psychology. Her main research interests refer to the meaning of working in school-to-university and university-to-work transitions, vocational guidance, career development, formal and informal learning, organizational identification, work values and organizational communication. She has taken part in many national and international research projects in the field of work and organizational psychology and published several research articles on different topics in the field. One of her most recent works are the volumes *Why human capital is important for organizations, The Social Organization and Digital HR* co-edited with Davide de Palma (2014, 2016; 2017 Palgrave Mac Millan). She is Delegate for the Rector of the University of Bari, Italy, for Job Placement and scientific member of the Board of the Center for Long Life Learning at the University of Bari, Italy, where she coordinates the validation, accreditation and certification of prior informally acquired learning of adults.

Serafina Pastore, PhD, is an Instructional Design and Educational Assessment and Fulbright Research Fellow and works as a researcher at the University of Bari, Italy, where she also teaches in PGCE courses. She was nominated in 2018 as an AERA Emerging Scholar in Measurement and Assessment in Higher Education (SIG 64). Her research interests include the study of assessment in higher education, formative assessment and feedback, teacher assessment literacy and assessment of student competencies. With considerable expertise in the educational evaluation field she is member of the quality assurance board of the University of Bari, Italy, and serves as the coordinator of Special Interest Group on Educational Assessment with the Italian Evaluation Association.

Dr. William H. Robertson is a Professor in the Teacher Education Department in the College of Education at the University of Texas at El Paso. His academic areas of expertise are in science education, curriculum development and technology integration across K-12. Additionally, he develops, research and teaching materials related to inquiry-based STEM Education, project-based learning, problem-based learning and action science. Dr. Robertson has received a number of prestigious awards including the UT Regent's Outstanding Teaching Award, as a Fulbright Scholar in Santiago, Chile, and the 2016 President's Meritorious Service Award. A long-time participant and performer in skateboarding with over 40 years in the sport, Dr. Robertson has developed Dr. Skateboard's Action Science (http://www.drskateboard.com), which addresses physical science concepts for middle school students utilizing skateboarding and bicycle motocross (BMX).

Roger C. Schank is the Chairman and CEO of Socratic Arts, a company that delivers Story-Centred Curricula to businesses and schools. He is also the Executive Director and founder of Engines for Education. He was the founder of the Institute for the Learning Sciences at Northwestern University where he was John Evans Professor of Computer Science, Education and Psychology (now Professor Emeritus). Dr. Schank is a fellow of the Association for the Advancement of Artificial Intelligence (AAAI), the founder of the Cognitive Science Society, and co-founder of the *Journal of Cognitive Science.*

Dr. Osvaldo Muñiz Solari is a Professor and Associate Director of the Grosvenor Center for Geographic Education in the Department of Geography at Texas State University. He holds a Ph.D. in Geography from The University of Tennessee and a M.A. degree in the same field from Michigan State University. He is an Honorary Professor of International Studies at Texas State and advisory member of the Commission on Geographical Education (CGE) of the International Geographical Union (IGU). His research interests in geography education are online education, geospatial technologies applied to geography education, and learning progression. He has been editor of two important books for international knowledge in geography education of the CGE-IGU Series: *Geospatial Technologies and Geography Education in a Changing World* and *Learning Progressions*, published by Springer. He has been engaged in geography education research projects to develop international collaboration in Asia and Latin America.

Dr. Daniel A. Tillman is an Associate Professor in Educational Technology at The University of Texas at El Paso (UTEP) and a Co-Director of the UTEP College of Education Makerspace. His research focuses on the diffusion of technology innovations into K-12 education, use of physical and digital multimedia within STEM (science, technology, engineering and mathematics) education, and the STEM career pipeline. He received his PhD in Instructional Technology from The University of Virginia (UVA), which is where he met his future wife, the amazing Dr. Rachel Boren. While at UVA, he served as a Graduate Fellow in the Center for Technology & Teacher Education and as the office manager for the Dynamic Media Research Laboratory. Prior to entering the PhD programme at The University of Virginia, he directed and edited documentary films for 8 years.

Cecilia Wallerstedt has a background as a teacher in music and mathematics in upper-secondary school. She has a PhD in Arts Education from the Academy of Music and Drama, University of Gothenburg, Sweden. In parallel to her PhD education she worked in a cross-faculty (Humanities, Arts and Education) xx *Contributors*

research project on young children's learning in the arts in pre- and primary school. During the last years, she has worked in a project funded by the EU (Framework 7) on technology-transformed musical improvisation and composition with young children and in a postdoc project on how young people learn to play songs in the new media ecology, particularly addressing the nature and functions of new notational systems shared among learners over the Internet. Her current position is as Head of Department at The Department of Education, Communication and Learning, University of Gothenburg, Sweden.

Judith Lloyd Yero holds a Master's degree in Curriculum Development from DePaul University, and completed doctoral coursework in a combination of Biopsychology and Education at the University of Illinois (Champaign-Urbana). She is the author of *Teaching in Mind: How Teacher Thinking Shapes Education* (2nd edition 2010), and is presently Director of MindFlight Education Resources. After 20+ years as a secondary school teacher and administrator, Yero presents teacher workshops on The Implications of Brain Research for Education. In recent years, she has travelled around the United States visiting learner-centred schools, and has served as a consultant on learner-centred education.

1 Towards a new educational contract

Javier Calvo de Mora

This book discusses the case for integrating informal learning in the daily life and work of schools. The recognition of informal learning is a step towards understanding that learning takes place in multiple ways, even before birth and throughout the life cycle. It can take place anywhere, anytime and anyhow. It is an essential feature of the human fabric. This creates a new educational challenge: Integrating formal and informal learning in schools in order to build social relationships and knowledge platforms that can meet the challenges of the 21st century.

The aim of this introductory chapter is to offer conceptual tools that help to define informal learning from different perspectives. The purpose is to enhance the school as a social institution that recognizes multiple sources of learning in the creation of knowledge. The following spaces of reflection will be discussed:

- The nature of informal learning.
- Features contributing to the development of informal learning in schools.
- Impediments and limitations of informal learning.
- Benefits of informal learning.
- Institutional challenges.
- Contents of the book.

The nature of informal learning

Learning is best seen as a natural human ability. The formation of society and the building of human capacity have been possible due to the continuous acquisition of knowledge. Yet knowledge in official school curricula focuses not on this natural learning process but on specified subjects and disciplines that are sanctioned by authorities. Natural learning, or everyday learning, that is not part of "official learning" tends to be seen as "informal": Creativity, entrepreneurship, problem solving and empathy, among other metacognitive abilities, have until recently not been recognized by the school system.

The precise specification of informal learning is difficult because it is embedded in daily social processes such as belonging to a community, social movements, gender identification, families, community regeneration, justice, health,

2 *Javier Calvo de Mora*

leisure, etc. The ethical qualities of this kind of informal learning are clear and are part of the intellectual profile of each human being and their lived experiences. At the same time, antisocial, xenophobic and violent behaviours are also often acquired informally and the elimination of such learning is an important role for schools.

The processes of acquiring informal learning involve basically personal experience and social influence: Observations focused on self-interest, reflections on misconceptions and successes, imitation and adaptation into a diversity of social groups, dialogue and languages between adults and children, social speech such as aesthetics or fashion, social networks, peer communication, collaboration between peer groups, etc. These processes of "natural learning" are often conceptualized in school contexts as *active learning methods*, and this concept starts to recognize the importance of informal learning.

The conceptual foundation of active learning methods is simple: Neither students nor teachers are symbolic institutions seeking rewards based on hierarchical position or institutional prestige (Weber, 1905). Rather, the basic assumption of this book is that both students and teachers are considered actors ("understood as human beings with their beliefs, feelings and emotions in their rationality") (Alpuche de la Cruz, 2015) capable of autonomous individual action. The justification of this basic assumption, focused on the freedom of individuals, represents a critique of social determinism favoured by functionalist approaches, where the origin and social context of each individual determines the itineraries and school destinations of students.

The concept of social relationship is implicit in informal learning. That is, learning (both formal and informal) is acquired through social relationships in which different human beings exchange meanings, complement knowledge, create new categories of or build necessary symbols to undertake communication processes. They may also engage in other actions which provide opportunities for mutual influence among different organizational actors in an institutional framework, such as schools.

The effects of autonomy of thought and social relationships among organizational actors are consistent with the idea of pragmatic complexity in schools (Ansell & Geyer, 2016; Cilliers & Greyvenstein, 2012). The central idea is that the interactions of organizations (and their members) with different local and global environments constitute self-organized learning spaces that consist of unique practical spaces of information as well as knowledge. Such spaces have their own "boundaries" that define the scope where each subject acquires his or her formal and informal learning. The organizational complexity lies in the fact that as far as schools are concerned, formal school subjects or specific groups of subjects have their own learning spaces compatible with the common space of the school as an institution. Such norms and rules characterize schools and will govern exchanges between formal and informal learning to reflect a particular organizational culture.

An organizational culture that encourages informal learning values the autonomy of different school actors who can express the diversity of their experiences learned, inside and outside the school space. All forms of knowledge should be the object of merit and appreciation within the social and cultural framework of each school space. This includes the formal curricula and the informal learning acquired by each student, with both being assessed. This double reality of value and merit constitutes the basis of social justice in the processes of schooling. This requires a balance between recognizing the objective value of acquiring available knowledge for each subject as well as giving credit for the acquisition of informal learning that takes place in the particular social and cultural contexts of the school and its community (Guba & Lincoln, 1994).

Schools as cultural organizations are characterized by the complexity of social relationships among their members, always subject to an exchange of meanings via the basic technology of institutional functioning: Teaching and learning. Additionally, reflective actions taken by the users themselves will always add value to formal learning (Adams & Gupta, 2017; Scheerens, 2011). Schooling is not a one-way process. Both students and teachers will reflect on the purposes of the organizations of which they are a part and the goals the organization has for them, and they may (or may not) modify them in terms of their individual objectives and purposes (Blaschke & Stewart, 2016).

What is informal learning?

The most common definition has been proposed by Livingstone (1999):

> any activity involving the pursuit of understanding, knowledge or skill which occurs outside the curricula of educational institutions, or the courses or workshops offered by educational or social agencies. (p. 51)

This definition has some shortcomings: It defines informal learning outside the institutional context, and it excludes the exchange between formal and informal learning. Other approaches locate the definitions of informal learning in more qualitative terms. For example, Michael Eraut (2004) proposed several definitions of informal learning. He focused on the education of adults, his *raison d'être* being that different cognitive actions shape the awareness of different organizational actors in different social environments: Memory of events, selection of information, building of expectations, reflection, focus of interest, recognition of important events, discussion, personal involvement in actions and strategic planning of actions. In this conceptual framework, informal learning includes the experiences that are acquired and learnt by subjects throughout the development of their own lives. This appeal to individual freedom is key in order to define informal learning: It is the unique and personal learning which is acquired by adults. Other approaches classify informal learning from the focus of the subjectivity of each organizational actor based on two variables: Intentionality and consciousness (Van Noy, Jacobs, Korey, Bailey, & Hughes, 2008; Van Noy, James, & Bedley, 2016). In other words, it is the learning of and from life that is distributed in the different actions undertaken by individuals in the social and cultural contexts in which they live (Foley, 1999).

Factors contributing to the development of informal learning in schools

According to neo-institutional theories, meaning structures and communication patterns are the framework for basic analyses of organizations. The structures of meaning (norms and rules) refer to the grammar or organizational language that prevails in each school. These involve the universe of concepts used by school members, the symbols used to establish feelings of belonging to a common reality, the rituals used to control organizational habits and the beliefs established to regulate the social order that allows the continuity of the school year with its regulatory characteristics. Communication patterns refer to the social climate that allows or prevents social relationships in schools; for instance, mutual trust, citizenship rights in schools, feeling of responsibility and belonging.

A neo-institutional organizational perspective

From a neo-institutional perspective, "structure of meaning" and "pattern of communication" provide the basic framework for explaining the organization of schooling. This framework regulates the organizational grammar of schooling. "Structure of meaning" refers to the interpretive processes of teachers and students in all aspects of school education. "Pattern of communication" refers to the social relations in which different school actors exchange knowledge and information related to formal and informal curriculum. A "direct pattern of communication" is characterized by the recognition of some level of hierarchy between information senders (usually teachers) and beneficiaries (usually students). This is how much traditional teaching and learning takes place. An "autonomous pattern of communication" acknowledges that from time to time actors in the education process will switch their roles from information senders to beneficiaries, regardless of their identity as a teacher or a student (Figure 1.1).

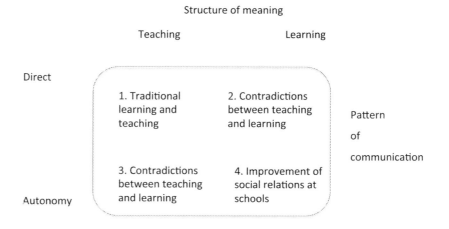

Figure 1.1 Structure of meaning and pattern of communication.

Traditionally, synchronizing the patterns of communication between different education actors has been regarded as a matter of efficiency. The maintenance of hierarchy in education relationships has also been regarded as a disciplining technique that creates a social distance between teachers and students. A contrary education organizational concept is being highlighted in this chapter. It is based on an education environment where all actors adopt autonomous patterns of communication. Transactions and responsibilities are assumed by all school actors, who consequently acquire cultural agency in schools. This concept will improve social relations among all actors who constitute a school. All members have the ability to create knowledge and produce content that is important for themselves as well as for other individuals or social groups.

The key for effectively developing this model is the creation of a "learning framework." This is an institutional process by which norms and rules of learning are fixed in each school site. It identifies the cognitive processes that are going to be recognized, validated and certified by a school community. Schools that are focused on their own "learning framework" develop a sense of ownership over it and value communication patterns based on dialogue and cooperation. Such schools are characterized by the creation of social capital creating stable learning environments characterized by educational qualities that are focused on reflective action, trust, social solidarity, feeling of belonging or collective action. This learning environment symbolizes the school reality where students and teachers together develop their learning activities. Beyond the physical space of each school there are new school "boundaries" that include informal learning as an important reality of schooling in this new educational system.

Impediments and limitation of informal learning

The consideration of students as having organizational agency is an *ideal model* that creates new social relationships needed to produce new knowledge which is broader than the academic knowledge prescribed in mainstream educational systems (Jeffs & Smith, 1990). One step forward for this institutionalized curriculum is the diversification of learning sources and the legitimation of learning acquired in the classroom and extracurricular activities. Yet this still maintains student dependency with regard to curricular prescriptions of the educational system. This raises the issues of what can be regarded as "authentic learning."

There are different views. Two conceptual tendencies can be identified in authentic learning. One is pragmatic (transfer of knowledge) and the other is practical (participation of students and teachers in real-life issues, as referents of knowledge). From the point of view of the transfer of learning to other different situations based on classroom experiences, school systems are currently in charge of this transfer task. On the other hand, there are those who defend the symbolism of real-life experience as the main source of learning, the result of daily practice, symbolized in the liberal myth of *the self-made person* (Renner, Prilla, Ulrike, & Joachim, 2016). In other words, authentic learning from this perspective is based on a need to learn something to cover a personal or collective

6 Javier Calvo de Mora

demand. This is the case of the self-employed worker who learns languages in his adult age to serve clients who demand his/her services, or the student who learns a sport in order to be part of a group and feel like a member of such group.

In fact, these two approaches of authentic learning are complementary. The reason behind such complementarity is the following. On the one hand, teachers learn their profession through real life, that is, in the process of their daily work. On the other hand, students learn through simulation, that is, through problem solving and practical examples that could be applied to their professional futures. "Authentic learning," in this view, is reflected in the complementarities between formal and informal learning (Annen, 2013) whose boundaries can be regarded as liquid. That is, the different learning processes are interchangeable as part of active learning and critical thinking (Karr, 2009; Natale & Ricci, 2006). Formal and extracurricular school knowledge can work together to build understanding of any effective action and reasoning that might be needed. For instance, individual ideas and thoughts designed to question reality can help to understand reality and the actions required to improve it (Zimmerman & McClain, 2016).

Teacher dependence on external constraints, such as educational policy and curricular prescriptions, is another important barrier and limitation when considering informal learning in schools. This area of dependence and external control of school learning represents a closed approach to schools and the processes of schooling, which involve considering teachers as technicians applying prescribed knowledge. On the contrary, if we consider school as a knowledge laboratory, a variety of information is available susceptible to collective learning, involving the spatial and temporal expansion of schools to the life of each student and teacher. Practical experiences can be transformed into knowledge through cognitive processes. This is a process of critical thinking that can be acquired and learned in the daily practice of school actors.

The most important focus of attention (from both practical and pragmatic points of view) is the lifeworld of each school actor. This concept, which stems from the sociology of knowledge, constitutes the cultural background of each individual reflected in his/her beliefs, behaviours, languages and practices of communication. This creates an important equality principle among different student populations (Bevan et al., 2010) when considering that each school subject is considered as an educational agent: A subject who has the ability to be a source of knowledge and learns from other subjects who are part of their educational space.

To conclude this section, informal learning depends on the social and cultural capital of individual lives (Cole & Vanderplank, 2016; Rehm & Notten, 2016). The former is located in the social, familiar, educational and economical networking of each individual's lifeworld. The latter refers to the communicative and discursive abilities of individuals which enable them to understand the intentions and messages of other individuals, as well as the capacity to express their ideas, intuitions, experiences or any other type of cognitive construction that must be transmitted to other individuals. This highlights the importance of formal and informal learning in the processes of individuals' social mobility, personal emancipation, exploration of new goals and life strategies. The accumulative learning acquired (intangible capital) builds the social culture of each individual and, obviously, of the communities of which they are a part. In other words, the commitment of schools can be to create learning environments (social cultures) (Sanders, 2007), that is, the cognitive, social and emotional space where students and teachers learn together.

Benefits of informal learning

School management is a key issue in understanding the benefits of recognizing informal learning at schools. Management action based on personal reflection and critical thinking is needed to support school improvement and build learning climates or environments characterized by five areas (Grosemans, Boon, Verclairen, Dochy, & Kyndt, 2015; Harrop & Turpin, 2013).

First, it needs to be recognized that students and teachers have their own educational beliefs and values. These are related to areas such as school learning, teaching, leadership, social relationships and the evaluation and classification of students.

Second, the interdependence between informal and formal learning contributes to the training of students and teachers. This collaboration can be understood from two different perspectives. First, there is the institutional collaboration between schools and cultural organizations—schools are not isolated from the societies in which they are embedded. Second, teachers and students will have different interpretations regarding the standardized teaching and learning patterns that are part of each system. Too much reliance on standardized testing can create less positive attitudes towards informal learning.

Third, school actors experience a diversity of social relationships with their closest reference groups (families, professional communities, teacher unions, social networks, etc.). These relationships contribute to the construction of individual and collective beliefs regarding the basic technology of school work: Teaching practices and evaluation of required knowledge by each student.

Four, innovative learning methods such as action research, problem solving, written productions or construction and design of learning provide different information sources from those of official school curricula. Additionally, such methodologies mean explicitly developing each school participant's capacity for expression. The tacit and unintentional learning implied in these types of learning helps to build knowledge profiles for each student as well as their teachers.

Finally, improving organizational contexts means expanding communication patterns between formal and informal educational agents and actors. In this context, the social and cultural collective of each school can contribute to the construction of knowledge. Strengthening the processes of self-organization and the design of new organizational structures can create new social relationships. This can facilitate the sharing of information and significant or relevant knowledge to strengthen the sense of belonging to the school.

8 *Javier Calvo de Mora*

Institutional challenges for informal learning

The methodologies of school work are the structural foundations for the permanent relationships between formal and informal learning. These permanent relationships contribute to the creation of a new institution for the schooling system, new working habits, learning environments and interactions among the different members of a school, and other learning technologies that are established for a better understanding of curriculum content. All in all, these relationships contribute to a new view of the organizational actor who is less institutionalized and more focused on the continuous improvement of the behaviour norms and rules of each school organization.

From a more practical point of view, the main institutional challenge for informal learning is its recognition. Such recognition of the value and merit of informal learning means adopting a flexible view of knowledge and getting close to an approach that is focused on the autonomous learning of each student oriented, guided and monitored by each teacher. As students learn in this way, they come to understand different epistemologies and they engage in deep learning (Singh, 2015, p. 4). Additionally, as students acquire new skills such as global education competencies (Ley et al., 2014), develop initiative for performing tasks, develop creativity for reflective actions, etc., these can also contribute to informal education. Such skills indicate the interaction that can take place between formal and informal learning.

Conclusion

The main effect of the institutional recognition of informal learning is an acceptance of the importance of school content that is informally generated by students and teachers. This can result in a greater sense of belonging to the organization on account of its recognition of each organizational actor's content and knowledge. This focus on individual contributions means that schools cease to be islands and the educational system ceases to be an archipelago. That is, there is horizontal continuity among different types of knowledge acquired by students and vertical continuity among different layers and levels of the educational system. These continuities can counter social exclusion on account of socioeconomic factors in different communities (Ramani & Siegler, 2015; Ramani, Rowe, Eason, & Leech, 2015), including migrant populations (Alenius, 2016) and at-risk adolescents (Keating & Janmaat, 2015).

Schools, perhaps implicitly, take decisions with regards to their learning priorities. In this framework of priorities, there are two sides. One visible side is the value given to learning as expressed in report cards. A less visible and more informal side is related to the subjective conditions in which students learn. The informal side can influence the decisions related to the reports given to a particular school population. This suggests a relationship between the formal and the informal and a recognition of the importance of informal learning in schools.

Finally, the stability of the interactions between different types of learning in schools is subject to the administration of each school. Political action changes in schools when the informal learning of their constituents is considered. School policy is typically understood as the power of taking decisions to improve both learning and education in the school population, and this is often about correction. Yet when political structures change to be more inclusive, the management and policy focus is on a community of professional learners and their multiple modes of learning and ways to enhance this learning, whether it is formal or informal. This change to school governance and management highlights the role of the school as an institution and the political decisions that need to be made to ensure that informal learning is recognized as an important part of the curriculum experiences of all students and teachers.

School governance focused on shared responsibility is a feature of schooling recognized by the European Union (Rogers, 2014). It not only assists in the recognition of informal learning but can also help to meet a broader agenda that could result in the design of a certification system that acknowledges the full range of learning in schools and systems. This would be both a practical and pragmatic outcome as mentioned earlier in this chapter and an important way to embed informal learning in recognized structures. The rationale for doing so has been given throughout this chapter, and it remains an important goal to which the remainder of this book will hopefully contribute.

References

Adams, J. D., & Gupta, P. (2017). Informal science institutions and learning to teach: An examination of identity, agency, and affordances. *Journal of Research in Science Teaching*, *54*(1), 121–138.

Alenius, P. (2016). Informal learning processes of migrants in the civil society: A transnational perspective. *European Journal for Research on the Education and Learning of Adults*, *7*(1), 44–55.

Alpuche de la Cruz, E. (2015). El actor, la organización y las instituciones: Un enfoque alternativo, en Pino Hidalgo, Enrique y Toledo Patiño, Alejandro (Eds.), Institucionalismo y Gobernanza, Biblioote Nueva, Universidad Autónoma Metropolitana, México, p. 47.

Annen, S. (2013). Recognising non formal and informal learning: Typology and comparison of selected European approaches. *Literacy Information and Computer Education*, *4*(1), 927–937.

Ansell, C., & Geyer, R. (2016). Pragmatic complexity a new foundation for moving beyond evidence-based policy making? *Policy Studies*, *38*(29).

Bevan, B., Dillon, J., Hein, G. E., Macdonald, M., Michalchik, V., Miller, D., … Yoon, S. (2010). *Making science matter: Collaborations between informal science education organizations and schools*. Washington, DC: Center for Advancement of Informal Science Education.

Blaschke, L. M., & Stewart, H. (2016). Heutogogy: A holistic framework for creating twenty-first century self-determined learners. In B. Gross (Ed.), *The future of a ubiquitous learning* (pp. 25–40). Berlin: Springer-Verlag.

Cilliers, F., & Greyvenstein, H. (2012). The impact of silo mentality on team identity: An organisational case study. *Journal of Industrial Psychology*, *35*, 1–10.

10   *Javier Calvo de Mora*

Cole, J., & Vanderplank, R. (2016). Comparing autonomous and class-based learners in Brazil: Evidence for the present-day advantages of informal, out-of-class learning. *System, 61*, 31–42.

Emirbayer, M., & Johnson, V. (2008). Bourdieu and organizational analysis. *Theory and Society, 37*(1), 1–44.

Eraut, M. (2004). Informal learning in the workplace. *Studies in Continuing Education, 26*(2), 247–273.

Foley, G. (1999). *Learning in social action: A contribution to understanding informal education.* Leicester: NIACE.

Grosemans, I., Boon, A., Verclairen, C., Dochy, F., & Kyndt, E. (2015). Informal learning of primary school teachers: Considering the role of teaching experience and school culture. *Teaching and Teacher Education, 47*, 151–161.

Guba, E. G., & Lincoln, Y. S. (1994). Competing paradigms in qualitative research. In N. K. Denzin, & Y. S. Lincolns (Eds.), *Handbook of qualitative research* (pp. 105–117). Thousand Oaks, CA: Sage.

Harrop, D., & Turpin, B. (2013). A study exploring learners' informal learning space behaviors. Attitudes, and preferences. *New Review of Academic Librarianship, 19*(1), 58–77.

Jeffs. T., & Smith, M. (Eds.). (1990). *Using informal education.* Buckingham, UK: Open University Press.

Karr, S. (2009). Critical thinking: A critical strategy for financial executives. *Financial Executive, Academic OneFile.* Retrieved April 4, 2019, from http://go.galegroup.com/ps/anonymous?id=GALE%7CA215465249&sid=googleScholar&v=2.1&it=r&linkaccess=abs&issn=08954186&p=AONE&sw=w

Keating, A., & Janmaat, J. (2015). Education through citizenship at school: Do school activities have a lasting impact on youth engagement? *Parliamentary Affairs, 69*(2), 409–429.

Ley, T., Cook, J., Dennerlein, S., Kravcik, M., Kunzmann, C., Pata, K., Purma, J., Sanders, J., Santos, P., Schmidt, A., Samdi, M., & Trattner, C. (2014). Scaling informal learning at the workplace: A model and four designs from a large-scale design based research effort. *British Journal of Educational Technology, 45*(6), 1036–1048.

Livingstone, D. W. (1999). *The education-jobs gap: Underemployment or economic democracy.* Boulder, CO: Westview Press; Toronto: Garamond Press.

Natale, S., & Ricci, F. (2006). Critical thinking in organizations. *Team Performance Management, 12*(7), 272–278.

Ramani, G., & Siegler, R. (2015). How informal learning activities can promote children's numerical knowledge. In R. Kadosh, & A. Dowke (Eds.), *Oxford handbook for numerical cognition* (pp. 1135–1154). Oxford, UK: Oxford University Press.

Ramani, G. B., Rowe, M. L., Eason, S. H., & Leech, K. A. (2015). Math talk during informal learning activities in head start families. *Cognitive Development, 35*, 15–33.

Rehm, M., & Notten, A. (2016). Twitter as an informal learning space for teachers? The role of social capital in twitter conversations among teachers. *Teaching and Teacher Education, 60*, 215–223.

Renner, B., Prilla, M., Ulrike, C., & Joachim, K. (2016). Effects of prompting in reflective learning tools: Findings from experimental field, lab, and online studies. *Frontiers in Psychology, 7*, 1–9.

Rogers, A. (2014). *The base of the iceberg: Informal learning and its impact on formal and non-formal learning (study guides in adult education).* Opladen/Berlin/Toronto: Barbara Budrich Publishers.

Towards a new educational contract 11

Sanders, D. (2007). Making public the private life of plants: The contribution of informal learning environments. *International Journal of Science Education, 29*(10), 1209–1228.

Scheerens, J. (2011). Indicators on informal learning for active citizenship at school. *Educational Assessment Evaluation and Accountability, 23*(3), 201–222.

Singh, M. (2015). *Global perspectives on recognising non-formal and informal learning: Why recognition matters.* Cham, Switzerland: Springer.

Van Noy, M., Jacobs, J., Korey, S., Bailey, T., & Hughes, K. L. (2008). *Noncredit Enrollment in Workforce Education: State Policies and Community College Practices. … of Community Colleges.* Retrieved from http://files.eric.ed.gov/fulltext/ED503447.pdf

Van Noy, M., James, H., & Bedley, C. (2016). *Reconceptualizing learning: A review of the literature on informal learning.* New Jersey, NJ: Rutgers Education and Employment Research Center. Retrieved April 10, 2019, from https://equityinlearning.act.org/wp-content/uploads/2017/07/Informal-Learning-Lit-Review-Final-April-2016-1.pdf

Weber, M. (1905). la ética protestante y el espíritu del capitalismo, México: Fondo de Cultura Económica.

Zimmerman, H. T., & McClain, L. R. (2016). Family learning outdoors: Guided participation on a nature walk. *Journal of Research Science Teaching, 53*(6), 919–942.

Part I

Schools and informal learning: Shaping the future

2 What we really learn in school?

Roger C. Schank

Introduction

A book about informal learning implies that there is such a thing as formal learning. I suppose that formal learning must refer to what goes on in classrooms, but real learning doesn't actually happen in classrooms, at least not about the subjects being taught. Real learning occurs whenever you have a goal, try to achieve that goal, fail and then seek explanations as to why you have failed. Real learning goes on all the time in our daily lives. It occurs at work. It occurs at home and on the playground. It occurs when we pursue a hobby. It occurs when we pursue relationships with other people, and it occurs when we sit down to think about something that is bothering us. In school? Not a chance, unless, of course, we are talking about what you learn when you ignore the teacher and let your mind wander.

For real learning to occur in a classroom, the subject matter would have to be of interest to the student, relating to a goal that the student actually has (as opposed to wanting a good grade). How many students wake up in the morning worrying about mathematics or literature? Only those who might have a test that day. How many 10-year-olds have math discussions with their friends? It seems absurd to even ask this question. What are they talking about with their friends? Whatever they are talking about is what they are actually learning. We learn through conversation, through asking for help and through trial and error. We all know this, but we like to pretend that we learned something in school. After all, we spent all that time in school. It must have been for something.

Here is what we really learn in school:

1 we learn to pay attention to what the teacher is saying. This does not mean we are really listening. We learn we are supposed to look like we are listening;
2 we learn to memorize truths that the school would like us to believe in. These are usually about what a wonderful country we live in, or some random science facts like $F = MA$ or all important quadratic formulas. We

16   *Roger C. Schank*

typically forget what we have temporally memorized, or if we don't, we can't apply it and have no use for it;

3 we learn to do what we are told. We know we will be punished if we don't, so we try hard to please the teacher;

4 we learn to sit still. This is actually a very bad thing to learn because it is only through active investigation of an interest of ours that we can learn anything;

5 we learn to try to succeed at whatever task has been put before us. But, what we really learn is to subjugate our own interests for things the school says we should be interested in;

6 we learn to parrot back what we have been told. "Columbus discovered America" is big in the Western world;

7 we learn to work hard for a meaningless credential. A high school diploma proves what? It proves that you played by the rules for 4 years and

8 we learn to retain meaningless knowledge. In Canada, students learn that Canada won the War of 1812. In the United States, students learn that the United States never lost a war and they never even find out that Canada was involved in it at all.

Why do we behave this way in school?

Formal learning originated with the Romans who evolved the Liberal Arts curriculum to train orators in the Forum. Rich kids learned to give speeches by sitting in a classroom and being lectured at. (Presumably at some point they had to give an actual speech and learned from that.)

Universities have copied the Roman model for 2000 years.

Why? Because, really, universities were never meant to teach actual job or life skills. They were meant to train the elite and keep them in power. It worked. Seven U.S. presidents had Harvard degrees and five had Yale degrees. People who attended these schools love to tell you that they went there. It is still the ultimate status symbol to have attended one of the elite universities in one's country. These schools don't want to teach people to work. (The President of Yale once told me, in response to something I proposed: "We don't do training, Roger.")

So if schools are not trying to satisfy curiosity, nor are they trying to teach job skills, what are they trying to do? The obvious answers are that schools are trying to prepare students for college, and the top universities are trying to do research and to train researchers. But there are already so many top research universities, and there are lot more schools pretending that they are teaching students to do research. How many researchers do we need?

Or, they claim they are teaching students to think. *Mathematics teaches you to think. Literature teaches you to think. Philosophy teaches you to think.*

This is nice nonsense. There is no evidence for it whatsoever. How would we define one's ability to think in order to test these outlandish claims? By giving students math problems? They mean that mathematics teaches you to

What we really learn in school? 17

think about math. Mathematicians aren't better than anybody else at thinking about their own lives.

Why do schools continue the formal learning model?

One way to understand this is to consider the lecture. Debate has been occurring recently on whether lectures are a good thing. No one really believes that you can learn from a lecture. If you don't believe me, ask yourself if you ever would give a 1-hour uninterrupted lecture to a child of your own. No one would even think to do that, and your child would try to leave the room if you did do it. No one believes that you can learn from lectures. But teachers, especially professors, defend lecturing all the time when it is being attacked. They like talking for one thing. And, good speakers can give an entertaining lecture. But entertaining is not about learning. Lectures started because those who could read were reading to those who couldn't.

Lectures matter a great deal in universities. If you have 1,000 students listening to a lecture, you are doing something that is financially important for the university. Students pay tuition and 1,000 students pay a lot more than 10 do. But the professor is paid the same amount either way. So universities love lecturing, as do professors who can satisfy their teaching requirement with little interaction with individual student.

We all know that one-on-one teaching is the best way to educate. In PhD programmes we actually provide one-on-one education. PhD programmes are one of the few parts of the education system that is not broken. Students pursue their own interests, and a mentor helps them think things out. Parents do the same thing. But, in between, being a 4-year-old at home and being a PhD student, education is a disaster. Why? Because your own curiosity and needs can't drive what you learn, and no one is really paying attention to what you are curious about.

Temporary memorization of knowledge that you likely will never use is not learning. It is school. It is "formal learning" which I contend is valueless.

Although I loathe school and find it incredible that we still make every kid go to school for 10 or more years, I do understand the major reasons why that is so.

The primary reason is, of course, day care. If you can send your kids to school, then you don't have to look after them yourself. Every parent needs help with day care. We could simply admit this and turn teachers into day care providers and move on.

The second reason is indoctrination. Every country devotes part of the school day to making kids believe that they live in the best country in the world. In the United States, we make every school child recite the *pledge of allegiance* every morning. They recite it, but at age 6 they could not possibly know what any of the words mean (except *flag* because they are staring at one while they recite it). We don't care. We are indoctrinating them. Indoctrination and understating are decidedly unrelated.

So keep the day care and eliminate the indoctrination. I often speak in Spain, and when I attack the various subjects that are taught in Spanish schools,

18 *Roger C. Schank*

I inevitably hear about the importance of learning Spanish history. I ask them if their history courses include learning about the Spanish Inquisition. Uh well, no they don't. The murder of all the Indians in Uruguay? Uh well, no. History as a form of indoctrination is the case in every country. The U.S. Civil War was about slavery. Uh huh.

Informal learning is a more effective model

To me, informal learning means the stuff we learn by doing. I know how to throw a (American) football very well. Can I tell you what I know? Of course not. I can just do it. I can drive a car. Do I know the answer to how much pressure I need to put on the brake pedal in order to stop the car when it is going fast? No. I can simply do it. I can listen carefully when someone talks to me so I can quickly diagnose what their real issues are. Do I know how to do that? Yes. Can I tell you how to do that? No.

So, how does informal learning really work?

About 40 years ago, I was having lunch with a Yale colleague (Bob Abelson—a famous social psychologist) who was also my closest friend at the time.

I complained to him that my wife couldn't cook steak rare. (I hate overcooked meat.) He replied that back in the 50s he was in the United Kingdom and he couldn't get his hair cut as short as he wanted it. (Crew cuts were in style in the United States then, but not in the United Kingdom.)

That's all there is to know about learning.

Huh?

1 often, learning just starts with a conversation;
2 the first speaker has a problem and wants help thinking his problem out;
3 the listener relates his friend's problem to a problem of his own;
4 the link is through an explanation that the listener thinks might be the explanation both parties are seeking and
5 so he replies to a story with a story.

Underneath all this are some simple truths.

1 Learning starts with confusion, which quite frequently is the result of an expectation failure. This is one reason that school is really not a good way to educate. If I need to be curious and confused in order to learn, school would have to try to relate to something I am already curious or confused about—but how could that happen with fixed curricula and many students in class each of whom is curious about different things?
2 Listening can only work if the listener is curious too. A listener may not be curious about what the speaker is curious about, but the speaker is trying to make the listener curious about something. If they succeed, the listener will

What we really learn in school? 19

attempt to find in their own memory something that they have experienced so the listener can respond to the speaker with a story of their own.

3 Explanations are the basis of understanding. Bob was searching for an explanation. He constructed one by matching my story to his story. But what was he matching exactly? He was matching on the plans and goals held by the actors in the story and his own curiosity about what their points of view might have been. He unconsciously constructed an explanation: Maybe the actor who didn't want to accede to the request because he thought that the request was too extreme.

4 When we match our stories to the stories of others, we do so in order to learn from them. When we think about a story we heard, we do so in order to construct an explanation of the events in the story. We can do this only by finding experiences we have had that relate to the experience being told to us. We pursue this path if we are curious about an explanation (typically because we think that explanation will help us to understand something we were curious about).

5 But what do we match on? Certainly not words or pixels. We match on high-level abstractions like goals, plans, and intentionality. My goal was to eat the way I like. Bob's goal was to look the way he wanted. When goals do not get realized when we thought they would, we wonder why and seek explanations. My goal was to get someone to do something for me and so was his. So the explanation would have had to have been about convincing other people to do what we wanted. That kind of goal (how to convince someone) was never actually discussed, but that is what we were both curious about, had been thinking about and matching on that is how Bob was reminded of his own experience.

If you are not curious, frustrated by not getting what you want, wondering why your predictions failed, why your diagnosis was wrong, you will not learn. We seek explanations and use them until they fail, and then we get confused again.

To put this another way: If you are not confused and curious you will not learn. This applies to every form of education.

How does this kind of learning take place in school? At first glance it would seem that it doesn't. But not all teachers are the same and not all courses are the same. A good teacher does not provide answers to students; they provide questions.

This is a pretty old idea. Socrates helped us all learn about what teaching should look like, but oddly enough we have ignored what he suggested in most schools. Don't answer a student's question—ask one back. *How might you do X? Why do you think that happened?* and so on. Answers don't matter. Questions do.

So why don't schools teach Socratically? That is an easy question to answer. So, what do you think the answer is? Of course, I have a viewpoint on the answer, but then so do you. Let's discuss.

But, of course this kind of interaction doesn't happen much in school. Classrooms tend to prevent one-on-one conversations. There are also tests to

20   *Roger C. Schank*

give and grades to assign and curricula to get through. In other words, teachers can't have the conversations with students that they should have. There is stuff to tell students that they must memorize and believe. No questions are acceptable (except when they are about facts) when there is information to deliver.

It is this "information delivery model" of education that makes informal learning impossible.

Teachers should confuse their students. They should not be giving them explanations. F = MA explains nothing your average student is curious about. They know already that the harder you hit a ball the further it goes.

How can we do this in a school setting?

It is impossible.

Or...

It is actually quite easy.

Huh? Have I confused you? Good. Now we can think together.

How would we do that? By having a conversation. Of course that cannot happen here because my writing and your reading are taking place at different times and places.

But what about school? Conversations could happen in school. And they do, when kids get the chance to whisper or text to each other.

Good conversations (from which one learns) start with curiosity, as I have said. But this cannot happen in school as long as there are subjects and curricula. What would the alternative look like?

Imagine that you are curious about how aeroplanes work. Who would you ask and what would you ask? You could ask a teacher, who would probably say that your question was not relevant to what needed to be taught that day. The teacher might also admit to not being an expert on aeroplanes. Maybe the teacher could find someone to answer your question. But any answer you might find would probably cause other questions to come to mind. If your curiosity isn't stifled by the teacher, their answers might lead you to want to design an aeroplane (if that is what you happen to have been thinking about). How would you get help with that?

My own children

By the age of 10 both my children knew what they wanted to do in life. The school was, at best, not helpful. But as I knew their goals, I helped them achieve them. My daughter wanted to be a writer. I helped her by telling her she could not be an English major in college and that she needed an employable skill. She taught herself to write, and she figured out a way to earn money. (Her latest book was just published.) My son was obsessed with subways, so I took him to places to try out new ones. I told him he had to study subways in college. He said there was no way to do that. I said to keep looking. He managed to get a PhD in transportation and is now high up in the Los Angeles County Transportation system.

But is this informal learning? Riding subways and learning about them is certainly not formal learning, so what is it? We need a different way of looking at learning. Formal learning doesn't exist in my opinion. There is school and most

What we really learn in school? 21

kids hate it except the ones who like winning and doing exactly what they are told. Informal learning cannot just be seen as "the other stuff." We need courses that enable going in whatever direction you choose and lead you towards accomplishing something you really want to accomplish. Going to "school" would be a lot more valuable and fun.

Can computers revolutionize learning?

This leads me to my main point. Remember how computers were going to change education? No really interesting changes have actually happened because of computers. Students can Google answers when this is allowed but mostly computers have replaced typewriters and made giving and grading tests easier. In other words, computers have not been very useful in education except in being used to make the administration of education easier. No one really cares about the student's learning experience.

Potentially the computer can change all this. It hasn't because we simply can't conceive of school in any way other than the way the Romans did it. Maybe we should reconsider.

What would an effective computer-based learning experience look like?

By computer-based education, I do not mean e-learning, MOOCs, personalized learning, computer-based training or any of the other nonsense that has appeared lately. They are all the same really. All are ways to "deliver content" and then test to see if you have memorized that content.

The computer can be a "doing device." We can change education by offering thousands of online experiences to students who are curious about something. We can propose things that they could try, mentor them one-on-one and look at what they actually accomplish.

What can a kid do on a computer? A child can enter a virtual world (or story), try to figure out what is going on there and try to accomplish things in that world. That is what kids do all the time, when they play with dolls or pets, or when they try to build things with blocks. It is the same basic idea except the experience would be previously designed by experts, gradually taking the child through harder and harder challenges. At the end of the experience, the child would know how to do something they couldn't do before that is something that they chose to accomplish, not to attain a grade but because they really wanted to do it.

What sorts of learning experiences should be delivered?

I propose eliminating every single subject taught in school after kids have mastered basic skills like reading, writing and arithmetic. (I would add to the 3 R's—getting along with others, learning to speak, learning to diagnose a problem and learning how to plan.)

22   Roger C. Schank

What do we do instead? We let kids pursue their own interests. Really? Suppose all they want to do is play video games or watch movies or kick a ball? Let them. At some point they will want do so something else.

What we can do is make the "something else's" very enticing. And we can suggest that kids talk to each other (they would be in the same school building after all since we haven't eliminated the use of that building as a drop off point—with supervision).

So what "something else's" should we build and what should they look like? Here are a few to consider:

1   criminal justice;
2   sports management;
3   the music business;
4   the legal office;
5   military readiness;
6   the fashion industry;
7   engineering;
8   computer networking;
9   homeland security;
10   medical technology;
11   construction;
12   computer technology;
13   television production;
14   real estate management;
15   landscape architecture;
16   computer programming;
17   the banking industry;
18   automobile design;
19   architecture;
20   biotechnology lab;
21   film making;
22   travel planning;
23   financial management;
24   parenting and child care;
25   animal care;
26   urban transit;
27   hotel management;
28   health care industry;
29   food industry and
30   graphic arts.

Just these 30? Of course not. How about 100 more? How about 1000 more?

We can't do that. Why not? It would cost a lot of money. A U.S. senator told me "it would cost as much as building a nuclear missile." "So build one less missile" I responded.

What we really learn in school? 23

We can easily find the money.

They will need help if they dive in. Our job as curriculum (really "story") designers is to make the story interesting and provide help as needed. This help can come in the form of stories gathered from experts delivered just in time. Or it could come from live people (expert mentors available on line, or experts who happen to be physically present or from other kids who are around).

Each curriculum would start with a story. ("You have been asked to help as an assistant in the next TV production, criminal investigation, computer art fair, etc. Here is a task you can do in a week if you learn some of the basics. Here is where to start. Here is some stuff to read and some very simple assignments. A mentor is available to help you. ("You have 10 days. Ask for help whenever you need it.") In such a project-oriented environment, students work with each other and with mentors (who may be teachers or may be experts from the community) to attempt the simplest of tasks in a given field.

Gradually the assignments get more complex. As the complexity increases, students have to learn a range of skills outside of the field they are specifically studying. For example, they may be asked to prepare a budget for a project, to do a cost benefit analysis, to make a presentation of a proposal they have created or to write up an idea. They would receive help in writing, reasoning, mathematics and so on in addition to the help they would receive giving specific advice about their field of inquiry. Thus, the on line experience allows for many mentors to give advice and for students to work in teams of like-minded students who may not be physically present.

Students would do one thing at a time. At the end of a full-year experience like this, graduates from a given curriculum will have had a year's worth of experience in a given field. Since these experiences would be designed with potential employers as part of the design team, the result could be immediate employment for those who seek it, or the beginning of curiosity about the next challenge for those who choose to go on in a given field. In other words, students would start at the beginning and choose to go as far as their interests and abilities take them.

Now we don't want 10-year-olds to be expecting to be doctors upon finishing a full-year course in how to be a doctor. But really that is not our purpose here. The idea is to get kids excited about something and help them learn more.

That is my version of informal learning: Drawing insights from the world around you, and planning what to do on the basis of the conclusions you draw.

What should we be learning informally?

- reasoning;
- human relations;
- communication;
- organization;
- creativity;
- taking initiative;

24 Roger C. Schank

- decision making;
- value judgments;
- ethics and
- prioritization.

Is that all? No. There are hundreds of things to be learned, thousands. No one can teach these things to us. I don't believe in teaching in any case. I do believe in mentoring, helping, challenging, setting goals, making plans, recovering if those plans don't work out, discussing what is on your mind, telling stories and hearing stories that shed light on the issues in your stories.

I once asked my 10-year-old grandson who his best teacher was. He replied "you?" (He does well in school. He wants to provide the answer that he figures you want to hear.)

"NO. YOU", I replied. We are all our own best teachers.

Informal learning is all there is really. Can parents of teachers help with informal learning? Yes, they can, by being there and seeing their job not giving information but as helping kids think things out better. But this cannot be done in a classroom. Online education allows the possibility of one-on-one teaching by having teachers be there when you need them.

Will we be able to shift over to that kind of education system? There is no reason we can't, except we need the money to build it, and we need governments, book publishers, test makers, teachers and nearly all the general public, to stop objecting to meaningful change in education. The Romans no longer need orators in the Forum.

3 Exploring the foundations of informal learning

Judith Lloyd Yero

Introduction

> *The illiterate of the 21st century will not be those who cannot read and write, but those who cannot learn, unlearn and relearn.*
>
> *~Alvin Toffler*

At the turn of this century, education theorists began talking about "21st century skills" that should be included in formal education. Beyond the "three Rs," these were often couched as the "four Cs." They included

- critical thinking/problem solving;
- communication;
- collaboration and
- creativity/innovation.

Assuming that learning requires teaching, educators began asking how they would "teach" these skills if they were added to the curriculum (Care, Kim, & Vista, 2017). But let's take a closer look at those skills by watching a group of 3-year-old preschool children engaged in play—the authentic foundation of a child's learning.

These children haven't been *taught* to think critically and solve problems. They haven't been *taught* to communicate. They haven't been *taught* to work together collaboratively. They haven't been *taught* to be creative. Yet, they are exhibiting all of these skills! These children have *learned* these skills by *doing* them—through trial and error, feedback and negotiation (Hobson, 2017).

While these skills will serve them well in the future, the children are focused on what they need "right now." This is a key feature of *informal learning*, which continues throughout our lives. Estimates suggest that more than 70% of our learning occurs informally (Cross, 2007, pp. 243–244). Yet informal learning typically is ignored in educational institutions.

26 *Judith Lloyd Yero*

In *The Necessity of Informal Learning*, Frank Coffield (2002) points out that,

> There is a strong tendency for policy makers, researchers and practitioners to admit readily the importance of informal learning and then to proceed to develop policy, theory, and practice without further reference to it. We must move beyond this periodic genuflection in the direction of informal learning and incorporate it into plans for a learning society.

Focusing education on the individual needs of learners is the antithesis of traditional knowledge-focused education. Trusting individuals to assume responsibility for their own learning may present a significant stumbling block. But the shift of focus from teaching to learning is imperative if education is to nurture a "learning society."

This chapter provides a foundation on which to build and expand the discussion of informal learning by revisiting the definition of learning, as well as exploring the elements of informal learning, self-determination theory (SDT) and the principles of individuality.

What is learning?

People often assume that when they use the same words to describe a concept or situation, they perceive that situation in the same way. This is rarely the case. Once we get beyond a dictionary definition, the meaning we assign to a word, such as *learning*, is largely an expression of a belief, not an absolute fact (Yero, 2010, pp. 37, 198–211).

Learn: *Gain or acquire knowledge of, or skill in, something by study, experience or being taught.*

Acquiring knowledge and skills by being taught (formal learning) is often accepted as the primary working definition of learning. However, think about the three or four most important things you have learned in life. Do they all fall in this category? Certainly formal learning is a *necessary* part of learning, but is it *sufficient* to characterize learning in its deepest form?

Here are a few other definitions that characterize learning in very different ways.

- Learning is a relatively permanent change in the behaviour or attitude of a person over time.
- Learning is the lifelong process of transforming information and experience into knowledge, skills, behaviours and attitudes.
- Learning is the advancement of understanding that enables the learner to function more effectively in the environment, improve and adapt behaviours, create and maintain healthy relationships and achieve personal success.

While all of these definitions are *true*, none is *complete*. Is a single definition of *learning* even possible?

What is knowledge?

If *learning* is the acquisition of knowledge or skill, what do we mean by the word *knowledge*?

Learning to solve an equation for x requires a different thought process than learning the chemical formula for salt or the definition of *alliteration*. Using alliteration in writing requires a different thought process than simply defining the word. There is, however, a tendency to group these processes under two headings—declarative and procedural knowledge. Simplistically, knowing the rules of chess is declarative knowledge, while the ability to play chess effectively is procedural.

Similarly, educators often divide knowledge into content and process. *Content* is the information that learners are expected to acquire. "*Process* is all the cognitive skills that the curriculum activities are intended to develop that are supposed to enable the student to do something with the content" (Bereiter, 2002, p. 133).

In his book, *Education and Mind in the Knowledge Age*, Dr. Carl Bereiter argues that the knowledge categories of content and process are too broad to be particularly useful. Bereiter suggests a potentially more useful breakdown of personal knowledge (Bereiter, 2002, pp. 137–148).

- *Statable knowledge:* Knowledge that the knower can pass on to others in some way, be it sentences, diagrams, formulas or stories. Such knowledge can be observed by others, evaluated and compared. This is the primary type of knowledge "assessed" in formal education, although it is often limited by tests in which students must select one "correct" answer from a list of choices.
- *Skill:* There are two parts to any skill: A cognitive part—the "knowing how"—and another part that can improve with practice. In formal education, students are taught *how* to do many different tasks, from solving a particular type of math problem to using reference materials. But with the proliferation of "hows" that students must learn, there is little time for practice that will improve those skills. Skills that remain at the level of "knowing how" are less likely to be used than skills in which the person feels some competence.
- *Implicit understanding: Understanding* implies a deep enough relationship with concepts, people or situations in the world to produce intelligent action on the part of the knower. "Implicit understanding is more like perception than like having propositions in the head" (Bereiter, 2002, p. 139). For example, the fielder who, at the instant the bat strikes the baseball, begins to run to the exact spot where the ball will land has *implicit understanding*. This is very different from someone who knows and/or can use the equation for calculating projectile motion. It is knowledge about projectile motion gained from *experience*, rather than a physics textbook. It can be assessed— but only by observing the learner in action!

28   *Judith Lloyd Yero*

- *Episodic knowledge:* Unlike semantic memory (e.g. knowledge about concepts, objects, people, facts and the meaning of words), episodic knowledge is something learned through personal experience that may later become useful in some other context. Walking past a high-rise building under construction may remind a person of having an acorn fall on his/her head in the woods. The recalled knowledge influences the person's behaviour. This knowledge is "selected" from a person's body of knowledge when an appropriate context arises, or when a person is asked to predict what might happen in a given context.
- *Impressionistic knowledge:* Bereiter (2002) asserts that all knowledge has an affective, or emotional, component. In fact, a growing number of neuroscientists propose that emotion is a necessary characteristic of human thought (cf. Brosch et al., 2013; Edelman, 1992; Gazzaniga, 1992). Neuroscientist Antonio Damasio (1995, pp. 43–45) suggests that, in the absence of emotions, higher thought processes are impaired. In the case of impressionistic knowledge, *the feeling is the knowledge.* It is the hunch, the intuitive sense, the gut feeling that may not be accessible, nor expressible, at a conscious level, but that influences our behaviour nonetheless.
- *Regulative knowledge:* In the acquisition and use of knowledge, the issue of "self" as learner has too often been ignored in education. Regulative knowledge is facilitated in an individual by opportunities for reflection. The more learners know about how they process information, the more effectively they can monitor and assess the products of their own thinking. Developed at an early age, self-reflection and metacognition may make a profound difference in a person's development.

Bereiter points out that formal education places the greatest emphasis on statable knowledge and the "knowing how" portion of skills—the only two forms of knowledge that can be directly conveyed from one person to another. Other forms are often neglected because traditional education has no mechanism to deal with knowledge that varies among students, can't be easily transmitted to an entire group, and can't be objectively assessed.

The remaining types of personal knowledge and/or understanding are acquired through *experience*—through what we now call informal learning. All types of knowledge are present in what most of us recognize as intelligent behaviour. "Competence in any domain will likely involve all six kinds of knowledge" (Bereiter, 2002, p. 148). In real life—in authentic learning—these forms of knowledge develop and function in parallel. They are interrelated parts of the system that encompasses the knower and the known.

What is informal learning?

If we employ the framework that learning occurs on a continuum, it's relatively easy to define *formal learning* as learning that is instructor-led, knowledge-centred, and covers an organized curriculum. It occurs in schools that award credentials of some type. *Success* in formal learning is typically measured by how comprehensively the learner can remember and/or use what the teacher had in mind.

Informal learning is not nearly as clear cut. In the literature, it is used to describe everything from extracurricular activities or electives within the formal learning environment to learning that occurs during the course of daily life. Theorists define informal learning in terms of the learner's intention, the location or situation in which the learning occurs, and/or whether or not the learning is "useful" or has "educative value." Terms such as *organized informal learning*, *incidental learning* or *tacit learning* further subdivide the realm of informal learning (cf. Coombs, 1974; Dale & Bell, 1999; Erhaut, 2000).

Even as more and more theorists insist that educators must address informal learning, there is a profound lack of agreement about what it entails and what kinds of knowledge it produces. Discussions of *how* this type of learning actually takes place rarely occur.

Learning from experience

From the moment of birth, and even before, informal learning occurs as a result of experience. In the infant and young child, interactions with the environment and with other humans support the accumulation of a critical database of information about the world. This database provides the learner with a matrix into which new experiences can fit, as well as providing prior knowledge that helps the learner make sense of new experiences.

David Kolb defined *learning* as "the process whereby knowledge is created through the transformation of experience" (Kolb, 1984, p. 38). Notice that Kolb uses the verb *created*, not *acquired*.

Success in experiential learning is demonstrated by interacting with the world in some way that is more effective or efficient than it was prior to the experience. But how does this type of learning take place? To what extent is it possible to recreate or support these elements within the formal learning structure?

Elements of informal experiential learning

Kolb's Experiential Learning Cycle theorized four stages that included doing/having an experience; reflecting on the experience; drawing conclusions/learning from the experience and testing/trying out what one has learned. While this is useful, it leaves much to the imagination in terms of how each of these steps occurs.

Lloyd Davies (2009) offers a model that identifies key elements in how we learn from experience. Many of the elements involved in unplanned experiential learning are equally useful for intentional learning.

Experiential learning has several characteristics that make it unique. (1) It is active in that it requires more than just remembering what someone else said; and (2) It typically leads to a change in behaviour (major or minor). For example,

30   *Judith Lloyd Yero*

when we touch something hot, we are motivated to observe and figure out how the object was different so that we won't make that mistake again. The time span for this learning may be very short, and may require only one experience to develop a new behaviour.

Unlike formal learning, which is typically future-oriented, informal learning is about meeting a present need. It is also personal to the extent that *the same experience* affects people in different ways, and the learning they take away from the experience ranges from none to highly impactful (Davies, 2009, p. 5).

Unpacking the elements

Davies' methodology centred on interviewing adults from different walks of life. He encouraged interviewees to recall an experience, or set of experiences, that caused them to alter their worldview in some significant way—in other words, to "make sense" of the world differently.

Davies distilled the information from the interviews into a new model for how people make sense of experience—how they learn. Learning is multidimensional, complex, and above all, personal! Here are a few of elements divided into related clusters.

A.   The experience itself
- *Expectations:* Depending on one's age, expectations may be based on prior experience, formal knowledge or the views of others. Formal learning tends to confirm expectations, while learning from experience often occurs when the experience produces results contrary to expectations.
- *Emotions:* When an experience fails to match one's expectations, what emotion(s) is/are triggered? Curiosity? Shame? Fright? Anger? Surprise? Obviously, this depends on the nature of the experience. However, the fact that the experience produces an emotion sets it apart from other more mundane experiences. "Emotions guide one's attention to things that are relevant to goals and concerns that are implicated in the emotional situation. ... Such processes ensure that what appears most relevant is attended to first" (Davies, 2009, p. 43).

  In the case of survival emotions, the evolutionary advantage is clear. Other emotions, such as shame or inadequacy, will prompt people to pursue the learning they need to avoid a recurrence.
- *Opportunity:* In essence, this refers to the time it might take to gather more information about the experience and reflect on it with the goal of learning from it. Whether a person has, or is willing to take this time, depends on a variety of factors.

  Example: A person drives the same route every morning. From prior experience, the expectation is for an unremarkable and incident-free trip. But on a given morning, a construction truck unexpectedly pulls into the road at an intersection that had previously been little used. The driver slams on the brakes to avoid an accident, producing a variety of emotions.

Some drivers may continue on with little or no thought about the incident, but for others, the emotions they experience may motivate them to spend at least a few moments reflecting on cause and effect, and potentially learning to be more cautious on that part of the road. Other drivers may go so far as to seek out information about construction in the area that may suggest selecting a different route.

B. **Learning orientation:** Elements that affect how a person responds to an experience

- *Personality:* Personality traits are generally defined as a person's characteristic thoughts, feelings and behaviours. There have been many attempts to classify personality, but the five-factor or Big Five approach to trait theory is widely accepted.

  > In this approach, personality traits are organized into five broad and relatively independent domains that include both positive and negative characteristics related to extraversion (sociable, energetic, withdrawn), agreeableness (helpful, cooperative, hostile), conscientiousness (hard-working, self-controlled, disorganized), emotional stability (calm, anxious, worrying), and openness to experience (curious, imaginative, unintelligent). (Hampson, 2017)

  People who are more open to new experiences, are persistent, and are confident in their own abilities, are typically more likely to learn from a given experience. This is not to say that they will learn the same things. For example, when people attend a workplace meeting, some may learn nothing, while others may learn financial lessons, social skills, technical lessons and/or organizational lessons.

- *Ability:* A combination of prior background and the extent to which an individual's capabilities have been developed contribute to what, and how much, a person may learn from an experience. The person's age, the strength of one or more of the intelligences described by Howard Gardner (2011) and the extent to which those intelligences have been developed contribute to the acquisition of learning from an experience.

- *Memory:* People often reflect on an experience by comparing that experience to others. Some people are less adept than others in retaining the essentials of an experience long enough to make those comparisons.

C. **Sources of information:** Assuming a person chooses to gather data, reflect on and learn from an experience, there are a number of potential sources of information.

- *Own observations and experience:* This information gathered through the learner's own observations. These observations may differ from person to person depending on prior experience, interest and other factors.

32   *Judith Lloyd Yero*

- *Fellow participants' observations:* When people share an experience, their observations often diverge.

  > It is a commonplace experience that two people attending the same meeting, football match, or witnessing the same road traffic incident, will have different, sometimes radically different, perspectives on what happened and why. So fellow participants' observations provide a potentially rich source of data on a shared experience. (Davies, 2009, p. 27)

- *Formal knowledge:* Knowledge gained in formal learning situations is another potential source of information in making sense of a new experience.

D. **Making sense:** These elements are involved in processing the information and arriving at a conclusion.

- *Reflection and insight:* Unexpected experiences produce cognitive dissonance. The natural tendency to reduce cognitive dissonance motivates taking the time (opportunity) to reduce the stress and add to learning so that the dissonance does not reoccur.

  Davies describes a number of ways in which people might use the data they have gathered to make sense of the experience. [This section of Davies' book is an excellent resource for developing deeper understanding of how informal learning occurs (Davies, 2009, Chapter 11).]

- *Learning:* The outcome of the learning process may include knowledge (facts), a deeper understanding, improved judgment and/or new skills. The new learning may result in a permanent change in the learner's ways of thinking about a situation, social interaction or choice of future action.

- *Credibility checking:* Once a learner reaches a conclusion, trying it out in similar situation helps to insure that the learning is reliable and the conclusion is credible.

- *Experience bank:* Once satisfied, the learner adds the learning to his or her experience/knowledge bank.

These elements may occur in any order and often require iterations. In some learnings, not all of them will occur. Typically, many take place at the unconscious level. Davies argues that, in the case of complex learning situations, the more we are able to bring these elements into consciousness, refine them and add them to our repertoire of learned behaviours, the more effective our learning may become.

Each element of experiential learning is unique to the individual. From the moment of birth, no two individuals, no two brains are, or can be, alike. Unlike formal learning, *experiential informal learning cannot be organized or structure by someone else.* No one but the learner can, or has the right to, determine which learnings are worth the effort and which are not.

Foundations of informal learning   33

On the other hand, educators can *facilitate* informal learning by helping learners bring the elements into consciousness. Instructors can model a variety of effective ways to think about an experience—how to ask questions, look for patterns and use logic and reasoning. However, this must be done against a background of respect for each learner's needs.

What about motivation?

> *Knowledge which is obtained under compulsion obtains no hold on the mind.*
> ~Plato

Educators the world over understand that the deepest learning takes place when the learner is motivated and engaged. As we saw in the last section, informal learning often depends on a person's willingness to take the time necessary to learn from an experience. Therefore, understanding what motivates a person to learn—either formally or informally—is essential.

Formal education in childhood is too often based on the underlying belief that young learners, left to their own devices, won't learn anything useful. This assumption comes, in no small measure, from "the Calvinist belief that children are inherently lazy and untrustworthy and that it is society's role to mold their minds and characters into a socially acceptable form" (Mercogliano, 2006, p. 21).

Since the days of Rousseau, theorists have argued against this assumption, particularly in the education of the young. Yet despite the warnings of names such as Pestalozzi, Froebel, Montessori, Dewey, Piaget and others, global education has moved in the opposite direction—towards one-size-fits-all standardized education that effectively eliminates opportunities for meaningful informal learning (Sahlberg, 2012; Zhao, 2015).

Self-determination theory

Contrary to the Calvinist view, extensive research supports the idea that humans have evolved to be inherently curious, physically active and deeply social beings.

> From infancy on (when in need-supportive environments), people manifest intrinsic tendencies to take interest in, deeply learn about, and gain mastery with respect to both their inner and outer worlds. (Ryan & Deci, 2017, p. 4)

One of the first things scientists do when studying plants or animals is to establish an organism's *physiological* needs for nutrients and support, as well as the observable effects of these needs on growth and functioning. SDT brings this same functional viewpoint to the study of the *psychological* growth and development of human beings, as well as investigating how environments do or do not support these needs affect social behaviour.

SDT's approach is based on the concept that optimal human development and organization requires specific nutrients from the social environment. These consist of:

> ... a set of *basic psychological needs* that may be either satisfied or frustrated. ... Need-supportive environments facilitate the development of integrated self-regulation, including capacities to manage the multiple drives, impulses, emotions, and motives that arise within every individual. If basic needs are thwarted, there is alternatively fragmentation and defense rather than integration. (Ryan & Deci, 2017, p. 9)

Drawing on years of empirical studies and inductive reasoning, self-determination theorists have identified three basic psychological needs without whose satisfaction optimal growth is not possible. Human beings are *intrinsically motivated* to take action to fulfil these needs. Their fulfilment provides satisfaction that sustains motivation.

Basic psychological needs

Several criteria must be met in order for a need to be identified as "basic." Among them,

- the satisfaction of a need must enhance psychological health, integrity and well-being, and its frustration must hurt wellness;
- it must facilitate healthy development in an ongoing way and
- it must be universal to people in all cultures and of all ages (Ryan & Deci, 2017, p. 251).

The three basic needs that SDT has identified include:

- *Autonomy:* Autonomy refers to the need to self-regulate one's experiences and actions. Autonomy does not necessarily equate to independence (self-reliance). While some cultures value independence, others value interdependence and harmony. An action one takes is *autonomous* if it is congruent with one's interests and values and is integrated into one's sense of self.

  Actions may be placed on a continuum from fully externally controlled to fully autonomous. "When acting with autonomy, behaviours are engaged wholeheartedly, whereas one experiences incongruence and conflict when doing what is contrary to one's volition" (Ryan & Deci, 2017, p. 10).
- *Competence:* This refers to the ability to interact successfully with one's environment, and is seen as a primary factor in motivating actions. Learners will gravitate to a context in which they have experienced success and mastery because it makes them feel competent. They tend to avoid those in which they have failed or feel less competent.

Competence is, however, readily thwarted. It wanes in contexts in which challenges are too difficult, negative feedback is pervasive, or feeling of mastery and effectiveness are diminished or undermined by interpersonal factors such as person-focused criticism and social comparisons. (Deci & Ryan, 2017, p. 11)

- *Relatedness:* This is the need to feel socially connected. Relatedness pertains "... to a sense of being integral to social organizations beyond oneself ... both by being connected to close others and by being a significant [contributing] member of social groups" (Ryan & Deci, 2017, p. 11).
  Environments that support relatedness are based on caring, respect and the opportunity to engage with others in meaningful ways.

In short, SDT research confirms that the satisfactions experienced in feeling autonomy, competence and relatedness

> ... reflect, in the deepest sense, the essence of human thriving, and they predict any number of indicators of wellness and vitality. Moreover, SDT research documents that in social contexts in which there is psychological support for these satisfactions, people's curiosity, creativity, productivity, and compassion are most robustly expressed. (Ryan & Deci, 2017, p. 5)

On the other hand,

> When individuals experience need-thwarting environments, such as contexts that are overly controlling, rejecting, critical, and negative, or that otherwise frustrate autonomy, relatedness, and competence needs, individuals are more likely to become self-focused, defensive, amotivated, aggressive, and antisocial. *In fact, the presence of these more negative human capacities is typically indicative of social contexts that are thwarting of fundamental or basic psychological needs.* ... In short, the support versus neglect of basic needs is critical in influencing the flourishing or diminishment of people's inherent capacities to fully function. [Emphasis added] (Ryan & Deci, 2017, p. 9)

One can't help but relate these words to the "discipline problems" that frustrate so many traditional educators. Is the problem really with the learners? Or with the learning environment?

SDT applied to schools

Identifying fundamental human needs offers a framework that allows us to identify and predict which aspects of a given social context will enhance versus undermine high-quality motivation, healthy development and well-being (Ryan & Deci, 2017, p. 12). To this end, many studies in educational contexts have examined how teacher and parent approaches to motivation can

36 *Judith Lloyd Yero*

be either controlling or autonomy-supportive (Ryan & Deci, 2017, p. 18 and Chapters 13 and 14).

Educational policies that enhance intrinsic motivation

Numerous studies support the idea that intrinsic motivation leads to deeper and longer lasting learning, as well as psychological wellness. "The pattern of findings has been relatively consistent across all ages of students and across diverse cultures, including Western cultures that tend to be individualistic and Eastern cultures that tend to be more collectivistic" (Ryan & Deci, 2017, p. 381).

- *Choice:* It is not surprising that participants in research studies who were given choice were significantly more intrinsically motivated than those who did not have choice. However, not all choice is created equal! Further studies distinguished between *option choice* (deciding what topic to discuss) and *action choice* (ongoing choice about when, where, how and with whom activities are carried out). Researchers found that *action choice* was more beneficial for eliciting a sense of autonomy, an internal locus of control and intrinsic motivation (Reeve, Nix, & Hamm, 2003).
- *Optimal challenge:* In terms of competence, succeeding at a task is not enough to sustain feelings of satisfaction if the task demands little or nothing of the person. Ryan and Deci believe that intrinsic motivation is a growth function. People with autonomy who are intrinsically motivated tend to select optimal challenges. The key to maintaining motivation is balance—experiencing success in the majority of tasks students undertake while undertaking modest challenges.

  Researchers found that children spent most free-choice time with, and rated as most interesting, tasks that were one step ahead of their ability levels. On the other hand, rewarding children for accomplishing those tasks shifted them to an external locus of control and undermined their interest and persistence at similar tasks (Ryan & Deci, 2017, p. 153).
- *Social interaction:* There is an unfortunate perception that students observed "sitting around talking" are wasting time that might be better spent on "real learning." Yet in many corporations, work environments have shifted from cubicles that isolate workers to communities of practice (Cross, 2007, p. 151). This addresses the need of relatedness that frequently generates a flow of ideas.

> Conversation is a meeting of minds with different memories and habits. When minds meet, they don't just exchange facts: they transform them, reshape them, draw different implications from them, engage in new trains of thought. Conversation doesn't just reshuffle the cards: it creates new cards.
>
> ~Theodore Zeldin. (Cross, 2007, p. 131)

Educational policies that diminish intrinsic motivation

A lack or thwarting of fundamental human needs during development frequently leads to fragmentation and defence rather than integration, resulting in interpersonal vulnerabilities, emotional dysregulation and compromised behaviour (Ryan & Deci, 2017, p. 10). It is discouraging to note that many of the traditional "motivational techniques" used in formal education have been shown by research to *diminish* intrinsic motivation and/or performance. These include, but are not limited to

- threats of punishment;
- external rewards;
- evaluations;
- surveillance (even when the purpose is benign or supportive);
- deadlines and imposed goals;
- high-stakes tests and
- competition (when the goal is to win or beat another person).

These techniques tend to introduce an external stimulus that causes a shift towards an external locus of control and leaves the person feeling controlled (Ryan & Deci, 2017, pp. 147–150).

Chapter 14 in Ryan and Deci's book offers a variety of fascinating information about the application of SDT in schools, as well as describing studies on the influence of teacher and parent behaviours. *Keep in mind that implementing the principles of SDT is focused, not on content or teaching, but on curating conditions that support intrinsic motivation, thereby increasing the potential for deeper learning.*

Teaching to the *average* learner

The complex factors that characterize informal learning, as well as the psychological needs identified by SDT, demonstrate that externally structuring informal learning that suits every learner is impossible. That conclusion is further strengthened when we factor in the physiological effects of experiential learning.

It is estimated that a baby's brain contains 100 billion neurons. Each neuron has about 2,500 synapses (connections to other brain cells). By age 2 or 3, the number has grown to about 15,000 synapses/neuron, and more than one million new neural connections are formed *per second* (Center on the Developing Child, 2009). The richer the infant's experiences, the more connections develop within the brain. By the age of 3, a child's brain may contain 1×10^{15} connections, and *no two children have the same sets of connections because they have had different experiences!* [Emphasis added] (Graham, 2011)

The brain continues to reshape itself throughout adolescence and adulthood, with connections forming, disappearing, strengthening or weakening based on experiential learning. How likely is it that any two brains will (or can) process

38 *Judith Lloyd Yero*

the same information at the same age, in the same way and in the same amount of time? And yet that is the foundation around which traditional public education is built!

We recognize that it is "normal" for human beings of a given age to differ in physical appearance, such as hair or eye colour, height, weight or athletic ability. We accept that children grow and mature at different rates—that their bodies are a complex product of genetics, activity and nutrition. Therefore, it would be unreasonable to expect every 14-year-old—male or female—to "measure up" to the same standard weight, height, muscle strength or athletic ability.

Why then, do we not see it as infinitely more unreasonable when policy makers impose one-size-fits-all standards on the *minds* of all learners of a given age? Any attempt to design educational programs for average learner is doomed to failure, simply because *there is no such thing as an average learner!*

The end of average

In his thought-provoking book, *The End of Average*, Dr. Todd Rose (2015), the head of Harvard's Mind, Brain, and Education Project, traces the development of the mental construct of "The Average Man", as well as further distortions of the concept based on the invalid beliefs of "scientists" such as Edward Galton, Frederick Taylor and Edward Thorndike (Yero, 2016). Together, these ideas formed the foundation of standardized education. Despite the fact that research has shown *every one of the ideas to be invalid*, education and other public institutions remain firmly in their grip.

> ... [T]here is no such thing as average body size, there is no such thing as average talent, average intelligence, or average character. Nor are there average students or average employees—or average brains, for that matter. *Every one of these familiar notions is a figment of a misguided scientific imagination.* Our modern concept of the average person is not a mathematical truth, but a human invention created a century and a half ago by two European scientists to solve the social problems of their era. (Rose, 2015, p. 11)

The End of Average isn't solely about education, but the scientific facts presented in the book should have put the final nail in the coffin of standardized education. In my opinion, it should be mandatory reading for all educators, and is highly recommended.

The principles of individuality

In *The End of Average*, Rose (2015) argues that, rather than an educational system that urges everyone to be just like everyone else, only better—a system that constantly compares learners to a non-existent, mythical average—education must move towards a system that focuses on the development of individual

Foundations of informal learning 39

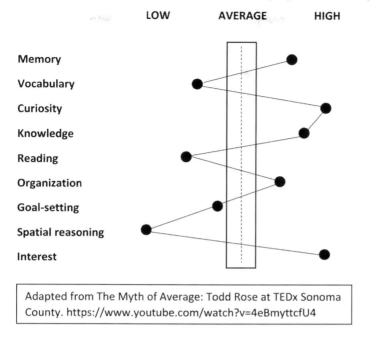

Figure 3.1 The jagged profile of one individual.

excellence. Rose has identified three principles of individuality to illuminate what must happen for this to occur.

The Jaggedness Principle: We cannot apply one-dimensional thinking to understand something that is complex and "jagged" (Rose, 2015, pp. 81–85). For example, *intelligence* is multidimensional. Yet it is common practice to assign a single "IQ" score based on some sort of test.

Figure 3.1 barely scratches the surface of the profile of a typical individual. Based on numerical data, either measured on some scale, or estimated using a hypothetical norm, this individual isn't "average" in a single category. Worse, the categories themselves are multidimensional. What would a comparable graph look like if we expanded the *Knowledge* category by asking "Knowledge about what? History? Math? Computer programming? Social media? Gaming? Music? Mechanics? Poetry?" And why stop there? If the student ranked high on knowledge about mathematics, can we assume that he would rank equally high on every type of math—algebra, geometry, probability theory, statistics, calculus etc.?

Yet, current educational policy insists that *all* students of a given age must "know and be able to do" the same things, at the same time, in a variety of disciplines! This is the scientifically invalid basis for primary and secondary formal education in many countries. And when it doesn't work, it is students and teachers who are blamed.

40   *Judith Lloyd Yero*

The selection and development of specific circuits in the mind of an individual are based, among other factors, on motivational, genetic and other cognitive dimensions of the mind. The mind of *every* individual is different—strong in some areas and weaker in others. The absence of a selected ability *does not* signify that a person is less intelligent.

Questions of which learner is *smarter, more talented, more creative* or has the *better character* are equally impossible to answer because, like IQ, each of those characteristics is not only subjective but multidimensional, and thus, outside the realm of statistics or comparison. By continuing to compare and rank students on a limited number of characteristics, educators necessarily discount the unique strengths of the individual.

The Context Principle: A person's behaviour always depends on the interaction of the person and the situation; it is meaningless to evaluate performance independent of the immediate context (Rose, 2015, pp. 103–106).

Systems such as The Myers-Briggs Type Indicator and the Enneagram suggest that human traits are "hard-wired." A person is friendly or unfriendly, industrious or lazy, introverted or extroverted. If this is true, then applying a label will allow us to predict how a person will behave in a given situation (Rose, 2015, pp. 101–102). Isn't this, as well as labelling students as *remedial, gifted, smart, aggressive* or *respectful*, the poster child for fixed mindset? (Yero, 2017)

In the 1980s, University of Washington professor Yuichi Shoda undertook a study of 84 children in a residential summer camp. For 6 weeks, Shoda and a team of 77 adult camp counsellors recorded more than 14,000 hours of observations—about 167 hours per child. After sifting through the findings, Shoda discovered that each child exhibited different personalities in different situations. Shoda found that individuals were consistent in their behaviour, *but only within a given context*. For example, one child was extroverted in class, but introverted on the playground. Another was introverted in math class, but extroverted in physical education (P.E.) (Rose, 2015, pp. 104–111).

Research has shown that the same variations are found in physical, mental, emotional or psychological traits or abilities. For example, a person may be honest when observed, but dishonest in private. You may be generous to someone who is truly needy, but not to a charity that you see as well-funded. You may not cheat on your taxes, but when a cashier unknowingly gives you too much change, do you return the extra?

The Pathways Principle: There is no single, normal pathway for any type of human development—biological, mental, moral or professional.

- In all aspects of our lives and for any given goal, there are many, equally valid ways to reach the same outcome.
- The particular pathway that is optimal for a given person depends on that person's individuality (Rose, 2015, p. 129).

Grouping learners by age, and the fixed pacing in public education, are perfect examples of how ignoring the importance of individual pathways inhibits

Foundations of informal learning 41

learning. Benjamin Bloom argued that the struggles many students had in schools "had nothing to do with their capacity to learn, and everything to do with artificial constraints place on them by the education process" (Rose, 2015 p. 132). To test this, Bloom devised experiments to see what would happen when students were allowed to learn at their own pace.

In one study, students were assigned to two groups and were taught a subject they had not learned before, such as probability theory. One group of students was taught in the traditional way—a teacher presented the concepts to all students at the same pace during fixed periods of instruction. A second group of students spent *the same total time* on the *same* material, but the tutor encouraged each student to move through the material at his or her own pace—slow in some places and fast in others.

When tested on the concept, roughly *20% of the fixed-pace group achieved mastery* of the material. In the self-paced group, *more than 90% of the students achieved mastery* (Rose, 2015, pp. 131–132).

Pacing is an artefact of one-size-fits-all schooling. Its primary purpose has nothing to do with enhancing learning, and everything to do with making teaching and testing more efficient. Worse, many teachers still believe that a student who learns faster is smarter! "Equating learning speed with learning ability is irrefutably wrong" (Rose, 2015, p. 133).

Every individual learns at a different pace, and the same individual learns at a different pace for different materials. Is it any wonder that so many students feel that they are "not good at" math, science or other subjects when subjected to the fixed-pace curriculum? "Were you really not good at math or science? Or was the classroom just not aligned to your learning pace?" (Rose, 2015, p. 135)

In informal learning, individuals create their own path, inventing as they go along. Every choice—every experience—changes the possibilities available to us. "This is true whether we are learning how to crawl, or learning how to design a marketing campaign" (Rose, 2015, p. 139).

> Almost everything in traditional educational systems remains designed to ensure students receive the same exact standardized experience. ... We continue to enforce a curriculum that defines not only what students learn, but also how, when, at what pace, and in what order they learn it. In other words, whatever else we may say, **traditional public education systems violate the principles of individuality**. (Rose, 2015, p. 188) [Emphasis added]

Looking ahead

As Albert Einstein reminds us, "The significant problems we face cannot be solved at the same level of thinking we were at when we created them." Information in this chapter about the kinds of knowledge, the elements of informal learning, SDT and the principles of individuality provide educators with a new, research-driven "level of thinking" on which to base their decisions.

42   *Judith Lloyd Yero*

Typically, formal learning is externally designed and directed, concrete, lock-step, future-oriented and top-down. By contrast, informal learning is situation dependent, self-paced, present-oriented and bottom-up. Each learner is responsible for his or her own learning. Because every learner is different, informal learning cannot be tacked on to an existing curriculum. Taking a break from formal instruction and "giving learners time" for informal learning does nothing.

While educators can't *structure* informal learning, they *can* curate environments that facilitate learning! This begins by shifting the primary focus from teaching to learning—from the curriculum to an analysis of the conditions that support optimal development and learning.

In 2009, brain theorists were asked to identify the characteristics of brain-compatible instruction. The overarching idea put forth by the theorists was that an *enriched environment* was the most essential component. This environment must include the following components (Radin, 2009, p. 44):

- *Emotional* involvement, from the standpoints of both teacher and student.
- *Lowered stress and threat levels.*
- *Experiences in the classroom*, including trial and error, exploration, practice, creativity and critical thinking.
- *Challenge, problem-solving and authentic work*, in which the students do the work of learning and create their own meanings.

Notice how these characteristics mesh with SDT! To what extent do today's classrooms reflect these ideas?

Begin with questions

In order to change our "level of thinking," we must begin by questioning our beliefs about the relationship between learning and teaching, and about how knowledge is acquired. We must question the many traditions that we have taken for granted.

Shifting priorities: For example, if 70% or more of an individual's learning in job-related work is acquired through some type of informal learning (Davies, 2009, p. 106), what does that suggest about the percentage of time (and money) allotted to formal (direct) instruction? Some theorists have begun to speculate about the appropriate percentage of direct instruction and opportunities to engage in informal learning related to the context (Clark, 2013).

Essential knowledge: What is essential knowledge? What is absolutely necessary and/or indispensable? Certainly, literacy and numeracy are essential, but does every learner need to "know and be able to do" the same things. Why?

> The basic premise of the new paradigm is that each individual ..., regardless of their backgrounds, comes to school with a unique set of strengths that can be developed into great talent, which can be of contribution to a society that values unique, innovative, and human products and services. ...

Foundations of informal learning   43

> Schools operated under the new paradigm are ... places where [learners] are provided rich resources and guidance so they can explore, experiment with, and expand their interests, passions, and potentials. (Zhao, 2016b)

When a concept or skill *is* identified as truly essential, the educator's role shifts from *giving* information to curating environments that offer learners access to the concept in many different ways, as well as the freedom to choose their own path! A scenario at the secondary level might start with a Socratic discussion to set the stage and provide the conceptual foundation. Identify related real-world issues and ask learners to suggest others. Then turn learners loose to choose what aspect of the topic they want to know more about, and how they want to learn it. The fundamental question should be "How can I use what I've learned to answer other questions or solve real problems?"

Assessment: Yong Zhao supports product-based assessment to demonstrate both cognitive and non-cognitive skills, as well as cultivating creative and entrepreneurial individuals.

> Product-oriented learning engages students in producing products or services that serve an authentic purpose—that is, that meet a genuine need of someone, including oneself. In product-oriented learning, the works of students provide evidence of learning, ability, and growth ... a more comprehensive assessment of a student. (Zhao, 2016a, p. 177)

Will all learners "know and be able to do" *all* the same things. No! But why should they if they have grown in their ability to ask and answer their own questions, and can successfully solve real-world problems?

Conclusion

If there is one message that comes through loud and clear, it is that deep learning is an *individual* process that can be facilitated, but not directed from outside. It can be *assessed*, but not measured! Informal learning can only be integrated with formal learning by shifting the focus from teaching to facilitating learning!

Other chapters in this book will describe a variety of ways in which educators are integrating formal and informal learning. Research offers many new tools for rethinking and transforming education. The possibilities are limited only by our imaginations and our determination to create supportive and purpose-driven learning communities.

References

Bereiter, C. (2002). *Education and mind in the knowledge age.* Mahwah, NJ: Lawrence Erlbaum Associates.

Brosch, T., Scherer, K. R., Grandjean, D., & Sander, D. (2013, May 14). The impact of emotion on perception, attention, memory, and decision making. *Swiss Medical Weekly, 143*, w13786. doi: https://doi.org/10.4414/smw.2013.13786

44 *Judith Lloyd Yero*

Care, E., Kim, H., & Vista, A. (2017, October 17). *How Do We Teach 21st Century Skills in Classrooms.* Retrieved March 28, 2018, from https://www.brookings.edu/blog/education-plus-development/2017/10/17/how-do-we-teach-21st-century-skills-in-classrooms/

Center on the Developing Child: Harvard University (2009). *Five Numbers to Remember about Early Childhood Development.* Retrieved March 16, 2018, from https://developingchild.harvard.edu/resources/five-numbers-to-remember-about-early-childhood-development/

Clark, D. (2013). *70-20-10 Versus the 3-33 Pervasive Learning Model.* Retrieved March 21, 2018, from http://www.nwlink.com/~donclark/hrd/media/70-20-10.html

Coffield, F. (2002). The structure below the surface: Reassessing the significance of informal learning. In F. Coffield (Ed.), *The necessity of informal learning* (p. 2). Bristol, UK: The Policy Press.

Coombs, P., & Ahmed, M. (1974). *Attacking rural poverty. How non-formal education can help.* Baltimore, MD: Johns Hopkins University Press.

Cross, J. (2007). *Informal learning: Rediscovering the natural pathways that inspire innovation and performance.* San Francisco, CA: John Wiley & Sons.

Dale, M., & Bell, J. (1999). *Informal learning in the workplace; DfEE research report 134.* London, UK: Department for Education and Employment.

Damasio, A. R. (1995). *Descartes' error: Emotion, reason, and the human brain.* New York: Avon Books.

Davies, L. (2009). *Informal learning: A new model for making sense of experience.* Aldershot, Hampshire, England: Gower Publishing Limited.

Edelman, G. (1992). *Bright air, brilliant fire: On the matter of mind.* New York: Basic Books.

Erhaut, M. (2000). Non-formal learning, implicit learning, and tacit knowledge in professional work. In F. Coffield (Ed.), *The necessity of informal learning* (pp. 12–31). Bristol, UK: The Policy Press.

Gardner, H. (2011). *Frames of mind: The theory of multiple intelligences.* New York: Basic Books.

Gazzaniga, M. S. (1992). *Nature's mind.* New York: Basic Books.

Graham, J. (2011). *Children and Brain Development: What We Know about How Children Learn.* Retrieved March 28, 2018, from https://extension.umaine.edu/publications/4356e/

Hampson, S. (2017, December). *Personality and Health.* doi: 10.1093/acrefore/9780190236557.013.121

Hobson, T. (2017). *Teacher Tom's first book: Teaching and learning from preschoolers.* Seattle, WA: Peanut Butter Publishing.

Kolb, D. (1984). *Experiential learning: Experience as the source of learning and development.* Englewood Cliffs, NJ: Prentice-Hall, Inc.

Mercogliano, C. (2006). *How to grow a school: Starting and sustaining schools that work.* Oxford, NY: The Oxford Village Press.

Radin, J. L. (2009). Brain compatible teaching and learning: Implications for teacher education. *Educational Horizons, 88*(1), 44.

Reeve, J., Nix, G., & Hamm, D. (2003). Testing models of the experience of self-determination in intrinsic motivation and the conundrum of choice. *Journal of Educational Psychology, 95*(2), 375–392.

Rose, T. (2015). *The end of average: How we succeed in a world that values sameness.* New York: Harper Collins.

Ryan, R. M., & Deci, E. L. (2017). *Self-determination theory: Basic psychological needs in motivation, development, and wellness.* New York: Guilford Press.

Sahlberg, P. (2012). *Global Education Reform Movement is here!* Retrieved March 14, 2018, from Blog by Pasi Sahlberg: https://pasisahlberg.com/global-educational-reform-movement-is-here/

Yero, J. L. (2010). *Teaching in mind: How teacher thinking shapes education.* Hamilton, MT: MindFlight Publishing.

Yero, J. L. (2016). *The Myth of the Average Man.* Retrieved March 30, 2018, from Learning in Mind: Rethinking the Purpose of Education: http://learninginmind.com/myth-of-average.php

Yero, J. L. (2017). *The Dangers of Labeling Learners.* Retrieved March 28, 2018, from Learning in Mind: Rethinking the Purpose of Education: http://learninginmind.com/dangers-of-labels.php

Zhao, Y. (2015). A world at risk: An imperative for a paradigm shift to cultivate 21st century learners. *Society, 52*(2), 120–135.

Zhao, Y. (2016a). *Counting what counts: Reframing education outcomes.* Bloomington, IN: Solution Tree Press.

Zhao, Y. (2016b, October 8). From deficiency to strength: Shifting the mindset about education inequality. *Journal of Social Issues, 72*(4), 716–735.

4 Inventing a public education system for the 21st century

John H. Falk

What should be the goals of public education in the rapidly changing world of the 21st century? How effectively does the current structure of public education support these goals? How could we reinvent public education in the 21st century so that it would more fully meet society's goals and aspirations?

This chapter is organized into three major sections, answering in turn each of the three questions posed above. The first section briefly describes the changing world of the 21st century and defines the educational goals that all societies will need to adopt in order to meet these challenges; strategies that make equity central so as to insure that none are left behind. The second section reviews the affordances and constraints of the current public education system, both within what most policy-makers, educators and the public currently think of when they hear the term "public education system"—formal K-16 schooling—as well as all of the educational opportunities that exist beyond schooling, at home, across the myriad learning organizations that exist within the informal/free-choice education sector and within the workplace. The third and final section describes an entirely reconceptualized 21st century public education system; one that more equitably and effectively accomplishes the ambitious goals set out in the first section by better accommodating the learning needs of all members of society while utilizing not just some but all of a community's available learning resources. In this final section I also address some of the major challenges that must be overcome in order to implement this re-envisioned approach to public education.

New goals for a changing world

Profound changes are occurring in virtually every critical area of life. Just a few notable examples include the explosion in computing, communications and other digitally derived technologies, the profound and relentless advances in bioengineering, neurobiology, materials science and genetics, and the on-going rapid and worrying changes brought about by climate change, population growth, urbanization and worldwide habitat destruction. Collectively, these alterations are disrupting all current societal systems and institutions, and particularly those related to education. Rapid change is making current approaches to public education totally obsolete as they are of insufficient resilience, scope and value to accommodate changing societal needs. Current efforts to tweak the existing system will only result in wasted time, effort and resources. Nothing short of a total reconceptualization and restructuring of public education is required.

Goals

In the 21st century, education needs to be reaffirmed as a right not a privilege. Accordingly, a 21st century public education system needs to fully meet *all* of the lifelong learning needs of *all* people, at *all* stages of life, *wherever* a person is and *whenever* s/he faces a learning need. Public education needs to have the capacity to support every possible learning for every learner at all times, regardless of economic or physical circumstances. The public educational system needs to be truly learner-centred, a system that begins and ends with the goal of serving the real-life needs, realities and motivations of all people, rather than the needs and requirements of only the most privileged few or those prescribed by a small cadre of institutional experts. Such a public education system does not currently exist anywhere in the world, but an understanding for what such a system might look like and how to create it does. The key to creating such a system is thinking systemically, outside of the current educational box. It requires moving beyond Industrial Age, top-down, one-size-fits-all, command-and-control approaches.

Current public education system

For more than a century, educators, policy-makers and the public have clamoured for education reform and improvement. However, when educational professionals, policy-makers and the public refer to a country's "public education system," they invariably refer to just one component of the educational ecosystem, that part represented by schools, the highly structured and regulated network of preschools, primary and secondary schools, as well as institutions of higher education. This approach to education expanded worldwide during the 20th century, and almost uniformly all nations now employ Western Industrial Age, top-down methods.

Schools

Although educational reformers have lambasted schooling for over a 100 years, variously finding fault with schoolings ability to teach basic skills like reading and mathematics, workplace competencies, insure equity of opportunity or adequately prepared people for meaningful lives, proposed solutions have always related to changing one aspect or another of school practice. Historically, the primary focus of educational reform has been on pre-college schooling, but in recent years, higher education too has become a target for "reform." The implicit assumption has always been that children and youth do most of their learning in school and thus the best, if not the only way to increase the long-term public value of educational investments is by making improvements in schooling. This "school-first" paradigm is so pervasive that few educational researchers or practitioners, let alone policy-makers

48 *John H. Falk*

or the public ever question its validity. The result worldwide has been a never-ending escalation in school change and spending (Roser & Ortiz-Ospina, 2018).

In reality, schooling is not really the major source of the public's learning. Schooling is not even the primary contributor to such school-focused outcomes as standardized test scores and graduation rates. Data from the United States has documented that only 20% of the variance in pre-college student success is related to teachers (13%) and school "quality" (7%). The remaining 80% of the variation in student achievement is related to prior knowledge (41%), home environment (33%), interest and motivation (14%) and aptitude (12%) (Goodwin, 2011). This is not to say that schooling in all of its many manifestations—from preschool through university—does not make important contributions to the public's learning, it does. However, schooling's contributions do not come close to living up to their current hype as the primary mechanism for insuring an educated society; nor are they the greater social leveller as many have claimed (Hahn, 2003). Schools as currently operating, even when they are at the top of their game, are woefully inadequate for fulfilling the full extent of 21st century learning needs. So if schooling is not the answer, where would people go to learn? Actually, most people already utilize a wealth of structured and unstructured learning resources to support their learning; learning that occurs in the more than 90% of their lives they spend outside of a school classroom.

Ecosystem view

The public education system goes far beyond schools and includes a vast array of learning resources (cf. Falk et al., 2015). Today's children and adults live and learn within a variety of settings and configurations that include the home, schools, informal/free-choice learning organizations and institutions and workplace environments, all shaped and mediated by a relentless and continuously evolving stream of digital and print media. Collectively these resources form a complex ecosystem of educational opportunities. This complex ecosystem of intersecting educational entities is not a mere "backdrop" for learners, it is in fact the true foundation of lifelong learning, and arguably always has been (Illich, 1971). There is increasing evidence that individuals develop their understandings of every critical concept, be it subjects like art, history, science or such 21st century skills as teamwork, communication, relationships or empathy, both in and out of school using a vast array of community resources and networks, through an accumulation of experiences from different sources at different times (cf. Falk et al., 2017). The educational ecosystem includes institutions like schools, museums, libraries and faith-based organizations, it also includes media sources life the internet, television, films, podcasts, books, newspapers and magazines, it includes the workplace and the home, and it includes networks of individuals—friends, family and those with shared interests. Some countries, particularly those in the developed world, have vast sprawling educational ecosystems, others more limited ecosystems. But in all countries, the boundaries of when, where, why, how and with whom people learn have always been blurred.

Parents and peers

Often acknowledged but rarely full appreciated, lifelong learning now and always has begun at home. Across a wide range of studies, parental support for learning has been shown to be the single greatest contributor to both children's success in school and their success later in life (Henderson & Berla, 1994). And over the course of a lifetime, parental support is replaced by support from peers and significant adults (Reeves, 2012). Family and friends support learners' interests and build self-efficacy towards learning; they also can provide critical mentorship to young learners about how to best take advantage of the educational ecosystem.

Informal/Free-choice settings

More and more data is emerging that shows that a range of informal/free-choice resources, for example, museum-like settings, broadcast and print media and the internet, are regularly utilized to support the public's learning (Falk & Dierking, 2010). Historically, most of these publicly available educational entities have been subsumed into a single broad category, generically referred to as informal or free-choice education; however, each of these various types of resources have their own affordances and constraints and perhaps surprising to those who have long accepted schools as the primary source of public education, each of these various sources of education currently makes as great a contribution to the public's learning as does schooling, and in some cases a greater contribution (Falk & Needham, 2013; Falk, Pattison, Meier, Livingston, & Bibas, 2018; Roth & Van Eijck, 2010).

Workplace

Although rarely considered part of the educational system, the workplace is in fact a significant contributor to the public's learning. Across all fields, the need for continuous learning has become an essential ingredient for 21st century success, with some of that learning happening on-the-job but much of occurring outside the workplace (Horrigan, 2016). Although companies regularly hope that schooling will provided new employees with reasonable background and skills, according to the U.S. Council on Foreign Relations, 60% of employers are having difficulties finding qualified workers to fill vacancies at their companies (CFR, 2018). The need for businesses to invest resources in training is nothing new, but compounding the problem is the fact that both the types of work as well as even the way people work now and in the future are dramatically different than the ways of work even a decade ago. In the future, all work-related learning is likely to be "on the job."

Summary of current realities

Many of the pieces of a future public education system already exist, but none are currently sufficient in themselves. Schools are making contributions, as are

50   *John H. Falk*

informal/free-choice learning experiences, parents, friends and family and the workplace. But currently the whole is considerably less than the parts. Lacking is coordination, connectivity and, increasingly important for the 21st century, any level of individual customization (Falk et al., 2016).

Some argue that the solution resides in more successfully pairing in-school experiences with out-of-school experiences. Certainly there is evidence to support the premise that marrying the assets of formal and informal education, parental support and the workplace results in improved outcomes (NRC, 2015). However, it is fair to say that currently the contributions of schools, the workplace and all of the various out of school educational institutions and situations combined currently fall short of satisfying the needs of 21st century learning as outlined at the beginning of this chapter.

At present, the current educational ecosystem is structurally incapable of supporting every possible learning need, from every possible type of learner, across every possible topic area and every type of learning situation or context, day or night, every day of the week and every day of the year. Currently not all people have equal access to, or support for satisfying their learning needs either inside or outside of school; despite the best efforts of educational reformers. In addition, the current educational system is not truly learner-centred. Even outside of school, most constituents of the education ecosystem remain largely institution-focused. The failure of the current educational ecosystem to fully meet the challenges of 21st century learning needs is due to the lack of systemically focused financial support and the absence of any structural coordination. In short, currently most of the assets required to create a 21st century public education system already exist. But to date there has been an almost total absence of the vision and political will required to capitalize on these assets and forge them into a single, coherent, Knowledge Age-appropriate, user-focused public education system.

Towards a public education system for the 21st century

In this final section I argue that building a public education system for the 21st century does not lie in tweaking the basic structures and functions of the current public education system. Yes, more frequent interactions between the formal, informal, home and business sectors would be great, but unless the basic assumptions and processes of public education are reformed, nothing is going to fundamentally change. Needed is nothing short of a total reconceptualization, one that begins afresh with first principles for what a fully functioning 21st century educational system needs to deliver to whom, how and in what ways. Even if it was desirable to totally blow up the existing system, it of course would not be possible nor totally practical to do so. It will be important to utilize existing structures and systems, but they need to be utilized in new ways with new priorities. Each of the current educational entities needs to be assessed for how it will help advance, rather than undermine, the needs of 21st century learners. The future requires not a single institution that does it all but rather myriad institutions that collectively do it all; not one solution that can be scaled up to

Public education for the 21st century 51

the millions, but millions of solutions that collectively serve everyone. In short, the public education ecosystem of the 21st century needs to be conceptualized as functioning more like a natural ecosystem and less like a 20th century factory.

In this reimagining I do not, as some before me have, begin by assuming that meaningful educational reform can only happen within the context of broad, society-level political reform (e.g. Socialist, Marxist, Capitalist). I understand why some believe this might be necessary but my approach is more pragmatic than ideological, and totally focused, to the extent possible, on singular realities of public education.[1]

Natural ecosystems as model

Over the past decades ecologists have studied how the complicated structures and patterns of interaction within natural ecosystems generate and sustain healthy, robust and resilient communities of life. All ecosystems are examples of what are referred to as complex adaptive systems (Holland, 2006). As ecologists have attempted to understand the nature of complex adaptive systems, ranging from deserts to coral reefs, from cities to rainforests, they have focused on a few key issues, in particular the relationship between the biodiversity and interactions of the inhabitants of the ecosystem and the overall dynamic functioning of that system. Complexity theorist John Holland (2006) identified several basic properties of healthy ecosystems: (1) Diversity and Redundancy; (2) Aggregation and (3) Flows. All natural systems experience a range of perturbations and occasional catastrophes. Some are large scale like a hurricane or volcanic eruption while others can be equally disastrous but very local such as a disease outbreak that kills only the oldest most important members of a species. System theorists call these potentially disruptive relationships/events "nonlinearities." Resilient natural systems accommodate, even thrive on nonlinearity. If what is true for a natural ecosystem like a forest or ocean were equally true for the ecosystem that supports public education, then we could ask what these properties might look like within this context and how might they be expressed.

Diversity and redundancy

The generation and maintenance of diversity and redundancy is fundamental to healthy systems. The essential challenge, though, is to understand what sustains diversity and redundancy at the level of an ecosystem. Understanding the complexity of an ecosystem is less about individual species and more about the diversity of niches that exist and how they interact (Morin, 1999). Thus, it is fair to say that the goal of any vibrant 21st century public education system should be to have an enormously rich and diverse set of educational niches serving an equally diverse set of learning needs. Education policy should be designed to encourage diversification both within and across educational sectors—schools, museums, community organizations, hobby groups and businesses—where a wide range of different types of learning needs, large and small could be supported. Inherent in

52 John H. Falk

such a diverse system would be a degree of redundancy too; the redundancy necessary to insure stability, resilience and ultimately equity since greater variability will increase the likelihood that the unique needs of every learner can be met.

In the Industrial, one-size-fits-all world, educators continually struggled to find the single solution that would work and then scale it up so everyone could have access to this single solution. As a consequence there has been a proliferation of bureaucratically manageable solutions that hone to the mean; think "monoculture." Lost is the vigour of the initial success and more often than not, once "to scale," few "solutions" actually really worked for anyone—national curricula and national standards are just the most conspicuous and egregious examples of these strategies. In the Knowledge Age, goods and services are increasingly only created when and as needed. No longer is it necessary to stockpile widgets in warehouses waiting for demand. This is true for books, bicycles, automobiles; why not education? Why should everyone wanting to learn French have to learn a single form of French only at pre-specified times in their lives? Why not allow people to choose between learning Parisian French, Canadian French, Haitian French and Malian French; learning French on the weekend, the evening or on Tuesday mornings, when they are young or when they are old? As it becomes increasingly possible to customize learning goods and services, why not create a marketplace of tens of thousands of educational goods and services; each educational offering capable of being customized to every person/group's specific learning requirements. Why shouldn't educational offerings be as plentiful and diverse as learner needs?

Creating a truly diverse and sustainable ecosystem of education providers is unlikely to come about through top-down mandates; certainly this is not how natural ecosystems evolved. This is a time where a two-pronged approach, coupled with patience, will be required. There needs to be an overarching policy regime in place that respects and fully supports diverse educational providers. And there also has to be a sufficiently *laissez-faire* approach to ecosystem management that acknowledges and encourages innovation and experimentation, and the time it takes for these to develop. The public education system of the 21st century should not try to emulate the command-and-control factory models of the 20th century. In other words, national curricula and the use of high-stakes testing to determine individual success are as obsolete as the horse and buggy. Ultimately, system management will require involvement of both "top-down," for example, government and private funders, as well as "bottom-up" stake holders, for example, key representatives from the delivery side of the system. Interestingly, it is exactly this kind of widely representative, community collaborative approach that has seemed to work best in efforts to manage complex human-influenced biological systems (Booker, 2005), and currently being experimented with in number of modest ecosystem-level efforts in places like Chicago, Portland and New York City.

Of course moving to a diverse, totally decentralized (i.e. non-warehoused) approach to educational delivery means that funding can no longer be centralized; disproportionately allocated to a single, large, factory-style institution, for example, schools. Each of these diverse and abundant educational resources will

Public education for the 21st century   53

need, in fact deserve to be publicly supported in some way. Currently, close to 100% of all government funding for education goes to the formal education sector but as suggested by the data above, these policies are totally out of alignment with current realities about where, when and how the public learns. Currently funding models encourage centralization and penalize diversity and redundancy. As will be discussed later in this chapter, future funding models need to be designed in ways that diversify and expand the number of educational providers and the range of services they provide.

Aggregation

This term refers simply to the ways individuals and groups within an ecosystem become grouped into populations, populations into species and species into functional groups/guilds, for example, of all the types of creatures that eat acorns in a forest such as squirrels, deer, birds, insects, etc. Within the context of an educational ecosystem this would involve collaborations and synergies between and within the major categories of educational players. Currently, many of these collaborations exist, and by and large are looked favourably upon by educational policy-makers, for example, when entities focused on a particular age-group or subject matter such as science, art or math get together to talk about how to best support and encourage learning both in and outside of school. However, in most current education systems, the relationships between the various entities are far from equitable.

Any complex system develops what ecologists call "inhomogeneities"— irregularities or inconsistencies in how resources are utilized or distributed (Booker, 2005). In terms of the current public education ecosystem, one such inhomogeneity is the fact that formal education institutions, at all levels, are too dominant, receiving not only virtually all of the financial resources but also commanding the support of virtually all other educational entities. Normally, the development of patterns of aggregation and hierarchical organization are both a natural consequence of the self-organization of any complex system and an essential element in the robustness and resilience of the community; however, historical and/or external factors can override these self-organizing principles. For more than a century, schools have been afforded primacy within the educational community. As an outgrowth of this history, reinforced by statutes and laws, formal education institutions have not had to compete with other sectors for resources and thus have effectively distorted the community that supports public learning (cf. Falk et al., 2015). This despite the fact that, as discussed above, formal education provides only a modest portion of a society's learning opportunities and actual benefits. In the future, all entities should be supported proportionate to their actual benefit.

Flows

All ecological systems can be characterized by flows. Ecologists have typically studied the flows of things like nutrients and energy, but in a human-dominated

54 *John H. Falk*

public education ecosystem, the critical flows are of people, things, information and money. Flows provide the interconnections between parts, and transform the ecosystem from a random collection of entities into an integrated whole, a community in which all of the parts are usefully interrelated and interdependent.

The current public education system has disproportionately focused on information and money—what is to be taught and how will the system be supported, but in the new 21st century public education system, the flow of people and things through the system—learners and teachers/facilitators as well as access to the "stuff" of learning, for example, tools, supplies, settings—need to take centre stage. Currently, the flow of learners and facilitators/teachers is severely constricted, particularly for those with limited economic, political and social capital (Archer, Dawson, DeWitt, Seakins & Wong, 2015). The young and the poor of all ages currently have limited educational options, and what options are available are often of poor quality. In a fully functional educational ecosystem, learners would be able to frictionlessly move between educational opportunities as their needs and interests demanded.

Meanwhile opportunities for teachers/facilitators are also restricted due to both conceptual and marketplace impediments. At the present, a large majority of the dedicated educators within the educational ecosystem derive their livelihood from teaching/facilitating; and so it is also likely to be in the future. However, most current educators are trapped within large bureaucracies because these are the only organizations that have the resources to pay them. In a fully functional educational ecosystem, teachers/facilitators too would be able to frictionlessly move between educational opportunities as the marketplace for their services demanded.

This marketplace dysfunction is responsible for the pervasive worldwide concerns about shortages of qualified teachers. If the system was restructured to permit free flow of both learners and teachers/facilitators, there would be no shortages. That is because every person is naturally both a learner and a teacher/facilitator. The real challenge is not about a lack of individuals with appropriate skills but rather one of coordination and matching—the challenge of connecting the person who has learning needs with the qualified person willing and able to satisfy those needs.[2] If this vision sounds unduly utopian, there are ample models demonstrating that such systems can and do work. Some of the most notable and frequently cited examples come from the information technology sector where open software and free technology "boot camps" are not only common but proven to be totally sustainable. Other examples include the Kahn Academy and MOOCs[3] where free lessons on a vast array of topics are made freely available to anyone.

"Things" too are key to the support of 21st century learning. Although understandably a great deal of educational emphasis of late has been focused on the availability of digital technologies, a vibrant educational ecosystem requires that learners also have access to other types of "stuff" as well. Learning theorists have for years (e.g. Illich, 1971) lamented the "locking-up" of the stuff of learning, for example, nature to play in, machines to take apart, spaces in which

Public education for the 21st century 55

real people can be seen working, laboratories and workshops where experiments can be conducted. If society's learning needs are to be fully supported then a whole host of tangible assets will need to be made readily available for not only facilitated groups but also individual, self-directed learning. The "do it yourself" (DIY) and Maker Movement represent growing counter-movements which have recently come to prominence in response to these issues with hubs springing up in libraries, schools and museums of all types (Rosa, Ferretti, Guimaraes Pereira, Panella, & Wanner, 2014).

Information is also a key flow within the educational ecosystem, and not surprisingly, currently information flows too are severely constricted. Increasingly, people's need for new and better information is growing exponentially, and this is true both at home and in the workplace. The pace of change is relentless and only the most informed are able to sustain an acceptable level of intellectual, emotional and economic comfort. As information resources have become increasingly global, people need to be able to access the best and most current information in the most efficient and effective manner possible. The current educational system actually inhibits the free flow of information. Sources of knowledge are becoming increasingly distributed and global, and so too needs be mechanisms for accessing that knowledge. Obviously much of this information acquisition will involve digital resources, including the use of ever more sophisticated artificial intelligence (AI) programmes. But ironically, the need for people as teachers/facilitators will not diminish, it will actually only increase. In this new system, the need for individuals with the know-how and commitment to support just-in-time learning will be at a premium, but these people will need to be appropriately remunerated for their services. In the Industrial Age, innovation was driven by companies, but in the new Knowledge Age, innovation will be driven increasingly by individuals (Friedman, 2016).

This brings us the fourth major flow in the system, money. As with the today's public education system, public and private funding of education will be required in order to fuel this new, 21st century educational system. Without question, if the 21st century goal of equally serving every age group, every population, every subject area and every community equally is to be achieved, changes in the distribution of resources will be required. Currently it is institutions, not individuals primarily in control. Institutions receive the funding and institutions set priorities for education. The public education system funding model needs to change, from top-down to bottom-up, from institutions to individuals. This single change would arguably be the single biggest catalyst to reforming the way education happens in the world. In this new model, societies would fund individual people—all people—with each person receiving sufficient funding to pursue their educational needs. It would make sense for funding to be skewed towards younger people, but everyone, every year of their life, should receive some financial support for their learning. Ideally monies would be distributed in ways that would restrict use to solely educational purposes, perhaps some kind of educational debit card.[4] Unlike the current

56 *John H. Falk*

school voucher systems advocated by some, primarily in order to divert funds from government schools to private schools, these educational supports would be spendable on ANY educationally relevant use. This would create something more akin to a real free market for educational services including individuals as well as organizations big and small. Such a system would absolutely need to be monitored; both from above to prevent abuse as well as from below to insure quality and service, presumably through some kind of individual rating and feedback system.

This is not as novel an idea as some might think. Ivan Illich (1971) proposed this solution decades ago, and a number of societies have flirted with variants of this idea. For example, recently the Italian government, in an effort to combat extremism, provided every 18-year-old youth in the country a "cultural allowance" which allows them access to any cultural resource—book, cinema, museum or archive. Similar ideas are inherent in the idea of a guaranteed minimum annual income explored by several countries and communities in recent years.

Thus, if the goal is to create a sustainable and resilient 21st century public education that has the capacity to meet the learning needs of all citizens—24-7-365-70+ years—then such a system must be designed as a system of the whole. In other words, every person needs to think of themselves as both a learner and an educator, and each individual needs to have sufficient funds to be able to secure the learning resources they need and be financially rewarded in turn when they support the learning needs of others. Equally, every institution in society needs to be involved—every business, every branch of government and of course every social service and community-oriented entity; all need to see themselves as part of the educational system and all must see not only how they can contribute but how they will benefit.

It also means that public education managers, whether public or private, need to attend to both the exogenous, for example, money, and endogenous flows, for example, people, things and information, within the ecosystem in ways designed to support and maintain a balanced, healthy and fair system. Currently the flows within the public education system are managed in a non-systemic way, with only some flows considered worth monitoring. Managers of a 21st century public education system will need to monitor the entire ecosystem for gaps and deficiencies in educational opportunities, for irregularities, abuses and dysfunctional aggregations. Their main goal will be to support efficient, effective and equitable flows of learners, facilitators/teachers, things, information and, of course, financial resources.

Nonlinearity

The property of nonlinearity is the change in the way the system interacts as the system evolves and develops. Complex adaptive biological systems change primarily through the reinforcement of chance events, such as mutation and environmental variation operating at local levels; the potential for alternative developmental pathways in such systems are enormous. In natural ecosystems,

Public education for the 21st century 57

these nonlinear events sometimes happen sufficiently infrequently that the system has time to evolve and recuperate but not always, as suggested earlier a new epidemic can wipe out key members of a species or even whole groups essential to the functioning of other parts of the system. In such cases, the system needs to be sufficiently complex and resilient to bounce back; in fact this is the definition of what it means to be resilient.

In the rapidly changing human world of the Knowledge Age, nonlinear events happen continuously and seemingly with ever increasing frequency. The current top-down, zero-sum, primarily school-first approach to public education management is woefully inadequate for dealing with continuous, rapid change. The time has come for all nations to mindfully encourage bottom-up, nonlinear approaches to public learning.

Inherent in the idea of nonlinearity is that changes initiated at one level, for example, learner needs, can often influence events at other levels, for example, institutional priorities. In the future public educational system envisioned here, these nonlinarites will actually be encouraged rather than discouraged, as happens currently, because the major driver of system-wide improvement will be the rapidly and ever-changing requirements and interests of individual learners rather than the glacially changing needs of institutional bureaucracies.

Thus another key innovation of this new system will be to not only put financial resources in the hands of learners but also systematically empower and support learners in the wise use those resources in ways customized to their own particular learning needs and interest. Every individual would be supported, from birth until death, in the development of their own personal learning projects and goals, and in the securing the information, human and material resources necessary for achieving those projects and goals. Obviously children and adults from poor or otherwise disadvantaged populations, for example, recent immigrants, minorities, individuals with disabilities would require additional support in this activity, but learning how to become a self-motivated, lifelong learner and having the support to accomplish one's learning projects and goals is actually first and foremost what this new public education system should be designed to accomplish.

Challenges

It is a reality of the current public education system that society has come to depend upon institutions like schools and universities to serve numerous, educationally unrelated functions, for example, pre-college schools provide "free" day care and many times free lunches and other social services, while colleges and universities provide a time and space for late adolescents to learn about independent living. Going forward, the importance to society of these functions are not going to go away. However, it is time that these critical societal concerns be resolved through their own 21st century solutions rather than conflating their solution with those of public education. It is time to directly tackle the critical

58   *John H. Falk*

task of insuring a quality 21st century education for all citizens and do so without encumbering its solution by weighing it down with a long list of essential, but educationally irrelevant problems that were, for purely historical reasons, appended to the institutional goals of schooling.

Equally important will be the task of assessing the quality of the 21st century educational system. Currently, high-stakes tests are failing to fulfil the assessment requirements of even the current limited definition of public education system. Going forward, such standardized testing would be totally inappropriate for assessing the greatly expanded—in scope and scale—public education system described here. Basically what's needed is a totally new, but equally robust process for measuring each person's unique educational progress. Required is a suitable short-term proxy for personal learning. A measure that is at the same time valid, reliable and generalizable and of course, one that is also relatively easy to implement. These new measures of educational progress would ideally be built into the learning process itself, a mechanism for providing continual feedback to the learner rather than, as in currently the case, assessment that is disconnected from actual learning and primarily designed to be judgemental and inform institutions rather than learners. This is a tall order but I would suggest it is possible if we really understood what is actually driving the vast majority of people to learn in the 21st century. It is not, as was assumed to be case for most of the last several hundred years, extrinsically driven needs such as grades and degrees leading to a good job, but rather it is the intrinsically driven needs of interest, curiosity and the desire to live a healthier, more secure and fulfilled life. With that end in mind I would like to suggest that the metric of choice for 21st century public education should be *satisfaction*.

The construct of satisfaction I am proposing is not the limited, almost trivial leisure attraction version of satisfaction, that is, "did you enjoy your time today?" Rather I propose using the broader, more robust measure of the satisfaction that derives from fulfilment of one's needs. As I have previously described (Falk, 2018), satisfaction in this context involves equal measures of cognitive, physical, social and affective dimensions. This needs-based measure of satisfaction highly correlates with not only deeply felt feelings of enjoyment, physical well-being and social and emotional fulfilment, but also with personal intellectual fulfilment. It also strongly correlates with expectations, including whether an individual has achieved his/her personal short- and long-term learning projects and goals. Ultimately, it also highly correlates with whether or not a person was pleased with the support they received from an educational provider. In other words, rather than merely measuring short-term changes in knowledge or understanding, a robust measure of satisfaction, if appropriately embedded into practice as a way of capturing authentic progress towards achieving some specific desired practice, skill or concept, would serve as an excellent proxy measure for nearly all of the types of much deeper, and ultimately more important dimensions of an educational experience that we know undergird long-term learning—emotion, commitment,

Public education for the 21st century 59

sense of accomplishment, cognitive growth, social mediation and personal choice and control. And if properly constructed, a measure of satisfaction would always be situated within the realities of a specific task or setting and always relative to each individual. In other words, consistent with proven social-constructivist notions of learning, a change-based model of satisfaction would take into account each individual's initial state as well as the unique context in which learning was occurring.

If such a robust measure of success existed, then each individual would be able to set their own criteria of "success" and continuously monitor their own progress to determine if they are making as much progress as they hoped. Collectively, the "success" of the educational system as a whole, or even that part being monitored by particular groups, could also be measured. But again, "success" would be dependent upon seeing that all individuals within the system were achieving personal growth and development, rather than as currently measured by standardized tests, that some individuals exceed and others fall below some arbitrary, predetermined threshold or mean. Armed with such a valid measure of success, teachers/facilitators could design and mediate educational experiences that keyed in on particular aspects of educational progress, for example emotional satisfaction, feelings of intellectual commitment and progress, heightened feelings of self-efficacy, enhanced perceptions of choice and control, and of course improved understanding, skills and competence. It would also provide targeted feedback to mentors and educational teachers/facilitators. Allowing them to see which pieces of the puzzle for each learner need improvement and how best to support learner accomplishments.

Finally, although an open, competitive system is desirable, like all fundamental systems this one too creates opportunities for abuse. There will absolutely be the need for some form of governmental oversight and regulation to prevent fraud, to monitor quality and insure personal safety. Advanced systems of information analytics will be essential to assuring equity and fairness in such an information-dependent system. However, information analytics will also be the Achilles heel of a system like this. Thus a key component will be the need for stringent and on-going, safeguards to insure individual privacy and data security.

Conclusion

Over the course of this chapter I have laid out a blueprint for what a truly responsive, vibrant and resilient 21st century educational system might look like, as well as some initial thoughts on what would be required to get from here to there. The primary goal for a successful, resilient 21st century public education system needs to be adaptability, but additional goals include a commitment to equity, effectiveness and some measure of efficiency. The exact details of how such system might actually operate can and likely will need to vary from society to society. All systems will need to be able to support diversity and redundancy, foster

60 *John H. Falk*

adaptive aggregations, insure that all the flows operate smoothly and accept and accommodate whatever nonlinearities might arise, but there is no reason that all such systems should or even could be identical.

I believe that we have no choice but to let go of the past and embrace a whole new future, one where the public education system is as diverse and complex as the most ancient rainforest. It is time to reinvent the functioning of the public education system so that it supports not only a handful of prescripted pathways but millions of unique, individually determined and supported lifelong educational trajectories. We must build a public education system that is sufficiently flexible and responsive to enable everyone to be successful; however, they might personally define success.

Will it be easy to create this kind of complex, adaptable public education system starting from where we are now? Of course the answer is NO. Is it essential? YES! The needs to overcome the current inertia and vested interests that impede significant change have never been clearer. The world's current educational systems are crippling societies, and even more damning, they are warping and wasting the lives and potential of billions of people. The reality is, this type of future is coming, sooner or later. Let's make it sooner!

Notes

1. I have designed a model that, for better or worse, builds on the reality that most of the day-to-day needs of most of the people within the world currently depend upon some variant of a government-regulated, free-market system where the availability and cost of goods and services are largely, but not exclusively driven by the rules of supply and demand.
2. A variation on this idea was first proposed by Ivan Illich (1971).
3. MOOC stands for massive, open, online course.
4. I will need to leave to another, longer chapter the details on how best to create, manage and enforce such a system.

References

Archer, L., Dawson, E., DeWitt, J., Seakins, A., & Wong, B. (2015). "Science capital": A conceptual, methodological, and empirical argument for extending bourdieusian notions of capital beyond the arts. *Journal of Research in Science Teaching, 52*(7), 922–948.

Booker, L. S. (2005). *Perspectives on adaptation in natural and artificial systems.* Oxford, UK: Oxford University Press.

Council on Foreign Relations Independent Task Force. Retrieved January, 2018, from http://www.cfr.org/united-states/us-education-reform-national-security/p27618

Falk, J. H. (2018). *Born to choose: Evolution, self and well-being.* London, UK: Routledge.

Falk, J. H., & Dierking, L. D. (2010). The 95% solution: School is not where most Americans learn most of their science. *American Scientist, 98*, 486–493.

Falk, J. H., Dierking, L. D., Osborne, J., Wenger, M., Dawson, E., & Wong, B. (2015). Analyzing science education in the U.K.: Taking a system-wide approach. *Science Education, 99*(1), 145–173.

Falk, J. H., Dierking, L. D., Staus, N., Penuel, W., Wyld, J., & Bailey, D. (2016). Understanding youth STEM interest pathways within a single community: The synergies project. *International Journal of Science Education, Part B, 6*(4), 369–384.

Public education for the 21st century   61

Falk, J. H., & Needham, M. D. (2013). Factors contributing to adult knowledge of science and technology. *Journal of Research in Science Teaching, 50*(4), 431–452.

Falk, J. H., Pattison, S., Meier, D., Livingston, K. & Bibas, D. (2018). The contribution of science-rich resources to public science interest. *Journal of Research in Science Teaching, 55*(3), 422–445.

Falk, J. H., Storksdieck, M., Dierking, L. D., Babendure, J., Canzoneri, N., Pattison, S., … Palmquist, S. (2017). *The learning system,* In R. Ottinger (Ed.), *STEM ready America,* Flint, MI: Charles Stewart Mott Foundation.

Friedman, T. (2016). *Thank you for being late: An optimist's guide to thriving in the age of accelerations.* New York: Farrar, Straus and Giroux.

Goodwin, B. (2011). *Simply better: Doing what matters to change the odds for student success,* Alexandria, VA: ASCD.

Hahn, J. (2003). Is public education really the great equalizer? Retrieved March, 2018, from http://www.studlife.com/archives/Forum/2003/11/07/Ispubliceducationreallythe greatequalizer/

Henderson, A., & Berla, N. (Eds.). (1994). *A new generation of evidence: The family is critical to student achievement* (a report from the national committee for citizens in education), Washington, DC: National Center for Law and Education.

Holland, J. E. (2006). Studying complex adaptive systems. *Journal of Systems Science & Complexity, 19*(1), 1–8.

Horrigan, J. B. (2016). Lifelong learning and technology. Pew Center for Research: Internet & Technology. Technical Report. Retrieved February 03, 2018, from http://www.pewinternet.org/2016/03/22/lifelong-learning-and-technology/

Illich, I. (1971). *Deschooling society.* London, UK: Calder and Boyars.

Morin, P. J. (1999). *Community ecology.* New York: Wiley-Blackwell Press.

National Research Council. (2015). *Identifying and supporting productive STEM programs in out-of-school settings.* Washington, DC: National Academy Press.

Reeves, E. B. (2012). The effects of opportunity to learn, family socioeconomic status, and friends on the rural math achievement gap in high school. *American Behavioral Scientist, 56*(7), 887–907.

Rosa, P., Ferretti, F., Guimaraes Pereira, A., Panella, F., & Wanner, M. (2014). Overview of the Maker Movement in the European Union. JRC Technical Report. Brussels: EU. Retrieved March 13, 2018, from https://ec.europa.eu/jrc/en/publication/overview-maker-movement-european-union

Roser, M., & Ortiz-Ospina, E. (2018). Our World in Data. Retrieved March 13, 2018, from https://ourworldindata.org/global-rise-of-education

Roth, W-M., & Van Eijck, M. (2010). Fullness of life as minimal unit: STEM learning across the life span. *Science Education, 94,* 1027–1048.

5 The relationship between formal and informal learning

Daniel A. Tillman, Song A. An, and William H. Robertson

Introduction

In this chapter, we investigate the relationship between formal and informal learning, first from a historical perspective, then from a contemporary standpoint and lastly as an attempt at predicting the future dynamic between formal and informal learning. Collectively, these three chief sections of our narrative provide a chronological outline of the evolving dynamic that exists among formal and informal learning. This chapter is thus an attempt to address the contemporary scenario in which educators find themselves, attempting to bridge the divide across prescribed formal education and the oftentimes student-preferred informal learning that occurs outside of the classroom.

It was during the European Renaissance period, lasting from approximately 1300 to 1700 A.D., that an optimal relationship between formal and informal learning began to take shape. In this section, we will trace the development of the relationship between formal and informal learning as it evolved from formative informal learning structures that were developed early on in civilization, and then transitioned via the more advanced pedagogical models created by the wealthy, the military, the monastery and the professional guilds. We will conclude the section with a discussion of how it took an Industrial Age mentality to fully implement formal education at the industrial scale, leading us to our modern predicament. Thus, this section will set up the discussion in the next section, which will use an academic approach to theorize the optimal relationship between formal and informal learning.

A brief history

For humans learning something in prehistoric times, there was no formalized education, only a rudimentary model of trying stuff out and then sharing the important discoveries (Gutek, 1972; Russell, 2004). Those who managed to develop some mastery of skills such as hunting or fire-making were probably keen to share it with their peers, and their peers were even more keen to learn it from the masters. So, in a basic sense, even during these early informal learning experiences, the rudiments of a formal learning model were beginning to

Formal and informal learning 63

form: Somebody had knowledge to share, and someone else wished to obtain that knowledge for themselves (Gutek, 1997). Some other features of this early learning model were as follows: (1) instruction was delivered primarily through projects focused on solving real-world problems; (2) because of the nature of the projects, the learning was internally motivated and (3) there was no formalization of roles such as "teacher" or "student," but rather there was mutual affinity for a meaningful project. Informal learning was happening everywhere during the early stages of civilization from nomads to farmers, an essential process to figuring out the world around us—and inherent within it were the seeds for growing the formal educational systems with which we would one day grow our own collective understanding of the world we are living in, and the universe around it (Russell, 2004).

In a sense, ancient history begins with the advent of systematic formalized education. Several different types of formal education seem to have each arisen independently of each other, and each of these models continues to guide us nowadays. For the upper class, the advantages of hiring professional one-on-one tutors for their children's edification led to some of the classic relationships of history, including that between Aristotle and Alexander the Great. Aristotle's own tutor, Plato, sought to create an academy wherein all learning could be codified, and the impact of this project continues to shape our direction today (Russell, 2004). But for the majority of those exposed to formal learning in ancient society, the choices fell among the various schools of professional apprenticeship that were developing. Foremost among these, at least in terms of bluster and braggadocio, was the military model of education, which focused to a great extent on maintaining discipline and structure (Foucault, 2012). Some of the more beneficial features of the military-education model persist with us today, and this will be discussed in greater detail later in the section focusing on transitioning into the scale-up of the Industrial Age formalization of education. Similar to the military model, various monastic schools aligned with the more organized religions began to develop their own pedagogical approaches, some of which were surprisingly similar to those generated by their military-minded counterparts. But it was within the burgeoning professional trades that the prevailing apprenticeship model perhaps best found its footing (Freeman, 2007).

With the development of specialized occupations, from butcher to blacksmith and winemaker to deep-sea fisherman, there grew a need for a formal learning model that did not require a deftly capable and prepared instructor—but instead employed the brute approach of extensive time-on-task work done by a student under the strict and watchful guidance of an expert (Freeman, 2007). The early stages of an apprenticeship within this model are notoriously merciless, as the student is subjected to years of labor at those tasks deemed beneath the master's station. This educational model constitutes the first wave of transitioning from informal to formal education because the role of the teacher and role of the student are clearly demarcated. And though the student-apprentice's work was often mindless, perhaps even dangerous, by demonstrating tenacity and commitment, the apprentice eventually earned the right to move on to

64 *Tillman, An, and Robertson*

more creative or even supervisory roles within the professional guild, and one day might even demonstrate themselves to be worthy of the title master craftsman, from whence they will be taking on the task of preparing apprentices of their own.

Each of these educational models for formalizing the learning process continues with us in various manifestations during the modern era, and their continued longevity is a testament to the legitimacy of their pedagogical foundations (Ferster, 2014). However, that is not to say that the road to the present has not been arduous and fraught with potential pitfalls—long periods of stagnant learning having punctuated the human experience, with the medieval period known as the Dark Ages serving as the most telling example (Russell, 2004). A troubling time lasting hundreds of years, this period was instantiated by the fall of Rome, and some historians do not consider it to have ended until the advent of the Renaissance. Yet while the lack of progressive learning seems to temporarily stymie humanity as a whole, there were of course pockets of creativity, and the formalization of the monastic educational model via the considerable growth of the Catholic Church is one such example. Likewise, the full formalization of the apprenticeship education model was developed during this era by the various professional trade guilds, each of which had their own specialized culture and requirements.

Yet it was not until the onset of the blooming creativity-driven age known as the Renaissance that formalized education exited its developmental slump and began once again to enjoy a period of impressive innovation and flourishing productivity (Pettegree, 2010). In particular, it was the onset of impactful hybrid education during this time that seems to have been a catalyst for the changes that we see occurring throughout society. During hybrid education, wherein the advantages of both formal learning and informal learning are leveraged to amplify each other, we see the onset of a genuinely modern attitude towards education, built upon the realization that the best models of education are those that encourage insightful creative productivity. The iconic notion of the well-versed "Renaissance Man" and "Renaissance Woman" serve as contemporary confirmation of the imposing impression that this period of ingenuity has had upon the modern mind.

As previously discussed, it was during the Renaissance that an optimal relationship between formal and informal learning began to shape—and perhaps no artifact from the era better represents this dynamic than the concept of a creator's portfolio. Regardless of whether the collection consists of colourful childhood drawings attached to a diligent mother's refrigerator, or the complete collected works of Leonardo da Vinci, a portfolio of the individual maker's best products is the fundamental demonstration of that person's understanding of the mediums through which they have chosen to express themselves. The modern professional's resume, with its quintessential bullet points condensing a lifetime of effort into finite, concisely expressed accomplishments, has in our present time become the equivalent standard for the creator's portfolio, essentially summarizing each person as a professional in their field.

To compartmentalize the entirety of humanity into individual mechanisms, each with a clearly stated role and rank, required nothing less than the brute ruthlessness inherent to the Industrial Age. The manufacturing of large-scale formal education was a non-trivial task, and though, as we have discussed, the formative structure was developed early on civilization, via pedagogical models from the wealthy, the military, the monastery and the professional guilds, it took an Industrial Age mentality to genuinely implement formal education at the industrial scale.

A survey of the current relationship between formal and informal learning

Within the historical context described, this chapter is an attempt to address the contemporary scenario in which educators find themselves—attempting to bridge the divide across prescribed formal education and the chosen informal learning that occurs outside of the classroom. One of the predominant modern attempts at optimizing the relationship between formal and informal learning environments is the entertainment-education (E-E) model. E-E pedagogy combines school subjects such as math and science with topics students find authentically engaging like popular dances, action sports and kid-friendly robotics.

Entertainment-education, also sometimes abbreviated as E-E or referred to as edutainment (e.g. Parker, 1990), is defined as "the intentional placement of educational content in entertainment messages" (Singhal, 2007; Singhal & Rogers, 2002). The E-E model strives to combine the genuine engagement that arises during informal education with the key learning goals that are the domain of formal education. The E-E strategy employs learning theories, including social cognitive theory, social learning theory, social constructivism, dramatic theories and diffusion of innovations (Singhal et al., 2006; Singhal & Rogers, 2002). The E-E strategy has resulted in numerous illustrative examples, including astronauts teaching science from outer space (An et al., 2016) and the use of 3D printers in STEM education (Tillman, An, Cohen, Kjellstrom, & Boren, 2014, 2015).

In this section of the chapter, we will discuss an E-E instructional model with clear steps for other educators to follow in order to create their own linkages between formal and informal learning. Two illustrative exemplars of the E-E approach that we will explore in depth during this discussion are dance-math and skateboarding-science.

Divided into the most fundamental components, the five steps for the E-E instructional model are

1 determine what educational content should be taught;
2 determine what entertainment context should be employed;
3 develop lesson integrating content into context;
4 implement and assess lessons with pilot group and
5 revise lessons to address any issues that arose.

66   *Tillman, An, and Robertson*

Restated in pseudo-algebraic notation, the five steps in the E-E model are

1   determine E_1;
2   determine E_2;
3   integrate E_1 with E_2;
4   pilot E-E and
5   revise E-E.

Within this sequence of steps, it is usually step 3, wherein the entertainment content is integrated with the educational context, that causes practitioners the most difficulty. As a practical solution to overcoming some of the common obstacles often faced at this stage, we offer the suggestion of employing a method similar to the approach used for planning to teach with problem-based lessons. Specifically, be sure to consider: Content and task decisions such as determining the curricular and content goals; considering your students' needs and interests; selecting, designing or adapting a task to fit the content and designing lesson assessments. As discussed in the 9th edition of *Elementary and Middle School Mathematics*, during the lesson plans, there should be preparatory *before* activities, planned *during* questions and extensions, as well as a strategy for the *after* discussion (Van de Walle, Karp, & Bay-Williams, 2016). Afterward, reflecting on the design and its implementation, there will be opportunities for improving the alignment within the lesson between the educational content and entertainment context, better anticipating student approaches and questions, as well as identifying the essential concepts (and potential misconceptions) that are at the core of the lessons.

Some further tips are that, during the before phase, it is important to make sure students understand the task they are undertaking, that you establish expectations about how students are to work and what products are to be created, as well as to prepare students mentally for the task by activating students' prior knowledge related to the problem. During the lessons, "let go" (Van de Walle et al., 2016)—meaning that you should give students a chance to (a) work with minimal guidance; (b) observe interactions and listen for group ideas, strategies and work processes to use in class discussions; (c) offer assistance when needed, either when members of a group raise their hands or if a group is not working well; as well as (d) provide an extension for groups that finish more quickly than others. In the after phase, an instructor should be sure to engage the class in productive discussion by encouraging student-student dialogue and not just student-teacher dialogue (which often excludes other class members); listen actively without evaluation, having students explain methods, solutions and justifications for their answers; as well as summarize main ideas and identify problems that could be used for further E-E explorations.

As the above discussion illustrates, the implementation of this "simple" E-E model can be deceptively difficult. Therefore, we will employ this section of the chapter to illustrate the E-E instructional model with clear steps, using "music-math" and "skateboarding-science" as examples.

Learning mathematics through music-themed contexts

In the past 5 years, we have developed and field-tested a number of informal mathematics learning modules that employ a music theme. The primary focus of these mathematics learning modules was on developing conceptual connections that leverage students' experiences with music, including listening, playing and composing music to help them construct new knowledge about real-world mathematics concepts. Through a collaborative effort, musicians and STEM specialists, including mathematicians, educational technologists and material engineers, worked together to develop music-themed informal mathematics learning modules. These were then used for facilitating elementary school students' comprehension, investigation and application of mathematical and scientific concepts through music creation, performance and the analysis of original music works as learning activities. The preliminary versions of the music-themed informal mathematics learning modules were designed and then tested at a 2013 summer camp in a university lab setting, and the revised versions of modules were implemented in classroom-based summer camps (2014–2017) with an aggregate of over 400 participants.

In our previous studies, which analyzed over 200 teachers' instructional designs (An et al., 2015; An & Tillman, 2014) and over 80 lesson implementations with students (An, Capraro, & Tillman, 2013; An et al., 2016; An & Tillman, 2015), we found that effective mixtures of informal music and formal mathematics learning requires that the student participants remain cognitively engaged with the mathematics tasks via the music-themed activities—by manipulating objects, performing activities and applying the skills that form the cognitive links between existing knowledge and new knowledge. Based on our research findings, the key standard to evaluate the quality of informal education's connections to formal educational goals is whether educators could use students' informal activity products (in this case, music-themed) as resources to examine mathematical concepts and assign math tasks based on students' own music activity outcomes. The following paragraphs describe five music-based informal learning module themes that we have found can serve to facilitate students' mathematical understanding through informal explorations.

Music performance observation

Students observed professional musicians' music production processes and interacted with musicians to discuss the relationships between music and mathematics. Students recognized that developing a music performance is a blend of mathematics and the arts and that there are important similarities in the kinds of problems, and approaches to problems, employed by both musical artists and STEM professionals. The World Music Ensemble, a band with undergraduate, graduate music majors and music professors, offered student participants opportunities to observe their individual practice sessions, rehearsals and performances. The World Music Ensemble demonstrated a variety of instruments and

68 *Tillman, An, and Robertson*

music from different cultures (e.g. Hispanic, Middle Eastern, Chinese) so that students observed similarities and differences across both musical products and the societies that produce them. Using a musical instrument classification system, students learned to identify and understand the mathematics relationships behind the sound production of idiophones, membranophones, chordophones, aerophones and electrophones. Such mathematical relationships included the structures of complex music forms, waveform shapes, frequency components, timbre, wave modulation (strike/attack, sustain, tremolo, fade), rhythm and dynamic patterns. For example, students explored arithmetic sequences in terms of overtone series and explore geometric sequences in terms of chromatic scale and guitar fret/flute figuring locations.

Music composition

Students understood how scientists and artists alike use an iterative creative process to arrange and combine pieces to delight their audiences. To facilitate novice students in composing and playing their own music, graphical notations were used as the main approach to represent music visually by using colours, shapes, numbers and letters to represent the music notes (An & Capraro, 2011). Based on this graphical notation system, students composed music by placing a group of colour cards on their desk and playing colour-coded instruments such as handbells and boomwhackers. This hands-on and visual-based music composition-playing system provided students with opportunities to (1) explore and analyze algebraic patterns and proportional relationships, (2) make geometrical transformations, (3) conduct measurement and design measurement instruments and (4) design and conduct experiments to explore probabilities such as permutation and combination within chords and melody development processes, in self-composed or professional music works. In addition to composing music, students also (1) analyzed relevance/accuracy of mathematical language in existing lyrics and (2) wrote original lyrics for their own composed melodies or existing songs.

Musical instrument making

Students learned to understand the principles of scientific inquiry and investigation by formulating hypotheses about how changing the properties of an instrument will affect its sound and testing their hypotheses. Students explored one-, two- and three-dimensional (3D) geometric concepts and relationships in different types of musical instruments (idiophones, membranophones, chordophones and aerophones) and explored acoustical physics to understand how the patterns of shapes, dimensions and materials affect instrument sound and tones. Specifically, students were offered opportunities to (1) use geometry and measurement concepts to design and construct different types of instruments, (2) fabricate musical instruments by using 3D printers with a variety of plastic, mental and hybrid materials, (3) use knowledge of sound production for basic acoustic instrument types to experiment with combinations of vibrating strings, pipes, bells, membranes and reeds, and to manipulate variables (length, size, volume, shape, material and tension), (4) recognize the iterative process by which a set of musical instruments was designed to produce a palette of music "colours," (5) determine the impact of such manipulation on the sound properties of pitch, tone quality or timbre, loudness and resonance time and (6) test how the combinations of sound waves with patterns of regular or irregular pitch intervals can cause different feelings or emotions.

Music video production

Students developed and produced music videos demonstrating STEM concepts, procedures and processes through a variety of representations. Supported by rapid prototyping design technologies such as green-screen chroma key compositing, students created music video productions incorporating composited video via a suite of student-friendly video editing software packages. This pedagogical approach presented an opportunity for students to cognitively construct STEM content knowledge, while simultaneously working in the real-world context of music video creation. Incorporating music video production-themed activities supported by rapid prototyping design technologies into maths pedagogy supported the objective of the NCTM to provide contextualized mathematics learning experiences to students as an opportunity to teach them about the real-world connections and applications of mathematical problem-solving skills. Using readily available and easily accessible technology, student participants learned to grasp fundamental principles of video making and editing technology, and video editing software let learners connect "what they hear" with "what they see" in multiple multimedia formats.

Collaborative music performance

Students were guided to prepare and perform a series of concerts in collaboration with aspiring professional musicians (undergraduate seniors with a major in music). Throughout this process, students learned to understand how constraints and objectives—such as artistic merit, cost, schedule and skillsets—help shape the design of a music performance. Specifically, as a part of a summative performance, students were directed to (1) apply arithmetic, geometrical and algebraic patterns in their music composition, arrangement and orchestration process to prepare a semi-professional instrumental ensemble for a group of musicians, (2) play existing and original music by using the instruments that they designed and fabricated individually and in groups and (3) upload and share their musical works as well as their mathematical findings through a video-sharing website.

The general framework across our research has been to build on the natural cognitive overlaps between the informal learning element (music) and the formal learning element (mathematics), so as to pedagogically develop such

70 *Tillman, An, and Robertson*

transdisciplinary contexts into opportunities for students to discover, recognize, analyze and apply mathematics in engaging learning settings. Positive impacts have accumulated across our studies investigating the effects of music-mathematics integrated education for preservice teachers and elementary and middle school students. For mathematics teachers, music-themed mathematics activities have served as a meaningful and accessible context for transforming traditional mathematics pedagogy. For mathematics learners, music has enabled them to represent their mathematical ideas from a different perspective, which supports their learning as they pursue conceptual understanding via multiple cognitive and affective experiences (An et al., 2013; An, Tillman, Boren, & Wang, 2014; An, Tillman, & Paez, 2015). Our studies have also indicated that music activities created an appropriate learning environment for supporting team work and minimizing language and culture barriers for English-language learners, and that such learning strategies can motivate students to undertake more challenging mathematical tasks (An et al., 2016; An & Tillman, 2015).

Learning science through action sports

Often, students will ask their teacher, "What is the point of this?" or "Why are we doing this anyway?" They want to know exactly how the material they're learning in class will apply to their everyday lives because, at times, it seems disconnected from what they do. Physical science concepts are often taught quite traditionally in school, and in an almost clinical manner, isolated to a specific circumstance within a classroom. This is what disconnects the tools and the content from the students' experiences. There is a real need for educators to explore and connect content in settings that are both authentic and relatable for students.

Each learner understands content and concepts differently based on his or her previous experiences, and the materials help to provide a context for understanding both science concepts and real-world connections. So much fascinating content is at the fingertips of learners everywhere, and with computer access and technology becoming more affordable, more information is accessible. The main emphasis is to engage students in the exploration of science and mathematics topics in a real-world context and to link education to delivery methods that integrate entertainment value and presentation. The students need opportunities to address misconceptions and to develop concepts in real-world situations. As Rutherford and Algren (1990, p. 198) stated: "Students come to school with their own ideas, some correct and some incorrect, about almost every topic they are likely to encounter." Learning is the responsibility of the learner, but the teacher guides the student into developing meaning from content material and classroom experience.

It is important to engage learners in learning situations that effectively integrate their own experiences and familiar materials that students can use to better understand specific concepts, especially in the science and mathematics fields

Formal and informal learning 71

(Eisenkraft, 2003). For example, students who enjoy skateboarding can be given opportunities to explore the concepts of velocity, acceleration, centre of gravity and moment of inertia. They may also use the skateboard and a local skatepark to investigate topics such as inclined planes, levers, fulcrums and screws. The purpose of this approach is to allow the students to explore meaningful science topics set in the context of something they enjoy doing.

An example: Scientific skateboarding

Dr. Skateboard's Action Science is a curriculum supplement for middle school (6–8) students that is designed to address content and process objectives in physical science for the Texas Essential Knowledge and Skills (TEKS). The video instruction and 20 classroom activities provide the teacher with a series of instructional tools and content information that can be used to explore and explain the concepts found in the areas of forces, motion, Newton's Laws of Motion and simple machines. It is the purpose of this research project to determine what impact Dr. Skateboard's Action Science has on a sample of middle school students in the area of physical science knowledge and skills.

Dr. Skateboard's Action Science maps to the physical science TEKS in which all middle school students need to be engaged. Dr. Skateboard's Action Science explores scientific concepts in a curriculum that is designed to address both physical science content and process skills. The video instruction focuses on the physical science concepts found in the areas of motion, forces, Newton's Laws of Motion and simple machines. The main purpose is to provide an interesting method of engaging students in the exploration of science in a real-world context. The overarching theme for Dr. Skateboard's Action Science is the appeal of action sports as teaching and learning vehicles for students, teachers and the community.

Dr. Skateboard's Action Science is an example of transformative education, a student-centred curriculum supplement built around interesting content linked to specific physical knowledge and skills in science. The videos and classroom materials provide the classroom teacher with an instructional series rich in science and including topics such as centrifugal and centripetal forces, inertia, centre of gravity and momentum. The purpose is to contextualize the classroom process of acquiring critical knowledge, developing proficiency in problem solving, engaging in self-directed learning and participating in collaborative teams.

Classroom activities and video content

The activities and materials are designed for students to interact in small teams, and this sharing within cooperative groups is a fundamental constructivist strategy that allows the teacher to facilitate the learning process. As a student-centred approach, it also helps to develop a common base of experiences to help students make connections to content. In the classroom,

72   *Tillman, An, and Robertson*

problem-solving strategies depend on the development of conceptual understandings, and hands-on explorations of simple topics combined with collaborative interactions among learners help to build an understanding of processes and concepts (Apple, 1993). It is important for educators to not merely regard the learner's point of view alone as fully complete and significant, but to guide the students in the analysis and synthesis of content information (Dewey, 1902). The learner is always defining meaning within the context of action and reflection, and the social situations, including discussion, explanations and hands-on experiences, provide the context for knowledge construction (Brooks & Brooks, 1993).

The video segments themselves do provide action, but also relevant content for the classroom, and complement the activities that teachers can implement in the classroom, and in tandem, can help reinforce the conceptual emphasis in a lesson. For example, the teacher can utilize the portion of "Newton's Laws" video that covers the concepts of force, mass and acceleration, which is designed as an effective introduction to the activity "Force Makes a Mass Move." This brief video segment serves as a hook in order to introduce the activity and additionally as a review for the content covered in class. In that sense, the materials serve both pre-activity and post-activity purposes, and allow the teacher the flexibility to have students explain fundamental physics as well as pursue inquiry extensions. Each activity contains both a teacher section and a student section. The teacher section provides standards alignment information, background knowledge, guiding questions with answers and extensions for student enrichment. The student section contains the classroom science activity, connections to real-world examples, explanations of concepts and actual photographs of BMX riders and skateboarders in action.

Making learning relevant and relatable

Action Science is designed to teach fundamental science concepts in physics in an approach that utilizes transformative educational strategies, which help students move from memorizing facts and content to constructing knowledge in meaningful and useful manners. The activities associated with Action Science address both the objectives and enduring knowledge of physical science in content and process skills for both the U.S. National Science Standards and the TEKS state standards.

The materials in Dr. Skateboard's Action Science were also designed to emphasize inquiry in classroom explorations. As a foundation for discovery, the teacher can use the video segment in the "Simple Machines" episode that relates to fulcrums and levers, and then have the students perform the classroom activity "Skateboards Have Levers and Fulcrums." After the activity, the teacher may revisit these ideas and then create an extension inquiry exercise for the students to do in teams. The teacher can provide the students with the same materials used in the activity such as rulers, tape, plastic spoons, rubber bands and modelling clay and challenge the students to design a simple

Formal and informal learning 73

machine made of at least three of the provided that uses a lever and a fulcrum and can propel a small marshmallow the farthest distance.

Active learning through facilitation

In making this transition in class, the teacher guides the students towards developing their own ideas and within a given time period, has the students create and test their unique designs. By engaging students in a design competition, there is a spirit of enthusiasm and excitement among the groups. There are also excellent opportunities to develop cooperative group skills and to have students use critical thinking to solve the problem presented. As Bruner (1962, p. 50) stated, "Students should know what it feels like to be completely absorbed in a problem. They seldom experience this feeling in school." Finally, the teams of students not only have to launch the marshmallow, but they also have to record the distances, calculate the average distances travelled and identify the lever and fulcrum within their machine. In this manner, the students have to present their ideas, justify their understandings and support their findings with experimental data.

Another classroom example in the design of the series is the use of the video segment in the "Forces" video that focuses on the concept of centre of gravity, which additionally bridges the concepts of gravity and lift. Prior to showing the video segment, the teacher can use open-ended questions with students in order to activate their previous knowledge concerning this content. Sample questions could include, "what do you do when you ride a skateboard or a bicycle?," "how do you balance on a skateboard or bike?" and "what forces are acting on you as you are trying to ride a bike or skateboard?" Additionally, previously marginalized students who have experience in these activities, but may struggle in science, can become experts in this discussion and contribute greatly to the classroom investigations.

Finally, the teacher should conclude the series of questions by asking, "what is the centre of gravity and why is it important?," and then facilitate the conversation in order to introduce the segment in the "Forces" video that covers gravity, lift and the centre of gravity. This approximately 4-minute segment of the video then serves as the engagement to the activity "Flatland BMX and the Center of Gravity" in which students create irregular cardboard shapes and determine the object's centre of gravity through a series of step-by-step procedures. Students exploring a concept should be given opportunities to work with hands-on materials so that they can have experiences that are real and fundamental. Hands-on learning plays a valuable role in the constructivist paradigm, as it is the process of learning by doing that is utilized in explorations and experiments (Dewey, 1902).

Next, students modify their shapes either by adding paper clips (which increases the mass) or by cutting off part of some of cardboard (which decreases the mass). In turn, they come to see that there is a fundamental relationship between the centre of gravity and the mass of an object, and that the centre of gravity will move in relation to an increase or a decrease in mass. After the

74   *Tillman, An, and Robertson*

classroom lesson, the teacher can revisit the activity by asking the students to explain their findings and the relationships they discovered. As students explore concepts, they develop a broader understanding of those concepts. When they relate what they are learning, seeing or doing to others, they can begin to see similarities in their understandings, as well as self-identify misconceptions they may have about content material (Bybee, 2006). Finally, there is a list of open-ended questions for students to answer, as well as extensions that they can engage in if there is additional time and motivation to explore these concepts. This entire activity can be done in the timeframe of a normal class period with minimal setup and clean-up and can provide both teachers and students an interesting alternative to exploring these fundamental physics ideas.

Learning requires risk and ambiguity

Learning happens when you go to areas of high risk and high ambiguity. Yet it's not just enough to learn—the goal should really centre on mastery. To master something takes a long time, which skateboarders at a local park know fundamentally. Recent experiences in the Information Age as it relates to the field of education continually reinforce the belief that it's less about what you know and more about what you can master. When you master something, you know what it takes to be successful, and then you can apply that ability to other aspects of your life. Whether a student is mastering skateboarding, painting, the guitar, a new language, science or mathematics, developing one kind of mastery can help him or her master something else. For teachers, we need to inspire others to use their gifts in their education, and thereby connect them to their dreams and aspirations.

In the classroom, constructivist curriculum must be designed so that it reflects real-life situations, and the use of relevant contexts helps to contextualize the concepts, as well as help provide connections across subject areas (Bentley, 1998; Hofstein & Yager, 1982). Research scientists and mathematicians cross over the barriers between academic disciplines all the time, and seldom operate solely on isolated areas of content, but integrate the use of language, knowledge and process application. Science education programmes that emphasize investigation give students the ability to retain facts through critical thinking by working through problems logically and making connections to the real world.

Future directions for the relationship between formal and informal learning

Within the education community, there has been a re-awakening of the need for hybrid education, combining the best of formal learning and informal learning. Most modern pedagogical frameworks recognize that the current state of formal education presents a K-12 system that is still designed for the Industrial Age (Mishra & Koehler, 2006). Higher education is trying to adapt to the Information Age but struggling, as online diploma mills scatter the landscape,

Formal and informal learning 75

further weakening the value of a post-secondary degree. Yet the current state of informal education is that it is thriving. Although after-school and summer programmes are often coopted by formal education advocates and their objective learning goals, other programmes like Upward Bound see increasing enrollment. And while museum-themed informal education has shown its limitations, online resources like YouTube and Wikipedia enable both kids and adults to take control of their own learning.

The current state of the relationship between formal and informal education is one of flux and unrest. Where we go from here will be determined by the priorities that we set and the discipline with which we pursue them. The E-E pedagogical model can serve as a prototype for our journey forward because it inherently acknowledges the dual importance of maintaining student engagement, while still focusing on key learning objectives. But it is not the only exemplar—other models like the flipped classroom can also provide insight into the potential for the relationship between formal and informal learning to be re-thought, and thereby made into a 21st-century appropriate pedagogy. We have entered the Information Age wherein accessible data destabilizes the formal education structure. What happens when the diffusion of innovations accelerates even further? Some scholars have already begun the investigation, but there is still much remaining to be discovered (e.g. Christensen, 2002; Rogers, 2003; Singhal & Law, 1997; Tillman, 2012; Zhang, Trussell, Tillman, & An, 2015).

The formalization of learning has been a long and arduous process, with many slips along the way (Education Alliance, 2006). Today, we find ourselves in a scenario where the disconnect between formal and informal learning is perhaps more pronounced than ever (Cross, 2001; Hill, 1998; Mishook & Kornhaber, 2006). If a single episode prior to the Industrial Age could be pointed to as the essential catalyst that caused and still defines our current predicament, perhaps it would be Napoleon's invasion of Prussia in 1806, which culminated on October 14th with the Battle of Jena-Auerstedt. Napoleon had developed a lightning-fast style of military campaigning, and the Prussian military was quickly overrun and defeated. French forces occupied Prussia, ruthlessly pursued the shattered remnants of the Prussian Army, and during the *Treaties of Tilsit* signed in 1807, much of Prussia's territory along the lower Rhine was claimed for France. The Prussian's had to do something, and so they introduced an obligatory 8-year schedule of primary education for all Prussian students, with a focus on the now standard subjects of reading, writing and arithmetic. During this process, they created the essential components of formal education, including subjects, classes and grades. Eventually, after witnessing the Prussian recovery from Napoleon's invasion, many other countries in Europe also adopted a formal primary school model for all national citizens of the appropriate ages, so as to prepare themselves for the complexity of a world where invading armies can move at lightning-fast speed.

When Horace Mann visited Germany in 1843, he was impressed with their formal educational system (Mann, 1848). He carried the idea of free but

76 *Tillman, An, and Robertson*

compulsory primary education back home with him to the United States, and then managed to convince some Massachusetts politicians that they should adopt tax-supported public elementary schools in their districts (Mann, 1857). It was a genuinely noble idea and spread throughout the country like wildfire. Yet it also set the stage for the "assembly-line model" that has become overly dominant in recent formal education and continues to thwart modern efforts at reforming pedagogical practice (Bull & Groves, 2009).

The "knowledge workers" envisioned in the late 1950s by Peter Drucker (1959) were perfectly suited for a world with lots of midlevel jobs requiring straightforward understanding. But the modern professional world seems to increasingly require high-level understanding of complex problems that have no obvious solution (Barak, Maymon, & Harel, 1999; Haier & Jung, 2008). Formal education must adapt to this chaotic, but creative contemporary environment, or face ruthless outsourcing, either to another country or even to a non-human. The machines are clearly coming for our jobs, and they are willing to do any job they are capable of accomplishing (Bostrom, 2014). They do not ask for vacation time, or better parking spots or a view of the lake. Which skills will continue to be employable throughout the 21st century is an essential question that any serious educator should be asking themselves, yet it is just one of many questions that we must both ask and answer as professional pedagogues (Jones-Kavalier & Flannigan, 2008; Lajoie, 2003).

Conclusion

In this chapter, we have investigated the relationship between formal and informal learning, first from a historical perspective, then from a contemporary standpoint, and lastly as an attempt at predicting the future dynamic between formal and informal learning. We determined that (a) informal enrichment programmes that shine a positive light on their formal education counterparts can have a positive effect in the classroom by increasing the comfort level of students learning the subject matter (Robertson & Lesser, 2013); (b) for students to become engaged by formal or informal learning, they have to be interested in the subject matter, otherwise the lessons are simply forgotten due to disregard (Parker, 1990); and (c) accordingly, student-centred pedagogies recommend that the curriculum should be connected to students' individual interests (Tillman, 2016). We completed this examination by recognizing that, collectively, outcomes from an integrated approach to informal and formal education infrastructure within the local region, as well as a better understanding of the transferability of these enhancements to areas outside of the geographic confines of the project, can be of great benefit to the community. As an illustration, informal enrichment programmes can provide activities that students find appealing and can therefore be used to direct their interests towards the more formalized lessons found in the classroom. This chapter has thus attempted to address the contemporary scenario, wherein educators are often attempting to close the gap between the informal learning that occurs outside of the classroom and the formal lessons they are expected to teach. We hope this chapter has provided a framework, and perhaps some insights, about how we might best approach this problem in our future educational practice and research.

References

An, S. A., & Capraro, M. M. (2011). *Music-math integrated activities for elementary and middle school students.* Irvine, CA: Education for All.

An, S. A., Capraro, M. M., & Tillman, D. (2013). Elementary teachers integrate music activities into regular mathematics lessons: Effects on students' mathematical abilities. *Journal for Learning Through the Arts, 9*(1), 1–20.

An, S. A., & Tillman, D. (2014). Elementary teachers' design of arts based teaching: Investigating the possibility of developing mathematics-music integrated curriculum. *Journal of Curriculum Theorizing, 30*(2), 20–38.

An, S. A., & Tillman, D. (2015). Music activities as a meaningful context for teaching elementary students mathematics: A quasi-experiment time series design with random assigned control group. *European Journal of Science and Mathematics Education, 3*(1), 45–60.

An, S. A., Tillman, D., Boren, R., & Wang, J. (2014). Fostering elementary students' mathematics disposition through music-mathematics integrated lessons. *International Journal for Mathematics Teaching and Learning, 15*(3), 1–18.

An, S. A., Tillman, D., & Paez, C. (2015). Music-themed mathematics education as a strategy for improving elementary preservice teachers' mathematics pedagogy and teaching self-efficacy. *Journal of Mathematics Education at Teachers College, 6*(1), 9–24.

An, S. A., Tillman, D., Robertson, W., Zhang, M., Siemssen, A., & Paez, C. (2016). Astronauts in outer space teaching students science: Comparing Chinese and American implementations of space-to-earth virtual classrooms. *European Journal of Science and Mathematics Education, 4*(3), 397–412.

An, S. A., Zhang, M., Flores, M., Chapman, J. R., Tillman, D. A., & Serna, L. (2015). Music activities as an impetus for Hispanic elementary students' mathematical disposition. *Journal of Mathematics Education, 8*(2), 39–55.

An, S. A., Zhang, M., Tillman, D., Lesser, L., Siemssen, A., & Tinajero, J. (2016). Learning to teach music-themed mathematics: An examination of preservice teachers' beliefs about developing and implementing interdisciplinary mathematics pedagogy. *Mathematics Teacher Education and Development, 18*(1), 20–36.

Apple, M. W. (1993). *Official knowledge.* New York: Routledge.

Barak, M., Maymon, T., & Harel, G. (1999). Teamwork in modern organizations: Implications for technology education. *International Journal of Technology and Design Education, 9*, 85–101.

Bentley, M. L. (1998). Constructivism as a referent for reforming science education. *Constructivism and Education, 13*, 233–249.

Bostrom, N. (2014). *Superintelligence: Paths, dangers, strategies.* Oxford, UK: Oxford University Press.

Brooks, J. G., & Brooks, M. G. (1993). *The case for the constructivist classroom.* Alexandria, VA: ASCD Press.

Bruner, J. (1962). *The process of education.* Cambridge, England: Harvard University Press.

Bull, G., & Groves, J. (2009). The democratization of production. *Learning & Leading with Technology, 37*(3), 36–37.

78 Tillman, An, and Robertson

Bybee, R. W. (2006). *The BSCS 5e instructional model: Origins, effectiveness, and applications* (Executive Summary). [On-Line] Retrieved September 9, 2007, from http://www.bscs.org/pdf/bscs5eexecsummary.pdf

Christensen, R. (2002). Impact of technology integration education on the attitudes of teachers and students. *Journal of Research on Technology in Education, 34*(4), 411–434.

Cross, N. (2001). Designerly ways of knowing: Design discipline versus design science. *Design Issues, 17*(3), 49–55.

Dewey, J. (1902). *The child and the curriculum.* Chicago, IL: Chicago University Press.

Drucker, P. (1959). *The landmarks of tomorrow.* New York, NY: Harper.

Education Alliance. (2006). *Closing the achievement gap: Best practices in teaching mathematics.* Charleston, WV: Business and Community for Public Schools.

Eisenkraft, A. (2003). Expanding the 5E model. *The Science Teacher, 70*(6), 57–59.

Ferster, B. (2014). *Teaching machines: Learning from the intersection of education and technology.* Baltimore, MD: JHU Press.

Freeman, C. (2007). *The closing of the western mind: The rise of faith and the fall of reason.* New York: Vintage.

Foucault, M. (2012). *Discipline & punish: The birth of the prison.* New York: Vintage.

Gutek, G. L. (1972). *A history of the western educational experience.* New York: Random House.

Gutek, G. L. (1997). *Philosophical and ideological perspective in education.* Needham Heights, MA: Allyn & Bacon.

Haier, R. J., & Jung, R. E. (2008). Brain imaging studies of intelligence and creativity: What is the picture for education? *Roeper Review, 30*(3), 171–179.

Hill, A. M. (1998). Problem solving in real-life contexts: An alternative for design in technology education. *International Journal of Technology and Design Education, 8*, 203–220.

Hofstein, A., & Yager, R. (1982). Societal issues as organizers for science education in the 80s. *School Science and Mathematics, 82*(15), 539–547.

Jones-Kavalier, B. R., & Flannigan, S. L. (2008). Connecting the digital dots: Literacy of the 21st century. *Teacher Librarian, 35*(3), 13–16.

Lajoie, S. (2003). Transitions and trajectories for studies of expertise. *Educational Researcher, 32*(8), 21–25.

Mann, H. (1848). *Twelfth annual report to the Massachusetts Board of Education. The republic and the school: Horace Mann and the education of free men.* New York: Teachers College, Columbia University.

Mann, H. (1857). *The republic and the school: Horace Mann on the education of free men.* New York: Teachers College, Columbia University.

Mishook, J., & Kornhaber, M. (2006). Arts integration in an era of accountability. *Arts Education Policy Review, 107*(4), 3–11.

Mishra, P., & Koehler, M. (2006). Technological pedagogical content knowledge: A framework for teacher knowledge. *Teachers College Record, 108*(6), 1017–1054.

Parker, L. (1990). *Edutainment.* New York: Jive/RCA Records.

Pettegree, A. (2010). *The book in the renaissance.* New Haven, CT: Yale University Press.

Robertson, W. H., & Lesser, L. M. (2013). Scientific skateboarding and mathematical music: Edutainment that actively engages middle school students. *European Journal of Science and Mathematics Education, 1*(2), 60–68.

Rogers, E. (2003). *Diffusion of innovations* (5th ed.). New York: Free Press.

Russell, B. (2004). *History of western philosophy.* New York: Routledge.

Rutherford, F. J., & Algrehn, A. (1990). *Science for all Americans*. New York: Oxford University Press.

Singhal, A. (2007). Entertainment media and social change discourses: Lessons from Peru, Mexico, and South Africa. *Brown Journal of World Affairs, 13*(2), 259–269.

Singhal, A., & Law, S. (1997). A research agenda for diffusion of innovations scholars in the 21st century. *Journal of Development Communication, 8*(1), 39–47.

Singhal, A., Papa, M., Sharma, D., Pant, S., Worrell, T., Muthuswamy, N., & Witte, K. (2006). Entertainment-education and social change: The communicative dynamics of social capital. *Journal of Creative Communications, 1*(1), 1–18.

Singhal, A., & Rogers, E. (2002). A theoretical agenda for entertainment-education. *Communication Theory, 12*(2), 117–135.

Tillman, D. (2012). Future directions for the AECT history makers video series. *Tech Trends, 56*(3), 7–8.

Tillman, D. A., Zhang, M., An, S. A., Boren, R., & Paez-Paez, C. (2015). Employing rapid prototyping design technologies to support contextualized mathematics education. *Journal of Computers in Mathematics and Science Teaching, 34*(4), 455–483.

Tillman, D. A., An, S. A., Cohen, J. D., Kjellstrom, W., & Boren, R. L. (2014). Exploring wind power: Improving mathematical thinking through digital fabrication. *Journal of Educational Multimedia and Hypermedia, 23*(4), 401–421.

Tillman, D. A. (2016). Not just consumers: Finding space for student creativity during mathematics instruction. *Journal of Mathematics Education, 9*(2), 1–3.

Van de Walle, J., Karp, K., & Bay-Williams, J. (2016). *Elementary and middle school mathematics* (9th ed.). Boston, MA: Allyn & Bacon.

Zhang, M., Trussell, R. P., Tillman, D. A., & An, S. A. (2015). Tracking the rise of web information needs for mobile education and an emerging trend of digital divide. *Computers in the Schools, 32*(2), 83–104.

Part II

Case studies of informal learning's potential

6 Asian students' informal civic learning: Can it enhance civic knowledge and values?

Kerry J. Kennedy and Xiaoxue Kuang

In liberal democracies schools have come to be regarded as important sites for the development of future democratic citizens. Equipped with structured curriculum and well-prepared teachers, subjects variously called Civic Education, Citizenship Education, Political Education or some other civics-related title have been slotted into the general teaching programme of schools. Where a specific subject has not been identified, citizenship education may be integrated into other school subjects or may take its place among the extracurricular activities of schools. The expectations of different societies about the education of citizens are usually very high with schools expected to produce regime-supporting students who will continue to support democratic institutions and values. Yet as successive studies have shown (Schulz, Ainley, Fraillon, Kerr, & Losito, 2010; Schulz, Ainley, Fraillon, Losito, Agrusti & Friedman, 2018; Torney-Purta, Lehmann, Oswald, & Schulz, 2001), students have access to multiple information channels of which schools are only one. What is more, civic learning takes place in many contexts outside of school—in families, with peers, in public debates and discussions in the media and recently over social media. The latter is of particular importance since, on the one hand, it has provided opportunities for mass democratic engagement, but on the other it has provided a platform for anti-democratic groups to promote their views that very often undermine the very democracy that schools and the community in general seek to support (Klein & Muis, 2018). While schools remain important agents of political socialization for young people, more needs to be known about informal learning processes that can also contribute to such socialization. The school's role in formal learning maybe enhanced if it can be integrated with informal learning processes in order to maximize the impact on students' civic learning.

The objectives of this chapter, therefore, are to explore informal learning opportunities available to young people and assess their relationship to formal civic learning. A model will be developed to show how different forms of learning are related and, based on this model, implications will be drawn for expanding our theoretical understanding of informal civic learning and improving current policies and practices for civic learning both in and out of school.

84 *Kerry J. Kennedy and Xiaoxue Kuang*

In order to achieve these objectives, the remainder of the chapter will focus on

- examining current issues related to informal processes of civic learning;
- describing the research methods used to investigate informal civic learning opportunities;
- presenting the results of the research and
- discussing the implications of the results for theory, policy and practice.

Informal civic learning—neither new nor surprising

Brooks and Holford (2009, p. 89) have pointed out that in the latter part of the 19th century, there was a debate about whether citizenship should be "taught" or "caught." The debate focused on whether the responsibility for citizenship education should be with schools or more informal groups such as youth clubs and movements. Ironically, it was not until the early years of the 21st century that a formal Citizenship curriculum was introduced in England. This suggests that teaching about citizenship, where it occurred, was either integrated into other subjects or was part of broader school activities that acknowledged the importance of the duties and responsibilities of citizenship since there was no formal citizenship curriculum. For John Dewey (1909, p. 9) in the United States, the lack of a school citizenship curriculum would not have been seen as a problem. His view was that schools should reflect the basic "relationships of citizenship" and, functioning as a democratic community, its principles would soon become known to students. His view was that the experience of citizenship and its values was the best way to develop those values.

Dewey, however, was not on the winning side of educational debates in the United States, and Civic Education became a firmly implanted component of the school curriculum and continues so today. In England, the Citizenship curriculum relied on school-based initiatives so has not quite created a new school subject since it is without a specified syllabus. Yet it has signaled that there are formal learning requirements around what is called "political literacy" and the demands of so called "active citizenship." Yet the idea that citizenship might be "caught," remains a powerful one. Informal learning has no boundaries. It does not need to be endorsed by educational authorities: It will happen in the course of daily living as the following examples show.

Scheerens (2011, p. 205) broke the formal/informal learning divide by showing how within schools there are many opportunities for informal civic learning: "dealing with conflict," "dealing with differences between cultures" and "peer interaction in collaborative learning." These examples might best be regarded as forms of informal learning for citizenship stimulated by "critical incidents" that provide opportunities for reflecting on and learning from day-to-day encounters. This kind of learning differs from what Scheerens (2011, p. 2014) refers to as "explicit teaching of citizenship" by which he means "formal learning experiences" that take place in lessons. This conception of multiple learning opportunities is consistent with the major studies of citizenship mentioned above in the sense that learning processes have figured prominently in these in an attempt to account for variation in students' civic learning achievements. Yet this incidental form of civic learning is not the only opportunity that students have to learn outside the classroom.

Schugurensky (2006, p. 166), for example, referred to "self-directed learning" that involves students in project work, that is, for the most part unsupervised, but may involve collaboration with others. He argued that informal learning in this context is intentional and conscious. The outcomes may be generic and related to citizenship (e.g. learning to work with others, respecting diverse opinions), but with more general academic-oriented projects there will also be outcomes unrelated to citizenship. In addition, there are forms of self-directed learning that might also be related directly to citizenship. School-based civic activities such as School Councils or Class Parliaments are explicitly citizenship-oriented activities where the process of participation itself is expected to yield important learning outcomes. This kind of informal learning, like more generally oriented project work, is both intentional and conscious. In a Deweyan sense it is designed to provide experiences that simulate democratic practices thus helping students better understand how democracy functions. It is the kind of experiential learning that Dewey often advocated.

There are also classroom activities that are experiential in nature rather than part of didactic teaching processes. Having students write a letter to a newspaper or a politician is, on the one hand, a technical task, but the very process of communication on a civic or political issue of importance also inducts students into real-world democracy. Encouraging a student to stand as a candidate for a school election or organizing students to develop a campaign around an environmental issue also engages students in the kind of decision-making they will encounter as adults. While all these activities are for the here and now, they also prepare students for the future and provide learning opportunities that transcend the formal curriculum. Yet schools are not the only place where students can experience informal learning opportunities.

Lauglo (2010) highlighted the important role of parents in discussing politics with their children to the extent that such discussions appeared to have a positive influence on formal learning outcomes irrespective of the socio-economic status of families. Wilkenfeld (2009) supported these results as far as the role of parents is concerned, and she also pointed to broader contexts in which informal political discussions can take place including in the community. Klofstad (2007, p. 856) referred to these kind of discussion as "civic talk" that highlights the informal nature of the discussions as well as the multiple contexts in which they take place.

In addition to parents, peers can also be an important source of informal civic learning, although it may not always be positive. Mellor (2010, p. 36), reporting the results of a national civics assessment in Australia, showed that the more civics-related activities in which students were engaged, the higher their scores on the national civics test. This linear relation held for Year 10 students (about 15 or 16 years old) but less so for Year 6 students (about 11 or 12 years old). Yet Torney-Purta et al. (2001, pp. 151–152), reporting the results of the IEA Civic Education Study, showed that students who spend a lot of time outside of home in the evenings are likely to have lower civic achievement scores. In both of these cases it is not possible to know exactly what kind of "civic talk" takes place, but what appears to be the case is that these informal learning opportunities influence civic understanding in different ways. The concept of the negative influences of informal learning deserves further consideration.

Social media has become an important tool for political communication. Klein and Muis (2018) have shown how fringe political groups, or anyone for that matter, can enter mainstream political debates simply by having access to social media. For young people, this has created both opportunities and potential problems. The concept of the "keyboard warrior" (Dennis, 2014) has been popularized in regard to youth. As "digital natives," they take naturally to a politicized social media and adopt political positions that best suit their values and are able to pursue it without barriers, and indeed without real civic engagement. Often this means they only talk to those who agree with them, and the only learning that takes place is what can be expected in a closed circle of like-minded people. This kind of informal learning will become more important and needs to be understood better and monitored closely.

It is against this background of multiple processes of informal learning that the present study was developed to explore how informal learning processes operate and how they impact on more formal civic learning that seeks to equip young people with the kind of knowledge and skills that can help them support their democratic communities.

The remainder of this paper will outline the research methods used, the results and their implications for citizenship education in general and society in particular. It will focus on students in Asia given that this is a strategic part of the world in terms of its economic growth, social values and its potential for influencing the future.

Research methods used for investigating informal learning

Samples

The study used secondary analysis drawing on the data from the International Civic and Citizenship Education Study (ICCS) 2016 dataset. Being the fourth IEA study, ICCS 2016 investigated youth preparation to "undertake their current and future roles as citizens" (Schulz, 2018, p. v). It collected information related to students' civic knowledge as well as their civic attitudes, perceptions, activities and intentions. Twenty-four societies took part in the survey. Among them, there were three Asian societies: Taiwan, Hong Kong and Korea, and they were chosen for this study. The total sample included 2,653 Hong Kong youth with 1,471 boys (51.7%) and 1,282 girls (48.3%); 2,601 in Korea with

1,414 boys (54.4%) and 1,187 girls (45.6%); 3,953 in Taiwan with 2,040 boys (51.6%) and 1,913 girls (48.4%).

Measures

Informal learning contained three subscales: "Traditional sources", "Social media" and "Friends".

Traditional sources (TRADSOR) was made up of four items which asked students how often they were involved in watching television (a) and reading newspapers (b) to be informed about national and international news; talking with parents about political or social issues (c) and what is happening in other countries (d).

Social media (SOCLMED) contained three items which asked students how often they were involved in using the Internet to find information about political or social issues (a), posting a comment or image regarding a political or social issue on the Internet or social media (b) and sharing or commenting on another person's online post regarding a political or social issue (c).

Friends included two items which asked students how often they involved in "talking with friends about political or social issues" and "talking with friends about what is happening in other countries".

Students' response categories were "never or hardly ever," "monthly," "weekly" and "daily or almost daily."

Other scales

Civic learning (SCHLEARN) contained seven items which asked students to what extent they have learned about the following topics at school: How citizens can vote in local or national elections; how laws are introduced and changed in <country of test>; how to protect the environment; how to contribute to solving problems in the <local community>; how citizen rights are protected in <country of test>; how political issues and events in other countries are handled; and how the economy works.

Students' response categories were "To a large extent," "To a moderate extent," "To a small extent" and "Not at all."

Community participation (COMPART) ask whether they had participated in ten different organizations, clubs or groups in the wider community either "within the last 12 months," "more than a year ago" or "never." For example, "an environmental action group or organization; a human rights organization; a voluntary group doing something to help the community; an organization collecting money for a social cause; a group of young people campaigning for an issue; an animal rights or animal welfare group; a religious group or organization; a community youth group (such as <boys/girls scouts, YMCA>) and a sports team."

School participation (SCHLPART) asked students if they had participated in seven different civic-related activities at school either "within the last

88   Kerry J. Kennedy and Xiaoxue Kuang

12 months," "more than a year ago" or "never." For example, "active participation in an organized debate; voting for <class representative> or <school parliament>; taking part in decision-making about how the school is run; taking part in discussions at a <student assembly>; becoming a candidate for <class representative> or <school parliament>; participating in an activity to make school more <environmentally friendly> and voluntary participation in school-based music or drama activities outside of regular classes."

Citizenship efficacy (CITZEFF) contained seven items, which asked students how well they thought they would perform several listed activities ("very well," "fairly well," "not very well," "not at all"). For example, "discuss a newspaper article about a conflict between countries; argue your point of view about a controversial political or social issue; stand as a candidate in a <school election>; organize a group of students in order to achieve changes at school; follow a television debate about a controversial issue; write letter or email to a newspaper giving your view on a current issue and speak in front of your class about a social or political issue."

Student interaction (INTACT) measured by three items, which asked students to rate their level of agreement with the statements about teachers and students at their school (ranging from "strongly agree" to "strongly disagree"). For example, "most students at my school treat each other with respect; most students at my school get along well with each other and my school is a place where students feel safe."

Physical and verbal abuse (ABUSE) measured by six items, which asked students how often did they experience six situations in their school during the last 3 months (ranging from "not at all", "once", "2 to 4 times", "5 times or more"). For example, "a student called you by an offensive nickname; a student said things about you to make others laugh; a student threatened to hurt you; you were physically attacked by another student; a student broke something belonging to you on purpose and a student posted offensive pictures or text about you on the Internet."

Analytic technique

Mplus8 was used for data analysis. Confirmatory Factor Analysis (CFA) was used to test the factor structure of the scales. Structural equation modelling methodology was used to test a model of the relationship between informal learning, formal learning, citizenship self-efficacy, participation experiences and civic knowledge. Model fit indices were used to assess the extent to which the data was a good fit to the proposed model. These include the comparative fit index (CFI; Bentler, 1990) and the Tucker Lewis index (TLI; Tucker & Lewis, 1973). Values above 0.90 and 0.95 indicate reasonable and good model fit separately (Bentler, 1990; Hu & Bentler, 1999). The values of the root of mean square error approximation (RMSEA) of less than 0.08 suggest adequate fit (Bentler, 1990; Hu & Bentler, 1999; Jöreskog & Sörbom, 1993).

The proposed model is shown in Figure 6.1.

Proposed model

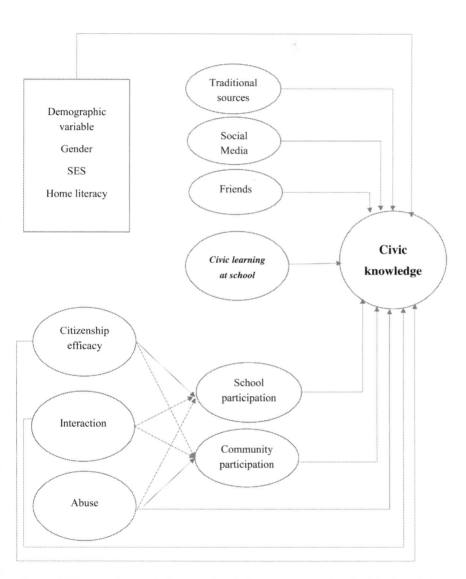

Figure 6.1 Proposed model for assessing influences on students' civic knowledge: Demographics, informal learning and social engagement.

90 *Kerry J. Kennedy and Xiaoxue Kuang*

Results

Fitness indices

Results of the CFA are shown in Table 6.1. They indicated that the CFI and TLI for most scales in Taiwan, Hong Kong and Korea were above 0.9, indicating acceptable model fit. For RMSEA, the values are less than 0.8 only for student interaction, school participation and community participation. The reliabilities of each scale in Hong Kong were above 0.7 ranging from 0.728 to 0.921.

Table 6.1 Reliability coefficients and CFA fit indices for each scale

Scale		Chinese Taipei	Hong Kong	Korea
Informal	CFI	0.933	0.951	0.956
learning	TLI	0.899	0.926	0.934
	RMSEA	0.118	0.137	0.115
		0.112–0.123	0.131–0.144	0.109–0.122
	Alpha	0.676	0.772	0.757
	Traditional sources	0.641	0.782	0.702
	Social media	0.740	0.837	0.722
	Friends			
Civic learning	CFI	0.927	0.968	0.949
at school	TLI	0.890	0.952	0.924
	RMSEA	0.153	0.106	0.120
		0.146–0.160	0.098–0.115	0.111–0.129
	Alpha	0.790	0.835	0.789
School	CFI	0.980	0.983	0.983
participation	TLI	0.970	0.975	0.975
	RMSEA	0.053	0.058	0.084
		0.046–0.060	0.050–0.067	0.075–0.093
	Alpha	0.693	0.728	0.743
Community	CFI	0.953	0.966	0.977
participation	TLI	0.940	0.956	0.971
	RMSEA	0.045	0.049	0.038
		0.040–0.049	0.043–0.055	0.032–0.044
	Alpha	0.729	0.766	0.830
Citizenship	CFI	0.943	0.956	0.960
efficacy	TLI	0.914	0.934	0.940
	RMSEA	0.202	0.261	0.250
		0.195–0.209	0.252–0.269	0.242–0.259
	Alpha	0.879	0.921	0.916
Student	CFI	1	1	1
interaction	TLI	1	1	1
	RMSEA	0	0	0
	Alpha	0.825	0.847	0.855
Abuse	CFI	0.973	0.966	0.958
	TLI	0.955	0.943	0.930
	RMSEA	0.084	0.111	0.087
		0.075–0.093	0.100–0.122	0.076–0.098
	Alpha	0.718	0.782	0.678

Asian students' informal civic learning 91

Table 6.2 Results of structural equation model (SEM) for measurement model shown in Figure 6.1

Civic Knowledge	Chinese Taipei	Hong Kong [β (standard error)]	Korea
Gender	0.170***(0.015)	0.145***(0.02)	0.164***(0.019)
SES	0.281***(0.021)	0.110***(0.026)	0.240***(0.027)
Home literacy	0.104***(0.021)	0.118***(0.025)	0.119***(0.028)
Traditional	0.230***(0.038)	0.291***(0.034)	0.252***(0.05)
Social media	−0.081**(0.029)	−0.145***(0.038)	−0.032(0.06)
Friends	0.033(0.038)	−0.055(0.044)	−0.049(0.055)
Civic learning	0.198***(0.015)	0.012(0.02)	−0.034(0.022)
School participation	0.285***(0.033)	0.265***(0.042)	0.416***(0.059)
Community participation	−0.041(0.031)	−0.138**(0.043)	−0.066(0.06)
Citizenship self-efficacy	−0.282***(0.026)	−0.06(0.034)	0.248***(0.045)
Interactions	−0.234***(0.047)	0.042(0.061)	−0.577**(0.209)
Abuse	−0.375***(0.057)	−0.146*(0.072)	−0.563**(0.203)

The reliabilities of most scales in Korea were above 0.7 ranging from 0.678 to 0.916. The reliabilities of most scales in Chinese Taipei were above 0.7, ranging from 0.641 to 0.879.

SEM results

Structural equation model (SEM) results are shown in Table 6.2. They showed that girls had higher civic knowledge than boys in the three societies (Chinese Taipei: standard error (β) = 0.170; Hong Kong: β = 0.145; Korea: β = 0.164). Socio-economic status (SES) and Home Literacy had a direct and positive effect on Civic Knowledge across the three societies (SES: Chinese Taipei: β = 0.281; Hong Kong: β = 0.110; Korea: β = 0.240; Home literacy: Chinese Taipei: β = 0.104; Hong Kong: β = 0.118; Korea: β = 0.119). This suggests that demographic influences on students' Civic Knowledge are important and need to be considered when other influences are being assessed.

Direct effects

There were medium to high correlations among three informal learning scales ("Traditional sources," "Social media" and "Discussion with friends," *r*: 0.527–0.751) across societies. "Traditional sources" were positively related to civic knowledge among the three societies (Chinese Taipei: β = 0.230; Hong Kong: β = 0.291; Korea: β = 0.252), while "Social media" was negatively associated with Civic Knowledge in Chinese Taipei (β = −0.081) and Hong Kong (β = −0.145), but not in Korea. The correlation between "Discussion with friends" and "Civic Knowledge" was not statistically significant.

92   Kerry J. Kennedy and Xiaoxue Kuang

"Civic learning at school" was positively related to civic knowledge only in Chinese Taipei ($\beta = 0.198$).

"Students' civic participation at school" was positively related to civic knowledge in the three societies (Chinese Taipei: $\beta = 0.285$; Hong Kong: $\beta = 0.265$; Korea: $\beta = 0.416$), while "Students' civic participation in the wider community" was negatively related to Civic Knowledge only in Hong Kong ($\beta = -0.138$). The relationship between students' "Citizenship self-efficacy" and "Civic knowledge" was negative in Chinese Taipei ($\beta = -0.282$) while positive in Korea ($\beta = 0.248$).

"Students' interaction at school" was negatively related to civic knowledge in Hong Kong ($\beta = -0.234$) and Korea ($\beta = -0.577$). "Students' feeling of abuse" was negatively related to civic knowledge across the three societies (Chinese Taipei: $\beta = -0.375$; Hong Kong: $\beta = -0.146$; Korea: $\beta = -0.563$)

"Students' citizenship self-efficacy" was also positively associated with "civic participation at school" and "participation in the wider community" in Chinese Taipei ($\beta 1 = 0.262$; $\beta 2 = 0.227$) and Hong Kong ($\beta 1 = 0.299$; $\beta 2 = 0.223$). In Korea, there was negative relationship between citizenship self-efficacy and community participation ($\beta = -0.128$).

Students' "interactions at school" was positively associated with civic participation at school (Chinese Taipei: $\beta = 0.423$; Hong Kong: $\beta = 0.556$; Korea: $\beta = 0.923$) and "participation in the wider community" (Chinese Taipei: $\beta = 0.287$; Hong Kong: $\beta = 446$; Korea: $\beta = 0.932$) among the three societies.

"Students' abuse at school" was also positively associated with civic participation at school (Chinese Taipei: $\beta = 0.507$; Hong Kong: $\beta = 0.605$; Korea: $\beta = 0.853$) and in wider community (Chinese Taipei: $\beta = 0.504$; Hong Kong: $\beta = 0.631$; Korea: $\beta = -0.939$) among the three societies.

Mediation effects

Mediation effects in the model are shown in Table 6.3. There were positive mediation effects between "Students' interaction at school"/"Students' abuse at school" and Civic knowledge through civic participation at school among the three societies (INTACT: Chinese Taipei: $\beta = 0.119$; Hong Kong: $\beta = 0.146$; Korea: $\beta = 0.383$; ABUSE: Chinese Taipei: $\beta = 0.143$; Hong Kong: $\beta = 0.160$; Korea: $\beta = 0.354$).

There were negative mediation effects between students' "interactions at school" ($\beta = -0.062$, $p < 0.01$)/students' abuse at school ($\beta = -0.085$, $p < 0.01$) and "Civic knowledge" through "Civic participation in wider community" only in Hong Kong

In Hong Kong ($\beta = 0.079$; $p < 0.001$) and Chinese Taipei ($\beta = 0.075$, $p < 0.001$), "Civic participation at school" plays a positive mediation role between "Citizenship self-efficacy" and "Civic knowledge." "Civic participation in the wider community" negatively mediated the relationship between "Civic participation at school" and "Civic knowledge" ($\beta = -0.031$; $p < 0.01$) only in Hong Kong.

Table 6.3 Mediation effects in the measurement model shown in Figure 6.1

	Chinese Taipei	Hong Kong [β (standard error)]	Korea
School participation			
Citizenship self-efficacy	0.262***(0.022)	0.299***(0.026)	0.025(0.045)
Interaction	0.423***(0.031)	0.556***(0.038)	0.923***(0.076)
Abuse	0.507***(0.031)	0.605***(0.038)	0.853***(0.067)
Community participation			
Citizenship self-efficacy	0.227***(0.025)	0.223***(0.027)	−0.128*(0.051)
Interaction	0.287***(0.036)	0.446***(0.039)	0.932***(0.083)
Abuse	0.504***(0.042)	0.631***(0.043)	0.939***(0.072)

Discussion

In this study we have been concerned with the relationship between informal and formal learning and whether the former can be utilized to assist young citizens with the knowledge, skills and values they need to negotiate increasing complex and volatile social and political environments. We have drawn on the data collected from three Asian societies in ICCS 2016 to explore this issue. The results have suggested that there is a great deal of value to be placed on different forms of informal learning, but these do not always seem to operate in the same way across the three societies. Thus, as argued previously (Kennedy, Kuang, & Chow, 2013), there is as much diversity in Asian students' attitudes to citizenship values as commonality and the current research has shown that this is the same with respect to informal learning. The following discussion will expand on this result.

The study defined informal learning in terms of multiple opportunities for civic learning available to students, but these different forms of informal learning exerted different effects on students' civic knowledge. Thus informal learning cannot be regarded as essentialist in nature, and it does not work in the same way in different societies. Traditional forms, as defined in this study, were positive across the three societies—social media exerted small but negative effect in all societies, though the effect was not significant in Korea. Talking with friends about social and political issues or about other countries, as a source of informal civic learning, did not affect students' civic knowledge in any significant way in any society.

These results suggest that educators need to be very cautious when relying on informal learning as a source for supporting students' civic knowledge. Given the salience of social media for young people, the negative finding here is of some concern and deserves further research. As for traditional sources of informal learning, teachers need to consider how these might be integrated into the school curriculum since these do have a positive impact on students' civic learning. It is of some interest that discussion with parents was included as an item in this scale since other research has also confirmed the importance of discussion with parents to civic learning (Kahne & Sporte, 2008).

94 *Kerry J. Kennedy and Xiaoxue Kuang*

School environments can be important to student learning of any kind (Blatchford, Pellegrini, & Baines, 2016) and in some cases can compensate for the effect of negative influences (Berkowitz et al., 2015). The school environment itself contains processes and experiences that in themselves represent opportunities for incidental informal learning. Students' experiences of abusive school environments in all societies in this study had a negative and significant effect on their civic knowledge. This result is consistent with the existing literature (Lacey & Cornell, 2013; Nakamoto & Schwartz, 2009). It suggests that whatever students learn from negative school experiences actually directly affects their formal learning. If, for example, the formal curriculum is teaching them to be "good citizens" but their experiences of life at school are negative, then the positive message is lost and this influences their civic learning negatively.

Following from the above result, it might be thought that a more positive friendship environment in school would have a positive influence on learning. Yet our results showed the opposite—the effect of a positive friendship environment on civic learning was either not significant, as in Hong Kong, or negative, as in Taiwan and Korea. This may seem counter intuitive but is consistent with literature that has argued "adolescents make friends with individuals with similar levels of academic achievement" (Flashman, 2012, p. 4). This suggests that friendship groups made up of low achievers are unlikely to have positive effects on student learning (whereas the opposite applies for high achievers). Thus positive friendships environments, as assessed in this study, do not necessarily have direct and positive effects on learning. Knifsend, Camacho-Thompson, Juvonen, and Graham (2018), however, have pointed to the importance of variables that mediate the effect of friendship on learning, and they identified the importance of school belonging. In their study, experiencing a sense of school belonging was likely to enhance student learning. In the current study, we also included mediating variables to explore further the influence of friendship environments in schools.

Students' participation experiences were assessed in this study (see Figure 6.1) both directly and as mediators because they are often an important part of civic education activities in schools. The results, however, were mixed. School participation exerted a direct, positive and significant effect on students' civic knowledge across the three societies ($\beta = 0.285$, 0.26 and 0.416 for Taiwan, Hong Kong and Korea, respectively). Community participation, however, exerted either no significant effect (e.g. in Taiwan and Korea) or negative effects as Hong Kong ($\beta = -0.138$). Thus the nature of participation experiences is important with school participation exerting more positive effect on formal learning than community participation. This maybe because school participation experiences are more directly linked to students' school lives, whereas involvement in community activities are more distal and, while important, do not feed into formal learning requirements.

School participation does act as a mediator for friendship experiences in Taiwan and Korea with the mediation effects being 0.12 and 0.38, respectively, based on data in Table 6.3 (there were no such effects for students in Hong Kong since the relationship between friendship experiences and civic knowledge were not significant in the first place). This reduced the direct effects of negative friendship experiences on civic knowledge, although not enough to overcome the negative nature of those experiences (from −0.23 to −0.11 in Taiwan and 0.58 to 0.20 in Korea). The same did not occur as a result of community participation with direct or total effects actually increasing as a result of the mediation. Thus mediated effects also differentiated significantly between the effects of different kinds of participation. Nevertheless, the study has highlighted the importance of school participation experiences both as a direct effect on civic learning and as a possible source of mediation to enhance friendship experiences. This may be because of what Marsick, Watkins, Scully-Russ, and Nicolaides (2017, p. 27) refer to as "incidental learning" that they see "as a by-product of some other activity...and may not be recognized as learning by the learner and others." In school participation activities students are likely to be involved with a broader range of peers than their immediate friendship groups, engage in different kinds of discussions and contribute to decisions about their day-to-day lives. Therefore any negative effects of friends may not be as students learn in this different environment. This is an important area for future study as the results of this study have shown that students who participate in school activities are likely to have better civic understanding.

Finally, an unusual finding from this study was that what students learn at school as part of their civic education was significant only in Taiwan ($\beta = 0.198$) and non-significant in the other two societies. This suggests that formal learning at school for Hong Kong and Korean students was unrelated to the requirements of the ICCS 2009 civic knowledge test, the results of which were used as the dependent variable in this study. These results suggest two main issues: various forms of informal learning seem unrelated to the requirements of internationally determined civic knowledge, as well as to what counts as civic education in Hong Kong and Korea. This requires a follow-up study to examine closely the curriculum requirements in these two societies as well as an examination of the international Civic knowledge test to assess the relevance of its requirements in local contexts.

Limitations

Marsick et al. (2017, p. 27) have made the point that "informal learning is challenging to study because it is neither highly conscious nor easily observable." Yet in this study we have sought to identify informal learning as students' behavioural characteristics (social media use, traditional media use and peer and family interactions). Thus, theoretically this study may not have tapped the full range of informal learning opportunities experienced by young adolescents but rather those that could be most easily captured in measurable latent constructs.

Measurement of any kind is always subject to measurement error and the study reported here will be no exception. Even though SEM was used to minimize such error, the psychometric properties of scales with just two or three items can be problematic in any analytic process. Thus, some caution needs to be exercised when interpreting the results in the light of possible measurement error.

96 *Kerry J. Kennedy and Xiaoxue Kuang*

The study drew its data from a cross-sectional survey and therefore causality of relationships cannot be inferred. For the causality issue to be addressed a longitudinal design is needed and multiple measures over time are necessary.

Conclusions and future research

This study has shown that informal learning is a multidimensional construct. Its influence on formal learning varies depending on which dimension of the construct is being examined. Social media have a negative impact on formal civic knowledge, while traditional media appear overall to have a positive impact. Peer and family influences are either not significant, as in Taiwan, or negative as in Hong Kong and Korea. Thus informal learning should not be regarded as an essentialist construct since its various manifestations can exert different influences on formal civic knowledge. This is in line with a sociocultural perspective as described by Marsick et al. (2017, p. 30) who suggest that "informal learning is *'contextually constituted'*... sourced by cultural material within the broader institutional setting."

Against this background, schools need to be aware of the multiple influences of informal learning and plan for them. For example, if social media is a negative influence, then social media education should attempt to address this by developing skills of critical and independent thinking. Since traditional media exerts a positive effect on civic knowledge, then it would seem helpful to incorporate these into the teaching and learning of civic education. This is particularly so in the light of the finding of this study that civic learning at school does not always positively influence students' formal civic knowledge (at least in the cases of Korea and Hong Kong). Both of these pedagogical initiatives need to move teaching away from direct instruction to models that can engage students more in the learning process since their purpose is to improve learning and not simply recitation of facts.

School participation emerged in this study as an important process that not only had a direct and positive effect on civic knowledge but also a mediating effect in relation to students' friendship experiences in school. This suggests that schools can place much more emphasis on developing participation experiences for students since whatever informal or incidental learning takes place can contribute in a very positive way to the culture of learning in a school. While these relationships did not seem to work in the Hong Kong context, this may be a good reason for taking time to improve both the nature and extent of such activities in that context. School participation's direct effect on civic knowledge in Hong Kong was relatively strong and its mediating effect with respect to friendship experiences was also positive. The direct effect of friendship experiences on civic knowledge in Hong Kong was marginally positive, but not significant. This suggests the mediating effect of school participation may not be effective. Yet this should not prevent Hong Kong schools from putting some effort into enhancing school participation activities.

Given the quantitative nature of the research reported here, it seems important to follow up with a series of qualitative studies to address significant issues that have been raised. One of those issues is concerned with the differential impact of school and community participation experiences on civic knowledge. Another is concerned with the role of friendship experiences and why they appear to have a negative or non-significant effect on civic knowledge. A third area has to do with school-based civic learning and its relationship with the international requirements of the ICCS Civic Knowledge test. What kind of curriculum do Taiwan's students experience that leads to a positive relationship between school-based learning and international requirements, and how does this compare with curriculum in Hong Kong and Korea?

As change becomes more rapid reflecting global growth and development, learning of all kinds will become more important. School learning is undoubtedly important, yet so too is the informal and even incidental learning that results from students' personal and social engagement in activities inside and outside of school. This study has made a small start in seeking to understand the complex relationships between informal and formal civic learning. Further work can build on these results so that more is known about multiple learning environments and learning opportunities can be translated into successful outcomes that can result in active, informed and engaged citizens.

Acknowledgement

The research work reported here was supported with a grant from the Central Reserve Allocation Committee and the Faculty of Education and Human Development of The Education University of Hong Kong for the project, "Big Data for School Improvement: Identifying and analysing multiple sources to support schools as learning communities" (Project No: 03A28).

References

Bentler, P. M. (1990). Comparative fit indices in structural models. *Psychological Bulletin, 107*, 238–246.

Berkowitz, R., Glickman, H., Benbenishty, R., Ben-Artzi, E., Raz, T., Lipshtat, N., & Astor, R. A. (2015). Compensating, mediating, and moderating effects of school climate on academic achievement gaps in Israel. *Teacher College Record, 117*(7), 1–34.

Blatchford, P., Pellegrini, A., & Baines, E. (2016). *The child at school: Interactions with peers and teachers* (2nd ed.). London & New York: Routledge.

Brooks, R., & Holford, J. (2009). Citizenship, learning and education: Themes and issues. *Citizenship Studies, 13*(2), 85–103.

Dennis, J. (2014, March 17). The Myth of the Keyboard Warrior: Public Participation and 38 Degrees. openDemocracy. Retrieved from http://www.opendemocracy.net/participationnow/james-dennis/myth-of-keyboard-warrior-public-participation-and-38-degrees

Dewey, J. (1909). *Moral principles in education*. New York: Arcturus Books.

Flashman, J. (2012). Academic achievement and its impact on friend dynamics. *Sociology of Education, 85*(1), 61–80.

Hu, L., & Bentler, P. (1999). Cutoff criteria for fit indexes in covariance structure analysis: Conventional criteria versus new alternatives. *Structural equation modeling: A multidisciplinary journal, 6*(1), 1–55.

98 Kerry J. Kennedy and Xiaoxue Kuang

Jöreskog, K., & Sörbom, D. (1993). *LISREL 8: Structural equation modeling with the SIMPLIS command language*. Lincolnwood, IL., Scientific Software International.

Kahne, J., & Sporte, S. (2008). Developing citizens: The impact of civic learning opportunities on students' commitment to civic participation. *American Educational Research Journal*, 45(3), 738–776.

Kennedy, K., Kuang, X., & Chow J. K. F. (2013). Exploring Asian students' citizenship values and their relationship to civic knowledge and school participation. *Educational Psychology*, 33(3), 240–261.

Klein, O., & Muis, J. (2018). Online discontent: Comparing Western European far right groups on Facebook. *European Societies*. [First online], doi: 10.1080/14616696.2018.1494293

Klofstad, C. (2007). Talk leads to recruitment how – discussions about politics and current events increase civic participation. *Political Research Quarterly*, 60(2), 180–191.

Knifsend, C., Camacho-Thompson, D, Juvonen, J., & Graham, S. (2018). Friends in activities, school-related affect, and academic outcomes in diverse diddle schools. *Journal of Youth and Adolescence*, 47(6), 1208–1220.

Lacey, A., & Cornell, D. (2013). The impact of teasing and bullying on schoolwide academic performance. *Journal of Applied School. Psychology*, 29(3), 262–283.

Lauglo, J. (2011). Political socialization in the family and young people's educational achievement and ambition. *British Journal of Sociology*, 32(1), 53–74.

Marsick, V., Watkins, K., Scully-Russ, E., & Nicolaides, A. (2017). Rethinking informal and incidental learning in terms of complexity and the social context. *Journal of Adult Learning*, 1(1), 27–34.

Mellor, S. (2010). Insights from formal testing of civics and citizenship learning in Australia. *Citizenship Teaching and Learning*, 6(1), 25–42

Nakamoto, J., & Schwartz, D. (2009). Is peer victimization associated with academic achievement? A meta-analytic review. *Social Development*, 19(2), 221–242.

Scheerens, J. (2011). Indicators on informal learning for active citizenship. *Educational Assessment, Evaluation and Accountability*, 23(3), 201–222. doi: 10.1007/s11092-011-9120-8

Schugurensky, D. (2006). "This is our school of citizenship": Informal learning in local democracy. *Counterpoints*, 249, 163–182.

Schulz, W., Ainley, J., Fraillon, J., Losito, B., Agrusti, G., & Friedman, T. (2018). *ICCS 2016 International report: Becoming citizens in a changing world*. Cham, Switzerland: Springer International Publishing.

Schulz, W., Ainley, J., Fraillon, J., Kerr, D., & Losito, B. (2010). *ICCS 2009 International Report: Civic knowledge, attitudes and engagement among lower secondary students in 38 countries*. Amsterdam, the Netherlands: International Association for the Evaluation of Educational Achievement (IEA).

Torney-Purta, J., Lehmann, R., Oswald, H., & Schulz, W. (2001). *Citizenship and education in twenty-eight countries – Civic Knowledge and Engagement at age fourteen*. Amsterdam, the Netherlands: International Association for the Evaluation of Educational Achievement (IEA).

Tucker, L. R., & Lewis, C. (1973). The reliability coefficient for maximum likelihood factor analysis. *Psychometrika*, 38, 1–10.

Wilkenfeld, B. (2009). Does context matter? How the family, peer, school, and neighborhood contexts relate to adolescents' civic engagement. *CIRCLE Working Paper #64*, Retrieved from https://civicyouth.org/PopUps/WorkingPapers/WP64Wilkenfeld.pdf

7 The Shanghai model for global geography education

Osvaldo Muñiz Solari and Lianfei Jiang

Introduction

Graduate students in geography, irrespective of subfields they are interested in, show a clear understanding of how environmental problems are being developed in the world. In fact, there is a sense of common preoccupation to find ways of resolving a variety of issues that affect land, water and the atmosphere. Students start their special connection with the Earth very early in their undergraduate years. The experiential activities they are exposed to in the fieldwork and laboratory practices are along with Kolb's experiential learning theory (Kolb, 1974). Even when Healy and Jenkins (2000) point out that both forms of learning are not prioritized, there are evidences that the latter has gained more adepts thanks to web-based platforms and accessibility to information technology. According to Perkins (2015), the increased power and availability of geospatial technologies (GST) in higher education have resulted in considerable multiplication in applications and users. Graduate students increasingly rely on remote operations for geospatial analysis. Geographic data is possible to obtain and interpret with enough accuracy by using Geographic Information System (GIS), Remote Sensing and Geographic Positioning System, among other GST. Furthermore, the worldwide availability of these technologies and devices connected to the Internet and to location hosted online, recognized as "cloud environment," facilitates activities develop by national and international practitioners engaged in networking operations.

If there has indeed been the kind of shift in learning in the sphere of cyber-networks that Kerski (2015) affirms, much of what is practised does not go along with traditional laboratories. Indeed, the growing influence of the Internet and the increasing number of devices to manage geographic information generate alternative modes of operations to study and resolve problems such as those related to environmental issues.

Similar environmental problems show repetitive characteristics and effects in different regions of the world, thus creating the need for sharing experiences and solutions. As young researchers, graduate students are eager to learn about similar environmental issues that occur in other parts of the world. Therefore, new communities of geographers tend to collaborate internationally to share knowledge through cybernetworks that impulse cooperation practised via online collaboration.

In the light of all this, it is reasonable to recognize how the term community of practice (CP) in the context of this chapter is understood given the influence of the cybernetworks. Knowledge reproduction seems to be the centre of communities as Lave and Wenger (1991) identify its evolution and reproduction. The situated learning theory emphasizes the relational attribute of individuals in permanent interaction with one another rather than a condition controlled by individuals. The cultural context in which each person is immersed and absorbs knowledge from it is a critical condition for knowledge development. However, the increasing influence of cybernetworks and the use of GST give a special condition to individuals who are part of a community that study the Earth. The legitimate peripheral participation by which learners enter this type of communities and engage with their practices is also combined with the independent work developed by individuals. It is this independency to think and look for new experience, information and practice that is translated into a constant informal learning (IL) process. Furthermore, Wenger, Trayner, and De Laat (2011) point out that the value of networks depends on individuals as independent nodes to act and evaluate the relevance of information flows for themselves and for the network. If we applied this approach to any CP that studies and tries to resolve geographic problems, such as those that involve environmental issues, it would be very logical to expect complex information flows. As a result, IL takes a dual form of operation influenced by the continuous action of the information communication technologies (ICT). A participant's IL about GST and resolving geospatial problems with GST faces the condition of being a user as well as a producer. Such practices have been identified by Budhathoki, Bruce, and Nedovic-Budic (2008) as "producers;" practitioners as informal learners and as informal contributors that in some occasions take global dimensions represented by crowd-collaborative communities.

The objective of this chapter is to demonstrate the value of IL within the context of a small CP in geography education. In this case study, several graduate students begin their journey knowing at front that they are part of a global community. Chinese students show a sense of responsibility to deal with environmental issues in their own country. They welcome foreign scientists to receive assistance and work together for some possible solutions. We will see that this CP shows a great disposition and willingness to overcome difficulties through special learning processes and find reasonable conclusions. Whether they work away from the real space or stay very close to it, the ability of participants to develop some effective results based on informal practice seems to indicate equal competence to deal with spatial thinking.

This experience should help to understand how a formal setting in geography education may create a good channel to IL. In fact, the most challenging aspect of this experience is to determine whether the IL takes its own course or requires some examination when dealing with a problem-based learning (PBL) situation.

Towards IL and global universities

We usually agree that the permanent improvement of ICT has created informed citizens who, with advanced or initial knowledge, are exposed to constant worldwide information over a multiple array of issues and problems. We also agree that population in various regions of the world is affected by the "digital divide;" phenomenon that is still a negative factor in the process of global integration (James, 2008) and even resulting in clear differences of digital dividends (World Bank Group, 2016).

Notwithstanding the fact of evident digital divides in various forms and conditions, the digital world integration is breaking down regional as well as territorial isolation. However, a great deal of people around the world are just part of what is recognized as social networks. Thus, people from different regions and countries have come closer through social contacts with the most diverse forms of platforms and channels. Apps and multiple devices play crucial roles in this increasing complex digital world. Besides social integration through the digital world it is equally important for the individual who takes advantage of both digital information and digital infrastructure to use and be an active participant of the digital world integration. Consequently, self-learning practice has been one of the evident benefits that people around the world have experienced with the development of ICT.

It seems to be obvious that an initial and very weak self-learning practice starts to take shape within the rudimentary digital network in the late 1970s. Usenet was created in 1979 by graduate students at Duke University. Hauben (1996) explains the creation of a simple network by three Unix computer sites at Duke University and the University of North Carolina at Chapel Hill. What follows is an increasing self-learning process practised by pioneers in networking with the creation of ARPANET and BITNET. The cyberinfrastructure was in its initial stage of development, far from territorial and global digital networks that are active today. Once Internet was built, as we currently know it, the IL activities accomplished by people on digital operations grew very fast and consistent with the exponential expansion of the cyberinfrastructure (Figure 7.1).

From citizens to netizens as Hauben (1996) introduces the latter concept and explains the initial evolution of information, he wrote:

> Net society differs from off-line society by welcoming intellectual activity. People are encouraged to have things on their mind and to present those ideas to the Net. People are allowed to be intellectually interesting and interested. This intellectual activity forms a major part of the on-line information that is carried by the various computer networks. Netizens can interact with other people to help add to or alter that information. Brainstorming between varieties of people produces robust thinking. Information is no longer a fixed commodity or resource on the Nets. It is constantly being added to and improved collectively. (p. 1)

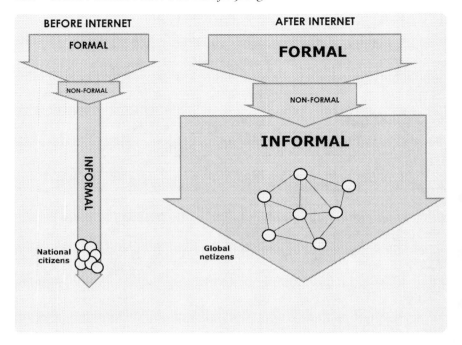

Figure 7.1 Cybernetwork and the expansion of IL.

Even when he described the Net society and the netizens in the late 1990s, it was a good perception of a global society closer to our present time. The concept of global inclusion has taken the world population to a new level of geographic integration that reduces the effect of borders among countries. However, the most profound significance of connectedness is the ability of individuals to expand their knowledge through informal education. Rogers (2004) clarifies that informal education is in fact IL; subsidiary and unstructured knowledge being the most extensive and intensive of all learning processes that each person practises every day. IL in this case study is consistent with the definition above. Furthermore, the model implies any knowledge assimilated by participants of a CP in geography that occurs inside and beyond the university environment, the latter mainly occurring through online operations.

Despite the influence of very active social networks and even individual experience of self-learning practices, it is argued in this study that the "global society" has not reached the stage of producing "global citizens." Muñiz Solari (2015) points out that there still are weak identification, responsibility and compromise with other global citizens. People are eager to watch events unfold in distant parts of the world, but they are easily disengaged when fellow citizens are seriously affected by environmental problems or even in great distress due to human conflicts and social tensions. When a natural disaster occurs such as earthquake, tsunami and nuclear radiation catastrophe, as we

Global geography education: Shanghai model 103

have observed in the past, social networks and crowd-collaborative communities actively respond with comments and suggestions. Moreover, the latter usually integrate data-sharing process to produce crowd maps to facilitate local and regional operations. Nevertheless, it is just a matter of time to observe how these expressions of global integration and mutual global responsibility tend to fade away and disappear.

Boni and Calabuig (2017) locate the formation of global citizens within the third imaginary (Marginson, 2011) represented by higher education institutions that can have an important role in national and international societies as places of interconnectivity. According to Nussbaum (2006) as cited by Boni and Calabuig (2017), cosmopolitan citizens are engaged with the global community of people to learn more about themselves, solve global problems through international cooperation and have obligations to the rest of the world.

Several studies demonstrate that the formation of future global citizens among university students has strongly been linked to the educational strategy of learning beyond the classroom (Brown & Cope, 2013; Burge, 2012; Singh & Sproats, 2005; Tallant, 2010). In the case of undergraduate and graduate students in geography and similar fields, three specific strategies are usually applied: International fieldwork, study abroad programmes and online collaboration. The first two are usually focused on one specific country with intensive activities yet they cannot create a wide and complex interaction as it is commonly seen with online collaboration (Muñiz Solari, & Coats, 2009; Ray, Muñiz Solari, Klein, & Solem, 2012). Online collaboration has increasingly connected universities as a result of constant and persistent innovations by researchers and students in the fields of online operations, digital platforms and network development. Regional universities have become global universities by sharing expertise and providing mutual information on educational technology, digital repositories and open sources. Bonamici, Huter, and Smith (2010) give a good example of online collaboration with the Network Startup Resource Center (NSRC), based at the University of Oregon. It was established in 1992 and for almost 20 years has leapfrogged the development of many campus networks in Africa, Asia, the Pacific Islands and Latin America.

The process of advancing in positions within the worldwide networks has been an important strategy to trigger networking in the digital world. Greater efficiency by reducing time and procedures to overcome language and cultural barriers, among others, represents one of the important goals in cyberinfrastructure implementation. This process can be demonstrated by stages from local network (intranet) to regional, national and international networks where interaction, cooperation and collaboration reach the level of permanent networking (Figure 7.2).

The sporadic self-learning practices developed by computer pioneers in the small networks during the 1970s have been transformed into permanent IL carry on by researchers, instructors and students alike in global universities. Among these digital IL activities are those performed by geography educators to study a variety of physical and human processes occurring in different

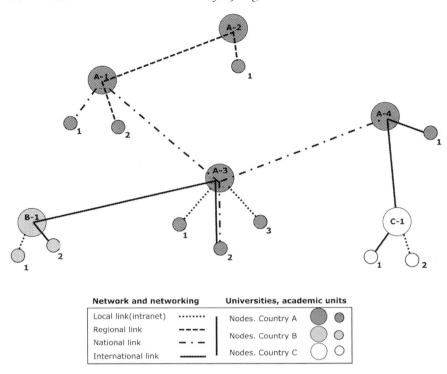

Figure 7.2 Reaching global university networking.

regions of the world. One group of geography educators are pre-service teachers who are also taking advantage of global universities through the principle of CP. So, on this view, participation is something that works its way into student's lives through their commitment to understand the Earth and be responsible for its environment. Their preparation to understand spatial phenomena is progressively combined with a shared responsibility for the well-being of their fellow netizens and nature. This new generation of geography educators are recognized by their willingness to work as global citizens with a netizen mind. However, their own strategies are based on IL practised with and increasing use and applications of digital geographic tools. They represent dynamic CP liberated from traditional formal education that is still disengaged from a "geo-enabled" world.

Technology-based IL

The increasing interoperability and user-generated content of the Web 2.0 has opened big channels for websites to enable community-based input, and content-sharing that facilitate interaction, cooperation and collaboration among participants. What is different with the new trend is the collaborative engagement of participants using geographic tools in this digital open environment.

Informal settings bring a new challenge when participants use technologies because the IL is socially and collaboratively developed in unorganized and non-administered form. Lai, Khaddage, and Knezek (2013) explain this special setting as opposed to formal education when dealing with blended activities in which digital technology presents some unification. In this regard, technology integration is defined as multiple combinations of computers, devices and apps to operate various software programs. Moreover, the use of devices and apps by individuals who are seeking for some solutions fulfil the critical function of generating coalescence among participants. This should be interpreted as the process of growing together in online learning communities via timely IL. The right moment to participate in the process of acquiring new knowledge and sharing information requires an effective digital integration. IL plays a precise mechanism based on the individual's good manipulation of data or information through electronic devices. Some of these digital devices are mobile in nature and are broadly used. Both these features have expanded instantaneous self-learning as well as cooperation and collaboration. Avci and Adiguvel (2017), citing Clough, Jones, McAndrew, and Scanlone (2008), remark on the reinforcing effect of both "opportunistic IL" and "collaborative IL" when participants use mobile technologies.

Higher education institutions and especially global universities with increasing digital integration are encouraging the use of mobile learning among their students to generate greater interaction and collaboration. Krull and Duart (2017) indicate in their research trends in mobile learning in higher education (2011–2015) that a significant proportion of studies focus on multiple devices. Here IL again has an important role due to the ubiquitous characteristic of wireless devices, such as smartphones and tablets, that have a liquid crystal display (LCD) flat-screen interface.

Technology-based IL practised by students who interact globally confronts some important barriers. Two of these barriers are related to the use of foreign languages and interaction with partners with different cultural backgrounds. Both create impediments for easy and fluent interaction that might hinder efficient communication. These obstructions tend to slow cooperation and collaboration, especially when IL is developed via mobile devices.

First, language abilities can be broadly defined as the capacity to read, search and communicate online in a different language. IL effectiveness might depend on strategies and skills to overcome difficulties to fully understand concepts and ideas. Cheng (2016) demonstrates that participants in an online learning process of reading in foreign language were able to show not only higher-order cognitive abilities in locating resources, evaluating materials, but also skills related to linguistic decoding and processing of materials. Moreover, online synchronous and asynchronous conversation like live chats and instant messages could improve language exchange. Baek, Yoo, Lee, Jung, and Baek (2017) explore this issue in a peer-tutoring environment with a positive impact of language exchange for students. Nevertheless, more sophisticated strategies are necessary to reach certain language proficiency threshold in an IL environment.

Second, differences in culture, such as values, norms, beliefs and basic assumptions, might create a variety of obstacles to develop efficient technology-based IL. Research results show strategies to reduce obstacles due to cultural differences in online settings. Cross-cultural understanding can be facilitated with self-introduction (Liu, 2007; Tu, 2004) to allow students to become acquainted with one another. A more refined strategy that falls into the management field with possible applications to online environment is innovation culture. Roffeei, Yusop, and Kamarulzaman (2018) develop a model based on undergraduate students in public research universities in Malaysia. The result of a structural equation modelling analysis demonstrates that self-efficacy, effective communication and innovation culture have significant effect on innovative behaviour.

Regardless of the situation or environmental conditions, the importance of self-belief in building innovation culture is evident. This strategy can be applied to online environment where technology-based IL requires strong initiative and innovation from participants working in community. Consistent with this approach, Karaseva (2016) has concluded that informal networking seems to be an important factor influencing teacher's self-efficacy. They learned their search skills without any formal training, by exercising the trial-and-error method. Particularly, self-efficacy and effective communication on the Earth's issues, such as environmental problems, tend to overcome cultural differences when graduate geography students develop geospatial thinking. This is commonly defined as a special and in-depth exercise of spatial thinking related to physical and human processes and patterns that occur on the Earth's surface and its atmospheric zone.

The geo-enabling world has accelerated the process of technology-based IL, and geospatial thinking practised by pre-service geography teachers through informal approach has equally been stimulated. Yet, for any successful work based on IL, it includes not only the efficient work accomplished with geo-enabled devices, but also the formal learning (FL) of a traditional setting that might also include the lab environment. Geospatial thinking needs the initial support of systematic analysis performed by an organized group of participants. In fact, spatial thinking and spatial literacy form two important pillars of spatial abilities that graduate students require to master in their preparation to become geography teachers. Jo and Muñiz Solari (2015) point out that a continuous exercise of basic and advanced concepts is necessary for good spatial literacy that allows the development of spatial thinking. Spatial abilities represent the first stage in the context of geospatial capacity building which is completed with geospatial integrative skills (i.e. data handling, data sharing) as a second stage (Figure 7.3). Nevertheless, the web-based platforms have introduced a new element of disengagement from FL. It is the inquiry process of asking geographic questions that increasingly relies on web-based GST. Baker et al. (2015) argue that the use of GST slowly expands to different learning settings, and both formal and informal procedures present a challenge in the teaching environment. Activities involving GST are already more often developed in digital IL settings enabling faster and more flexible research projects.

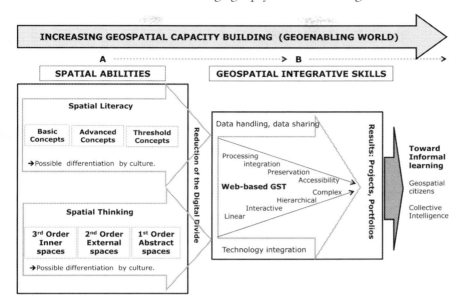

Figure 7.3 Integral geography education with GST in a geo-enabling world.

Adapted from Muñiz Solari (2014) as cited by Jo and Muñiz Solari (2015)

The Shanghai model for geography education

The need for an initial common ground to activate digital learning of world problems has brought together geography educators and students from distant countries creating several intercultural experiences (Muñiz Solari, 2009; Muñiz Solari & Coats, 2009; Ray et al., 2012). Intercultural Internet-based learning strategies represent one of the initial stages for global interaction and cooperation (Keane, 2005; Liu, 2007).

As an expression of global interaction and cooperation this geography education research experience has been conducted with a group of master and doctoral students in the School of Geographic Sciences at East China Normal University (ECNU), Shanghai, under the guidance of a professor and expert in online education from the Department of Geography at Texas State University. The international experience constitutes the first step of a Memorandum of Understanding in geographical studies between the two higher education institutions. ECNU Academic Community of Geography Education took the initiative to open the opportunity to develop this experience (East China Normal University, 2016). It represents a model for international collaboration in geography education with a strong emphasis on IL.

The increasing influence of technology integration has a more advanced manifestation with collaboration among participants who work in a CP (Meier, 2007; Warf, Vincent, & Purcell, 1999) yet they are not free of impediments such as

108 *Osvaldo Muñiz Solari and Lianfei Jiang*

language and cultural norms (Muñiz Solari, 2009; Warf et al., 1999), which might eventually discourage not only formal online education but also IL. Consequently, it was important to find procedures or verify the benefit of some strategies to reduce the effect of language barriers and cultural differences that Muñiz Solari (2009) points out as critical obstacles for collaboration.

What is interesting about global interaction, or for that matter the construction of collaboration among participants who understand global geographic issues, is the collective exercise of cooperation as a response to a common responsibility with world problems such as environmental impacts.

This case study is about a special blended learning (SBL) process performed by Chinese graduate students that in their condition of pre-service teachers work collaboratively in geography education. As stated by Cuesta Medina (2018), the blended learning creates an increased level of student flexibility that is also conducive to self-direct learning in which "they are exposed to multiple options to access and produce [online] content both synchronously and asynchronously, with or without the assistance of an instructor" (p. 48).

The SBL is a synergic action that starts with individual and group performance in geospatial thinking based on lab activities guided by a facilitator. The face-to-face activities of phase one are complemented by phase two activities that take each individual and teams away from the lab environment to pursue full digital IL. Even when there is a blended learning setting, both phases are characterized by technology-based IL and digital integration. Overall, the facilitator takes a secondary role in initiating an inquiry-based learning (IBL) or the exploration of academic content by presenting questions and requesting some answers. Each group of students is engaged in the "inquiry" process that is transformed in a more advanced learning when the groups are collapsed into one team to initiate and develop PBL. PBL is the study of a "real world" problem or situation as a context for learning once the IBL process gives the students some elements for analysis of a specific problem. In the process of implementation and development of both IBL and PBL, some barriers are tackled by special strategies to reduce inefficient acquisition of geographic knowledge (Figure 7.4).

The formal setting that guides the IL process

The first phase of this experience began in 2014 with a formal education setting for 15 graduate students organized in three groups for a 3-day workshop in the Geography Education Lab. The objective was twofold. First, learn the basic procedures that guide a CP to study global climate change based on IBL. Second, develop an inquiry process on factors that create climate change in China to initiate the process of problem analysis based on PBL during the second phase of this international collaboration.

The activities during the first phase focused on the mechanisms of global collaboration that is increasingly executed with an IL approach. Nevertheless, the initial stage of this phase required a guidance through an international project in

Global geography education: Shanghai model 109

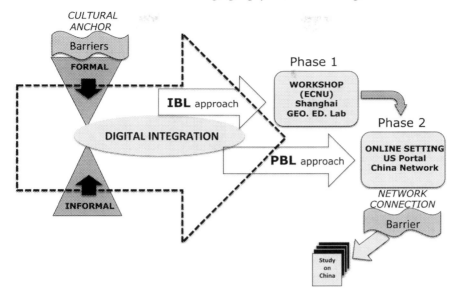

Figure 7.4 The Shanghai model for learning and collaboration.

geography education. We started with the international contributions of scholars who had worked with the Center for Global Geography Education (CGGE); a project funded by the National Science Foundation to develop a collection of course modules exploring important geographic issues (American Association of Geographers, 2010). CGGE modules use different platforms or Learning Management Systems (LMSs) to link students in countries around the world for collaborative learning, inquiry and comparative analysis. For this experience we used the global climate change modules (Solem, Klein, Muñiz Solari, & Ray, 2010) to guide the Chinese students as a CP for interaction and cooperation. The structure of a formal setting during the first phase demonstrates a new form of interaction and cooperation to set the guidelines for IL (Table 7.1).

The workshop was conducted in English because of both the facilitator's guidance and the CGGE materials published online by the American Association of Geographers (AAG). Consequently, it was advisable to select a strategy to overcome the language barrier confronted by the Chinese students who had very basic English preparation. Among the groups, three students had good English language proficiency to perform as mediators and allow each group to speak Chinese while English was also used for completing the activities. This strategy was very effective during the first 2 days that were devoted not only to understand the CGGE experience, the process of collaboration and the IBL approach, but also the initial IL operations within an FL environment.

Concerns about global climate impacts were already built in every participant's mind by the beginning of the third day when activities took a clear path towards the identification of problems in China. It was the time for initial PBL

110   *Osvaldo Muñiz Solari and Lianfei Jiang*

Table 7.1 Structure of formal setting (a 3-day workshop)

Time	Activity		Participants
Day 1			All (FL)
Morning	1	Introduction. The CGGE experience	All (FL)
Afternoon	2	Theory and methods for collaboration	All (FL)
	3	CGGE Learning modules. Form and structure	3 groups (FL)
	4	First practice. Working collaboratively	
Day 2			All (FL)
Morning	5	LMS. Working with platform	All (FL)
Afternoon	6	Guide. Facilitator and students. Operation	3 groups (FL)
	7	International collaboration. Strategy	3 groups (IL)
	8	Second practice. Working with IBL	
Day 3			Group 1 (IL)
Morning	9	Preparation of case study. Proposition 1	Group 2 (IL)
Afternoon	10	Preparation of case study. Proposition 2	Group 3 (IL)
	11	Preparation of case study. Proposition 3	Group 1 (IL)
	12	Working with PBL. Presentation 1. Discussion	Group 2 (IL)
	13	Working with PBL. Presentation 2. Discussion	Group 3 (IL)
	14	Working with PBL. Presentation 3. Discussion	All
	15	Final selection of one case study	

Note: CGGE, Center for Global Geography Education; FL, formal learning; IL, informal learning; IBL, inquiry-based learning; LMS, learning management system; PBL, problem-based learning

operations that were developed by each group of participants with an increasing IL approach. Thus, computer work in the lab and the constant use of digital devices such as iPhones and tablets by this CP characterized its work to create potential case studies and final propositions (Figure 7.5). The goal for each group during this phase one was to present a feasible environmental problem to be investigated in China with its most plausible analysis. The result was a final selection of one case study after the three presentations were delivered with a complete discussion about pros and cons of the study projections. For this environmental experience the final selection focused on the effect of haze and how to deal with its impact in China. Even when each group started a different project to study environmental issues related to global climate change in China, the whole community of geography educators finally formed one team. It was recognized as the "Shanghai Team" to study the effect of haze. After that action the team was ready to enter the second phase.

IL through online operations

In the light of the foregoing, we would like to press the point that the PBL approach is firmly rooted in the IBL initiative. The IL is structured with IBL as the first learning strategy to analyze the environmental issues. Although the two learning processes look like they are unrelated, PBL takes a special new road for IL operations that are only possible to accomplish when the main findings resulting from the IBL exercise are fully considered. In doing so, the second

Figure 7.5 Formal setting towards IL environment.

phase started with the IBL conducted by the group that presented the potential study on haze in China.

The Chinese team initiated the second phase with full international online operations supported by a LMS identified as TRACS at Texas State University. The LMS platform is based on Sakai; a fully customizable, 100% open-source LMS that allows participants to use more than one language for interaction, cooperation and collaboration within a research environment. TRACS-Global Climate Change platform (TRACS-GCC) was designed in Chinese and English with multiple functions such as core tools (e.g. calendar, email, resources, forums), content delivery (e.g. drop-box, learning modules) and collaboration (e.g. chat room, meetings and wiki).

The SBL strategy that characterized the first phase is transformed into a complete digital IL during the second phase. The IL process associated with the TRACS-GCC started with the Shanghai Team uploading their personal PowerPoint presentations, which were necessary to introduce themselves to the American counterpart. The latter was a Chinese advance geography doctoral student completing her GIS graduate program at Texas State University. She was asked to serve as a liaison for the Shanghai Team to facilitate the interaction process and reduce any language barrier that might inhibit the IL process. She also uploaded a personal presentation to initiate the interaction with the Shanghai Team and invited them to follow some procedures with IL strategies to explore the problem of haze.

112   *Osvaldo Muñiz Solari and Lianfei Jiang*

The networked interaction necessary to analyze during the second phase was more concentrated in the transformation of knowledge rather than the transmission of it. We were interested in the process of IL evolution under the influence of full online operations; therefore, it was quite interesting to observe how the IL practice by each participant took a new form influenced by the spatial disaggregation of the whole Shanghai Team. In other words, the cohesion that characterized the process of IL during the first phase of the SBL was totally transformed when each participant moved to different locations. Some of them left Shanghai to relocate in nearby rural areas or even stay far away from the metropolitan area for vacation or to work as new in-service teachers in high schools. As a clear consequence of this disaggregation several participants experienced new forms of IL influenced by the availability of electronic devices, Internet reliability, electronic information and time constraint.

Interaction and cooperation were required at this stage of the collaboration process to complete the PBL strategy. At this point, we need to remember that the CP had been engaged in geospatial thinking with an IBL strategy and they were now required to explore, understand and resolve the problem of haze in China. The PBL operations entail a special strategy to maximize the IL among participants. Thus, one member of the Shanghai Team took the leadership position to coordinate the interaction among members of the team that worked separately in mainland China. On the other side of the international project, the American counterpart maintained a direct interaction with the leader of the Shanghai Team through the TRACS-GCC. She offered and shared with the Shanghai Team another approach on haze in China by conducting IL based on both Chinese and English open sources.

Barriers are not only limited to language and cultural differences but also to technological reliability of the cyberinfrastructure. China is still affected by unstable connections, and this is a complex problem for an aspatial CP that is disseminated in different geographic areas. Unreliable connections inhibit the process of efficient knowledge transmission. Consequently, when the Shanghai Team faced the problem of unstable Internet to reach and proceed to interaction and cooperation based on the TRACS-GCC, the solution was to use a native resource for communication and keep a stable interaction among members of the Shanghai Team. The use of Tencent QQ as an instant messaging software allowed members to create TRACS-GCC-Texas; a QQ site to generate synchronous contact and keep working in the preparation of a report to study haze in China. Meanwhile, the Chinese leader maintained asynchronous communication with the American partner through TRACS-GCC to function as a link and update results of the IL process developed by the Shanghai Team. Another alternative solution was the use of regular emails to complete the process of data and document exchange.

We illustrate the whole IL online operations by a consecutive two-stage strategy of group and teamwork completed with individual IL to keep the process of building knowledge in permanent continuity. The initial aggregation created clusters of participants working together in the IBL process that is transformed

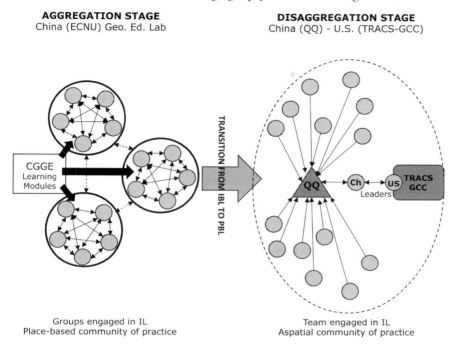

Figure 7.6 The Shanghai Model (a two-stage strategy for online IL).

into a disaggregated stage of participants working together remotely to develop the PBL process. During both stages, the IL progression is transformed to maintain an efficient knowledge transmission conducive to a final report on haze in China (Figure 7.6).

Results and discussion

Even when there are studies that still consider collaboration among universities and online learning in geography education a difficult enterprise (Clark & Wilson, 2017; Donert, Hay, Theobald, Valiunaite, & Wakefield, 2011), Clark and Wilson (2017) conclude that "due to its inherently global outlook, the discipline of geography is particularly well placed to capitalize on collaboration and online learning" (p. 501). However, the most promising global online collaboration among universities must be identified as a spontaneous work developed by researchers and students within an IL environment rather than formal settings through course delivery.

Global collaboration in geography education is an important responsibility because it creates among participants, as in the case of pre-service teachers, a clear compromise to prepare and guide global citizens. Learning beyond the classroom placed online collaboration as an excellent bridge between the formal setting and the informal one, expressing the latter as an amplification of opportunities offered by the cyberinfrastructure. Consequently, networking was translated into dynamic knowledge through IL transformed by digital technology. This case study has shown the evolution of a CP engaged in global collaboration after transitioning from a formal setting to a complete informal environment.

As an SBL process, this case study helped to initially understand how a formal lab setting in geography education created a good environment to develop IL among pre-service teachers who participated in an active CP. The most challenging aspect of this experience was to determine whether the IL could take a special course of action or being controlled by the initial FL practiced in the Geography Education Lab. In fact, it can be affirmed that the IL practiced by members of the CP organized in groups and working individually generated its own form and evolution characterized by a combination of IBL and PBL. This is particularly important when each participant learned to cope with uncertainty to resolve geospatial problems. They used their geospatial thinking acquired during previous geographic formal training to overcome difficult tasks. Consequently, the IL process took a typical exercise of selecting problems that focus on physical and human conditions; two fundamental directions that any geographer takes to analyze a geographic problem. Furthermore, and consistent with Karaseva's findings (Karaseva, 2016) they searched skills without any formal training by exercising the trial-and-error method.

The effectiveness of such endeavour was very early demonstrated by the need to overcome the barrier of language to develop effective IL. The special efforts made by each group and individual working in the geography education lab to use a foreign language besides their own was successfully accomplished with the assistance of some local leaders. Moreover, each member of this CP attempted to succeed in dealing with cultural differences to understand various perspectives on research approaches to analyze geographic problems and find adequate results. Yet the argument of this chapter was that however intimate the CP with subsequent IL, the latter took a special dimension activated by individual work based on a geo-enabled world. Thus, because of an aspatial setting during the phase, most of the participants worked separately in IL; therefore, building a personal knowledge construction related to the problem of haze in China. Even when the integration of knowledge was finally translated into a common report, the individual IL evolution was difficult to verify and measure.

During both phases, the IL progression was evidently transformed to maintain an efficient knowledge transmission, but some distortion and reduction of knowledge assimilation affected the outcome of this online experience at the end. To estimate the impacts of the transition from group activity during the aggregation stage to individual initiative during the disaggregation stage (Figure 7.6) will require a special assessment of the full online IL operation in the future. This assessment must be the initial point to start a new research project that might measure the succession and translation of geographical knowledge.

Undoubtedly, the effect of the opportunistic IL, as cited by Clough et al. (2008), became weaker as participants got increasingly immersed in IBL and later in PBL benefited by collaborative IL. In fact, it is fair to admit that technology integration played an important role because the use of computers, devices and apps helped to build knowledge through good manipulation of data.

Spatial thinking and geospatial thinking were evident among participants, yet the insufficient experience and ability to use GST reduced the effect of efficient geospatial analysis conducted not only by each group but also by each participant. The merit of this experience is based on the effort made by this CP to use technology integration through IL; however, GST in the form of GIS, Remote Sensing and Geographic Positioning System were not completely utilized. We expected to reach a process of IL about GST and with GST. Nevertheless, this process requires a more advanced stage where the CP reaches the level of a specialized scientific community.

Conclusions

This case study demonstrates the importance of a CP in geography education that takes advantage of the cybernetwork to get engaged in the SBL process based on IL to investigate an environmental issue in China.

The most challenging aspect of this experience was to verify that the IL on the selected environmental problem took its own course during the transition from IBL (first phase) to PBL (second phase). Equally important was the issue of experimenting with the notion of global citizens. The language barrier was resolved with a very smart strategy based on the natural selection of leaders with better proficiency in English. The solution of this problem that has always been a problem for Chinese students working either in formal or informal environments paved the way to facilitate the process of cultural difference when they studied similar western environmental issues.

Interaction, cooperation and collaboration were evident during each phase of this experience in which IL practices increased through time. It was easy to observe all the members of this CP interacting very efficiently to go through the IBL experience. Nevertheless, the cooperative emphasis of the initial stage of phase two represented by the PBL experience did not translate into strong collaboration among participants who develop their IL on haze in China. It was not the transmission of knowledge but the transformation of it that captured our attention. Still this critical issue was not resolved completely despite an organized IL experience during the aggregation stage. Probably the aspatial condition of all the members during the final stage of phase two played against the opportunity to measure the transformation of knowledge acquired through IL.

Finally, the great value of this case study is the informal experiential learning process developed with digital technology integration and its initial networking activities conducted by a CP in geography education.

116   *Osvaldo Muñiz Solari and Lianfei Jiang*

References

American Association of Geographers. (2010). *Internationalizing the Teaching and Learning of Geography,* Center for Global Geography Education (CGGE). Retrieved February 25, 2018, from http://www.aag.org/cs/cgge/modules

Avci, H., & Adiguvel, T. (2017). A case study on mobile-blended collaborative learning in an English as Foreign Language (EFL) context. *International Review of Research in Open and Distributed Learning, 18*(7), 45–58.

Baek, J., Yoo, Y., Lee, K., Jung, B., & Baek, Y. (2017). Using an instant messenger to learn a foreign language in a peer-tutoring environment. *The Turkish Online Journal of Educational Technology, 16*(2), 145–152.

Baker, T., Battersby, S., Bednarz, S., Bodzin, A., Kolvoord, B., & Moore, S., et al. (2015). A research agenda for geospatial technologies and learning. *Journal of Geography, 114,* 118–130.

Bonamici, A., Huter, A. G., & Smith, D. (2010). Cultivating global cyberinfrastructure for sharing digital resources. *Educause Review, 45*(2), 10–11.

Boni, A., & Calabuig, C. (2017). Education for global citizenship at universities: Potentialities of formal and informal learning spaces to foster cosmopolitanism. *Journal of Studies in International Education, 21*(1), 22–38.

Brown, S., & Cope, V. (2013). Global citizenship for the non-traditional student. *Journal of Community Engagement and Scholarship, 6*(1), 28–36.

Budhathoki, N. R., Bruce, B., & Nedovic-Budic, Z. (2008). Reconceptualizing the role of the users of spatial data infrastructure. *GeoJournal, 72*(3–4), 149–160.

Burge, L. (2012). Infinite possibilities: Exploring opportunities for no-traditional students to become global citizens. *Widening Participation and Lifelong Learning, 13,* 6–18.

Cheng, R. (2016). Reading online in foreign languages: A study of strategy use. *International Review of Research in Open and Distributed Learning, 17*(6), 164–181.

Clark, C., & Wilson, B. (2017). The potential for university collaboration and online learning to internationalise geography education. *Journal of Geography in Higher Education, 41*(4), 488–505.

Clough, G., Jones, A. C., McAndrew, P., & Scanlone, E. (2008). Informal learning with PDAs and smartphones. *Journal of Computer Assisted Learning, 24,* 359–371.

Cuesta Medina, L. (2018). Blended learning: Deficits and prospects in higher education. *Australasian Journal of Educational Technology, 34*(1), 42–56.

Donert, K., Hay, I., Theobald, R., Valiunaite, V., & Wakefield, K. (2011). International collaboration in organizations promoting geography education: Exploring success and acknowledging limitations. *Journal of Geography in Higher Education, 35,* 445–455.

East China Normal University. (2016). Academic Community of Geography Education. Shanghai: China Standard Serial Number (CN) 31-1022/G4. ISSN 1000-078X.

Hauben, M. (1996). *Netizens: on the history and impact of Usenet and the Internet.* Retrieved January 10, 2018, from http://www.columbia.edu/~hauben/netbook/index.html

Healy M., & Jenkins, A. (2000). Learning cycles and learning styles: Kolb's experiential learning theory and its application in geography in higher education. *J. Geography, 99,* 185–195.

James, M. J. (2008). *The digital divide across all citizens of the world: a new concept.* Social Indicators Research. Tilburg: The Netherlands. Retrieved January 7, 2018, from https://pure.uvt.nl/ws/files/917495/fulltext.pdf

Jo, I., & Muñiz Solari O. (2015). An agenda of GST in geography education for the future. In O. Muñiz Solari, A. Demirci, & J. Van der Schee (Eds.), *Geospatial technologies and geography education in a changing world* (pp. 205–221). Tokyo: Springer.

Karaseva, A. (2016). Relationship of internet self-efficacy and online search performance of secondary school teachers. *Procedia—Social and Behavioral Sciences, 231,* 278–285.

Keane, M. C. (2005). Geography forum: Intercultural learning online. In K. Donert, & P. Charzynski (Eds.), *Proceedings of the changing horizons in geography education* (pp. 236–240). Torun, Poland: HERODOT Network.

Kerski, J. (2015). Opportunities and challenges in using geospatial technologies for education. In O. Muñiz Solari, A. Demirci, & J. Van der Schee (Eds.), *Geospatial technologies and geography education in a changing world* (pp. 183–194). Tokyo: Springer.

Kolb, D. A. (1974). *Toward and applied theory of experiential learning.* Cambridge, MA: MIT Alfred P. Sloan School of Management.

Krull, G., & Duart, J. M. (2017). Research trends in mobile learning in higher education: A systematic review of articles (2011–2015). *International Review of Research in Open and Distributed Learning, 18*(7), 1–23.

Lai, K. W., Khaddage, F., & Knezek, G. (2013). Blending student technology experiences in formal and informal learning. *Journal of Computer Assisted Learning, 29*(5), 414–425.

Lave, J., & Wenger, E. (1991). *Situated learning: Legitimate peripheral participation.* New York: Cambridge University Press.

Liu, Y. (2007). Designing quality online education to promote cross-cultural understanding. In A. Edmundson (Ed.), *Globalized e-learning cultural challenges* (pp. 35–59) Hershey, PA: International Science Publishing.

Marginson, S. (2011). Higher education and the public good. *Higher Education Quarterly, 65,* 411–433.

Meier, C. (2007). Enhancing intercultural understanding using e-learning strategies. *South African Journal of Education, 27,* 655–671.

Muñiz Solari, O. (2009). Educación geográfica internacional por aprendizaje virtual. *Apertura, 9*(10), 89–103.

Muñiz Solari, O. (2014, October). *Geospatial technologies in geography education.* Shanghai, China: Keynote speech at the School of Geographical Science, East China Normal University.

Muñiz Solari, O. (2015). Geography education is a global responsibility. It is all about the earth. *Turkish Journal of Geography Education, 1*(1), 14–20.

Muñiz Solari, O., & Coats, C. (2009). Integrated networks; national and international online experiences. *International Review of Research in Open and Distance Learning, 10*(1), 1–19.

Nussbaum, M. (2006). Education and democratic citizenship: Capabilities and quality education. *Journal of Human Development, 7,* 385–395.

Perkins, R. (2015). Applied geospatial technologies in higher education. In O. Muñiz Solari, A. Demirci, & J. Van der Schee (Eds.), *Geospatial technologies and geography education in a changing world* (pp. 77–88). Tokyo: Springer.

Ray, W., Muñiz Solari, O., Klein, P., & Solem, M. (2012). Effective online practices for international learning collaborations. *Review of International Geographical Education Online—RIGEO, 2*(1), 25–42.

Roffeei, S., Yusop, F., & Kamarulzaman, Y. (2018). Determinants of innovation culture amongst higher education students. *The Turkish Online Journal of Educational Technology, 17*(1), 37–50.

118 *Osvaldo Muñiz Solari and Lianfei Jiang*

Rogers, A. (2004). *Looking again a non-formal and informal education—towards a new paradigm*. Retrieved January 12, 2018, from http://www.infed.org/biblio/non_formal_paradigm.htm

Singh, M., & Sproats, E. (2005). Constructing local/global pedagogies: Insights into the learning experiences of international students. *Education & Society*, *23*(2), 43–61.

Solem, M., Klein, P., Muñiz Solari, O., & Ray, W. (Eds.). (2010). Global climate change: A module for the AAG Center for Global Geography Education. Retrieved February 25, 2018, from http://www.aag.org/cs/cgge/modules

Tallant, M. (2010). A conceptual framework for exploring the role of studies abroad in nurturing global citizenship. *Journal of Studies in International Education*, *14*(5), 433–451.

Tu, C. (2004). *Twenty-one designs to building an online collaborative learning community*. Westport, CT; Greenwood.

Warf, B., Vincent, P., & Purcell, D. (1999). International collaborative learning on the world wide web. *Journal of Geography*, *98*(3), 141–148.

Wenger, E., Trayner, B., & De Laat, M. (2011). Promoting and assessing value creation in communities and networks: A conceptual framework. Ruud de Moor Centrum. Open Universiteit. Report number: 18.

World Bank Group. (2016). Digital *dividends*. World Development Report. 2016. Retrieved January 7, 2018, from http://documents.worldbank.org/curated/en/896971468194972881/pdf/102725-PUB-Replacement-PUBLIC.pdf

8 Academic family and educational *Compadrazgo*: Implementing cultural values to create educational relationships for informal learning and persistence for Latinx undergraduates[1]

Alberta M. Gloria, Jeanett Castellanos, Mary Dueñas, and Veronica Franco

Family understanding and support of one's educational journey is central to Latinx students' transition from high school to college and from college to graduate school. Questions and concerns about how long, how far away, and with whom Latinx student spend time are central to family concerns and subsequent decisions to pursue and engage higher education. All too frequently; however, this process is inaccurately and aculturally perceived by university personnel with family considered a limiting structure and force for Latinx students. Yet, when understood within a cultural framework consistent to the worldview and cultural orientation of values, beliefs and practices, Latinx families and communities are a substantive source of informal educational support and strength that culturally nurture Latinx students propelling them to graduation.

It is from a positive strength-based cultural perspective (Castellanos & Gloria, 2016) and generational transmission of values (Gloria & Castellanos, 2012), as well as community cultural capital (Yosso, 2005), that the processes of **academic family** and **educational** *compadrazgo* is addressed for Latinx students' academic wellness, persistence decisions and ultimate success. More specifically, these two dynamic familial processes are described within the context of core Latinx values and their role, function, and utility on college campuses. The chapter addresses how the systems of academic families and relationships inherent to educational *compadrazgo* address the psychological (e.g. self-beliefs, empowerment, motivation), social (e.g. networks of personal and professional connection, peer mentorship), and cultural (e.g. validation of values, beliefs and cultural practices) needs for Latinx students' professional development and educational persistence (Castellanos & Gloria, 2007; Gloria & Rodriguez, 2000).

To elucidate the processes of academic family and educational *compadrazgo*, this chapter includes our educational experiences as four Latinas who have

120 Gloria, Castellanos, Dueñas, et al.

individually and collectively created educational relationships and systems of informal and formal learning. Having known and worked together, our interactions span different academic relationships (e.g. faculty–student; mentor–mentee, colleagues) and contexts (e.g. different academic institutions, classrooms, in-person and long-distance research teams). Central to the processes are our layered and dimensionalized identities as cultural beings (i.e. *poderosas Latinas*; Gloria & Castellanos, 2012) and who we are as part of a larger collective or "academic family" (Castellanos & Gloria, 2007; Gloria, 1997). This chapter provides the conceptual bases and cultural processes by which we propose the informal workings of infusing the dimensions of Latinx family systems into higher education for student success. The chapter includes our narratives and composite vignette to elucidate the processes of living through the concepts of academic family and educational *compadrazgo* as salient to our dimensionalized identities (Gloria & Castellanos, 2012).

Theoretical approach to Latinx student's educational experiences

Having an understanding of the interplay of the person and environmental context in which Latinx students *sobreviven y prosperan* (survive and thrive) is a first step to support student success (Gloria & Rodriguez, 2000). Designed as a meta-model, the psychosociocultural approach considers the "whole" student in-context as a means to understand Latinx students' educational experiences and address their needs and concerns (Castellanos & Gloria, 2007; Gloria & Rodriguez, 2000). Centralizing the learning environment (e.g. predominantly White institution or historically White institution, community college that is primarily a commuter school, Hispanic Serving Institution), the approach individually and collectively focuses on three core dimensions, the psychological, social and cultural, to inform and contextualize Latinx students' educational experiences (Castellanos & Gloria, 2007).

Self-beliefs and perceptions: The psychological dimension addresses the self-beliefs and perceptions that Latinx students hold about themselves as scholars and persons in an educational learning setting that may or may not welcome, reflect or seek to know them. For example, Latinx students' sense of confidence or efficacy to succeed (Gloria, Castellanos, Lopez, & Rosales, 2005) or perceptions that they matter and belong (Dueñas & Gloria, 2017) inform how they engage learning and time in higher education. All too often, Latinx students' self-efficacy (i.e. one's belief in their ability to succeed) is compromised by subtle and overt messages from the context "telling" them they cannot succeed or somehow they must change their core being in order to be successful (Gloria et al., 2016). Indeed, having strong positive self-beliefs that they can and will succeed while knowing that their learning environment equally believes and is structured for their success is of essence for Latinx students' personal and professional wellness.

Social connections and relationships: The social dimension involves the scope and depth of those relationships and connections within the educational context

Academic family and educational Compadrazgo 121

that provide resource, promote success and allow Latinx students to persist academically. As Latinx students are infrequently reflected within the higher education system (Reyes & Nora, 2012), having connections and establishing relationships serves a key role. Latinx students often seek academic units, "counterspaces" (Nuñez, 2011, p. 639), or formal student organizations (Delgado-Guerrero & Gloria, 2013) that promote cultural connection, physical belonging or reflect perspectives and values. Through the development of meaningful student-faculty relationships, first-generation Latino undergraduates often manage key college transitions, from community on campus (Nuñez, 2011) to increased achievement (Anaya & Cole, 2001). Whether formal or informal, connections and relationships are central to Latinx students' successful educational experiences.

Cultural values, beliefs and practices in context: The cultural dimension focuses on the values and worldview orientations that Latinx students hold as they engage the university setting, of which values, practices and beliefs are frequently at odds with Latinx culture (Castillo, Conoley, & Brossart, 2004; Gloria & Segura-Herrera, 2004). Latinx students' sense of cultural fit (i.e. congruence of their values with those of the university) comes into play as they frequently experience a cultural clash and marginalization of their values as they negotiate the educational setting (Castillo et al., 2004; Gloria & Robinson-Kurpius, 1996). For example, Latinx students who have an increased sense of congruity reported increased academic persistence decisions (Aguinaga & Gloria, 2015). Engaging in a learning space of cultural reflection provides educational sustenance and supports wellness and meaning for continued persistence decisions (e.g. family advancement; Gloria & Castellanos, 2012).

Collectively, the PSC dimensions inform Latinx students' processes such as educational coping (Gloria et al., 2016), etic and emic wellness (Castellanos, Gloria, Rojas Perez, & Fonseca, 2017), psychological well-being (Gloria, Castellanos, & Orozco, 2005), and academic persistence decisions (Delgado-Guerrero & Gloria, 2013). In combination, the dimensions are informed by and play out within the educational learning contexts (e.g. classrooms, research labs, residential halls), providing a fuller view and insight into Latinx students' experiences. Using an integrative whole person–environment approach, Latinx students' strength-based processes and cultural and spiritual *patrón* (i.e. historical blueprint of generationally transmitted values and process; Gloria & Castellanos, 2012) are brought fully into the educational context.

Setting the cultural foundation—Core Latinx values and cultural *patrónes*

It is the interconnection of family and community values that Latinx values emulate (Castellanos & Gloria, 2016) interactions, relationships and practices are unified (Santiago-Rivera, Arredondo, & Gallardo-Cooper, 2002) and engaged via a cultural *patrón*. A positive (re)framing of Latinx values acknowledges and draws upon the historical and contemporary transmission and

122   Gloria, Castellanos, Dueñas, et al.

socialization of values as the basis of strength and "foundation of self-care and wellness within the family" (Castellanos & Gloria, 2016, p. 64). Specifically, a *patrón* is the:

> cultural and spiritual blueprint that Latina/os can draw strength and meaning from those beliefs, processes, and values, which have been transmitted across time (from generation to generation) and have allowed for survival, growth, and meaning (Castellanos & Gloria, 2016, p. 64).

Familia es todo (Family is everything)*: Familismo* engages the social and relational connections one has with their family, whereby the group needs supersede individual needs (Arevalo, So, & McNaughton-Cassill, 2016; Falicov, 2013). Within both biological and fictive kin, Latinx family often involves extended responsibilities, consistent loyalty, reciprocal obligation and care and concern for others. Family is considered the most central and salient unit, "the primary natural support system that provides physical, emotional and social support" (Gloria & Castellanos, 2009, p. 14). Further, family is often the main venue of socialization and enculturation of values and practices that are framed within social, environmental and political contexts (Cauce & Domenech-Rodriguez, 2002).

Yet, Latinx families have been unequivocally pathologized within psychological, social and educational literatures (Castellanos & Gloria, 2018). Thus, returning to the deep-structure meaning and interactions inherent to family is needed (Castellanos & Gloria, 2016). Drawing on the collective, Latinx have distinctive styles of engagement that address demographic, normative, structural, behavioral (Baca Zinn, 1994) and attitudinal (Sabogal, Marin, Otero-Sabogal, Marin, & Perez-Stable, 1987) familism. *Demographic familism* involves characteristics, such as number of persons or family members involved, whereas *structural familism* addresses the involvement and patterns of Latinx generations and extended family (Baca Zinn & Pok, 2001). *Normative familism* focuses on the centrality or value given to the collective and *behavioral familism* is the extent to which kin structures and family are in contact and interact with each other (Cauce & Domenech-Rodriguez, 2002; Hernandez & Bamaca-Colbert, 2016). Finally, *attitudinal familism* is the process of accessing family for emotional support, obligation to family needs and referent for decision-making (Hernandez & Bamaca-Colbert, 2016; Sabogal et al., 1987). Latinx *familismo* is multidimensional (Hernandez & Bamaca-Colbert, 2016) and involves psychosociocultural dimensions (Gloria & Rodriguez, 2000) that can be applied and integrated within higher education.

Siempre en mi mente y corazon (Always in my mind and heart): The self-referents and beliefs engendered from family are the affectual or attitudinal process of family within the psychosociocultural conceptual approach. The consistently identified source of emotional support and survival, family is at the center of existence and purpose for many Latinx (Falicov, 2013; Lopez, 2010; Santiago-Rivera et al., 2002). Helping to solve crises, managing challenges and

Academic family and educational Compadrazgo   123

coping with daily struggles, many Latinx look to family as the driving force for persistence and success. Family is the primary source and reason that Latinx perceive themselves as capable of moving through hardships (e.g. immigration, loss, discrimination, financial and physical struggles) and venue for relaying *dichos* (sayings) and *cuentos* (stories) of familial knowledge, cultural lessons (Zuniga, 1991) and historical wisdoms that emphasize endurance, perseverance and ability (Gloria & Castellanos, 2013).

Tu eres mi otro yo (You are my other me): The opening line to a historical poem (*In Lak'Ech*) prompts ethnic solidarity and collective understanding. The notion of *In Lak'Ech Ala K'in* is a timeless Mayan belief that espouses connection, relationship and community. Specifically, Latinx often believe they are inherently part of systems of networks, kinships and families that provide interconnected purpose and meaning (Cervantes, 2010). It is the connections and relationships within the context of the psychosociocultural conceptual approach that families and communities are based. Through the value and distinctive style of *personalismo* (Ortiz, 2009), connections and relationships within and across families and communities fulfill social needs and obligations through fictive and nonfictive kin (Gill-Hopple & Brage-Hudson, 2012). The care and concern for the relationship upon which family is preserved and maintained through *confianza* (trust) (Gloria & Castellanos, 2016). Indeed, by focusing on "other" versus self (e.g. allowing other's needs, others take precedence over one's needs; Falicov, 2013), Latinx are in effect helping and supporting themselves within the familial structure.

Bien educadxs (Well-educated persons): It is this dimension of cultural values, attitudes and worldviews within the context of the psychosociocultural conceptual approach that identity and enculturation of cultural values and practices are most evident. With a focus on family and historical transmission of processes, Latinx are socialized into a cultural and spiritual *patrón* (Gloria & Castellanos, 2012). Through the conscious and unconscious transmissions of values and cultural learning of customs and practices, Latinx are in effect "educated" and importantly "well-educated" by their families (Gloria & Castellanos, 2016). By understanding and having consciousness of the interconnection of past, present and future, Latinx can have an increased awareness and purposed sense of self that is culturally and contextually connected to themselves, families and communities (Comas-Díaz, 2013).

Creating family through *Compadrazgo*

How family and community are defined and created is a critical element in shaping individuals' connections, relationships, responsibilities and in turn the very ties and bonds "hold" and uplift, embrace, encourage and support. As many Latinx hold a collective identity regarding family, there is the often-held belief that one's community is stronger through connections. Specifically, the relational processes of *compadrazgo* or the process of taking on "co-parents or fictive kin" is a frequently engaged process to strengthen and extend family.

124   *Gloria, Castellanos, Dueñas, et al.*

In essence, the process of choosing *madrinas* (godmothers) and *padrinos* (godfathers) serves to broaden one's social network(s) (Gill-Hopple & Brage-Hudson, 2012) and collective responsibility to fictive family members through lifelong relationships (Mintz & Wolf, 1950).

By way of cultural milestones (e.g. *quinceaneras*, graduations) and religious and spiritual events (e.g. baptisms, first communions, confirmations, weddings), *madrinas* and *padrinos* are selected to care and assume responsibility for the well-being of others children and build familial relational bonds (Gloria & Castellanos, 2016). Ritual fictive kin are formed outside of biological family or marital ties who have cultural and symbolic commitment of family (Comas-Díaz, 2013; Ebaugh & Curry, 2000; Gill-Hopple & Brage-Hudson, 2012). Creating community to care for the spiritual, financial, social and physical of others, individuals are "considered chosen family with the same rights and obligations as biological family members" (Gill-Hopple & Brage-Hudson, 2012, p. 118).

Importantly, the process of choosing or implementing *compadrazgo* has historically occurred vertically and horizontally. Vertical *compadrazgo* involves selecting *madrinas* and *padrinos* who have more resources (e.g. are wealthier) or are powerful in relational status (e.g. have access to useful relationships), whereas horizontal *compadrazgo* involves selecting closely related or trusted persons who are "within" the family structure (Lopez, 1999; Mintz & Wolf, 1950; Nutini, 1984). *Madrinas* or *padrinos* "provide additional resources that may be called on in times of emergency, during celebrations, and for sharing daily life" (Gill-Hopple & Brage-Hudson, 2012, p. 118). Indeed, it is ability to shift with flexibility and fluidity that Latinx families implement cultural practices to expand and transform themselves to meet their needs and manage sociocontextual challenges (e.g. immigration, economics; Baca Zinn & Pok, 2001).

Community cultural capital of family

Drawing on the Latinx value, function, strength and resiliency of *familismo*, applying *compadrazgo* within higher education is a direct way to implement one's cultural and spiritual *patrón* (Gloria & Castellanos, 2016) and subsequent community cultural capital (Yosso, 2005) in the academic realm. In particular, familial capital are those processes that are nurtured and transmitted within family and "engages a commitment to community well-being and expands the concept of family to include a more broad understanding of kinship" (Yosso, 2005, p. 79). Bringing familial processes into higher education calls upon the "pedagogies of the home" (Delgado Bernal, 2002, p. 109) by which Latinx students can implement their relational connections and collective values inherent to family and community via consistent and congruent ways. Indeed, it is the *patrón* and generational transmission of cultural processes and interactions (Castellanos & Gloria, 2016) that begets the basis for (re)creating family in higher educational setting.

Academic family and educational *Compadrazgo: ¿Qué es la familia académica?*/What is academic family?

With similar yet contextualized roles and obligations, an *academic family* is most simply defined as those persons and chosen family who an individual has emotional ties and intellectual perceptions; social roles, connections and obligations; and culturally rooted values orientations within the academic environment or context (e.g. residence hall, classroom, research lab, student organization). Finding, creating and maintaining one's "academic family" (Castellanos & Gloria, 2007; Gloria, 1997) and educational *madrinas* and *padrinos* while in college is a specific process steeped within Latinx values and cultural and spiritual *patrónes*. Through creating one's academic family that Latinx students can find a sense of emotional connection and belonging on campuses (Dueñas & Gloria, 2017), find needed mentors (Castellanos, Gloria, Besson, & Clark Harvey, 2016), like-minded others (Delgado-Guerrero & Gloria, 2013), spaces of support (Nuñez, 2011) and feel culturally validated and reflected (Gloria & Castellanos, 2012).

How academic families inform Latinx students informal learning is perhaps best described through integrative narratives of two of the chapter authors. First, Franco describes nuanced feelings associated with being part of an academic family as well as the importance of being rooted to cultural values and processes that promote educational connection and meaning.

> My mentor and peers first introduced the concept of *academic family* in my third year of undergraduate school. When I first heard the concept, I recall thinking, "of course I have an academic family—my family has been supportive all throughout" and, while an unknown realm to my family, they have continuously served as a system of support. However, as a first-generation student of color navigating educational barriers, I soon learned the importance of forming a community within the educational realm. While the support from my family has been integral to my educational success, forming an *academic family* has been central to my perseverance in academia. As a student of color, I experienced the importance of becoming part of a network of peers and mentors who could help me navigate academia and who also understood the hardships, challenges and barriers I faced as a student. Through my *academic family*, I have created a sense of belonging, community, validation, cultural awareness and found a space where I proudly honor my cultural identity as a Latinx *mujer de color* (Latinx woman of color).
>
> Although I first heard the term *academic family* later in my undergraduate career, this concept and practice first emerged when I was in high school. As a high school student, I was involved in the Associated Student Body committee where I formed a tight-knit community with my peers and advisor. It was these individuals who introduced me to new possibilities after high school and who invested their time to help me apply to universities.

126 *Gloria, Castellanos, Dueñas, et al.*

In reflecting on my educational community *(academic family)*, I had the privilege to be part of a group where my peers and my advisor collaborated to form a community where we shared resources, practiced our cultural values and heard and learned from our advisor's experiences in academia. A sense of belonging, community and cultural appreciation helped me thrive in high school and it is these same elements that influence my success through undergraduate and graduate school.

Academic family symbolizes more than chosen family; it is more than a simple academic concept. I learned about the meaning of academic family, not by what I read in research articles or heard in courses, but by the experiences I encountered through my schooling. Yes, I had my parents and siblings support, yet there was often a barrier between my academic life and my personal life due to the unknown realm of academia my family did not understand. Thus, while pursuing a higher education was an early childhood instilled value; in reality, navigating the academic realm was challenging—a more complex and unknown process.

My first year of college, I faced academic probation due to the challenges I encountered in my courses and the transition from a low-income community to an affluent city. Belonging and being a part of the community campus felt unattainable. As feelings of isolation and loneliness rose, so did doubts about my presence on campus. It was my second year that I met a group of Latina women who embodied what to me meant and signified being Latina. Not only did they proudly speak their native language on campus and eat the traditional Latinx cuisine, they also navigated their academic journey through instilled values of *respeto, comunidad, personalismo,* and *perserverancia*. It was this group of women who welcomed me into a network of sisterhood, community, academic excellence and culture. Through my integration of a Latina Chicana based sorority, I found my academic family. My academic family consisted of *mujeres* who were older in age and served as mentors, helping me navigate through higher education. Through these lived experiences, I learned *academic family* is a form of social network in which I express, honor and value my identities, and most importantly it has served as a place in which the intersection of my identities are understood, valued and appreciated.

Next, addressing identity, Dueñas expands on how having an academic family provides a space of meaning and validation to persist academically.

As a Latina, the concept of family has been part of my cultural upbringing and how I find comfort, gratitude and happiness. I was raised in a home that valued spending quality time with others, contributing to the well-being of my nuclear family, while also acknowledging our family struggles. I knew that my family would support my endeavors while also provide guidance when I needed, but little did I know these qualities were possible in an academic setting.

Academic family and educational Compadrazgo 127

The concept of *academic families* allows me to integrate both my academic, cultural, and ethnic identities in ways that helps me succeed academically and feel connected as a student. Having an academic family created a community and a space where I felt valued particularly at a place where other students did not reflect my own identities. My academic family shared educational and professional interests, and common familial values. I feel that my academic family just knew who I was; they understood the challenges of being a person of color, the responsibility of attaining a bachelor/graduate degree, and they were invested in my overall success. Unequally, being in such community expanded my social capital to and greater sense of awareness and knowledge. This particular type of social capital helped me gain social networks that I would not have otherwise created and facilitated higher levels of growth that was not always accessible in other settings.

In retrospect, my first academic family was a High School Puente Program that helped first-generation, underrepresented students attend 4-year colleges and universities. However, it was not until my junior year in college that I felt a sense of belonging when a peer referred me to student organization that had an active Latinx faculty advisor. I took the initiative to enter into a counter-space of other Latinxs who shared the same identities and interests as I sought connection. It was here that I became involved in different professional development activities and gained the sense of efficacy to envision my continued education for my undergraduate and graduate studies. The relationships of my academic family gave me a sense of *compadrazgo* and connection that I could succeed and "would be okay" in academia.

Upon entering a predominately and historically white institution in graduate school, I was surprised to be among many Latinas, all of whom were strong, intelligent lived away from home, and willing to engage in education as a collective process. Both the formal and unstructured time of engagement had great influence and reminded me of "home." Knowing that my mentors were there for me, while creating a place among others made me feel safe to be myself and embrace my cultural identities. Speaking Spanish, gathering for home cooked meals, and reminiscing about shared cultural narratives were all familiar ways of engagement that connected us as family. As a Latina who values spending time with others and recognizes the power of collaboration, I found a culturally-grounded support system that offered support, confidence, mentoring and validation—a process that was critical for my growth as a Latina scholar. Being part of multiple academic families has provided me cultural-meaningful environments to manage challenges, deepen my educational agenda and empowered my identity as a first-generation Latina student and scholar.

Siempre hay lugar para uno mas/Always room for one more: Much like Latinx families, the ability to engage flexibly to incorporate and take on new family members (Falicov, 2013), so too does an academic family. By flexing to include new academic family members, the network of psychosociocultural interconnections

128 *Gloria, Castellanos, Dueñas, et al.*

yields an increased capacity for learning and success. Thus, the emergent question is: *¿Por qué tener una familia académica?*/Why have an academic family? Likewise, the complementary and perhaps more important question is: *¿Cómo promueve una familia académica el aprendizaje informal?*/How does an academic family promote informal learning? To answer these questions, we draw from our lived experiences and interactions within our academic families and conceptual- and data-supported reasons from educational and ethnocultural literature. Although listed within a specific psychosociocultural dimension, each process is clearly informed and influenced by the other dimensions (Castellanos & Gloria, 2007; Gloria & Rodriguez, 2000). Table 8.1 provides a list of how academic family promotes informal learning across the psychological, social, and cultural dimensions for Latinx students.

Table 8.1 How academic family promotes informal learning for Latinx students

Psychological	Social	Cultural
• Provides sense of belonging and mattering shared by others who understand the complexity and challenges of being a Latinx student (e.g. emotional toll and psychic cost of assumptions, microaggressions). • Offers emotional spaces of psychological protection from challenges and disenfranchising beliefs that invalidate Latinx experiences and values. • Allows for a sense of validation and value as someone who contributes to others on campus, in the classroom, and in the generation of knowledge. • Creates a sense of active resistance and social advocacy to advance one's community by being in higher education.	• Creates a space for shared experiences (both positive and negative). • Provides spaces and practices that reinforce the importance of family-like systems, which reflects the values of investment, care, responsibility and understanding. • Promotes exchanges that emphasize or are centered in *personalismo* and other salient Latinx values. • Allows connections and supportive ties regardless of whether one accesses it (i.e. to know that one is not alone or isolated). • Provides a baseline of normative experience (i.e. knowledge that others are having similar experiences). • Creates a space in which access to needed resources are available via established networks.	• Allows a system of protection within an oftentimes unwelcoming or hostile learning setting. • Provides systems of connection and rootedness of values and beliefs that reinforce and (re)position practices aligned to one's *patrón* within higher education. • Instills sense of pride and larger meaning of cultural reflection that is valued. • Provides a supportive and welcoming "space" in which one's values and *Latinidad* (identities as a Latinx) can be redefined, understood and valued. • Unifies students who share challenging cultural experiences and offers solutions and alternatives to navigating isolating and often non-inclusive educational spaces. • Engages in a value-based coping system that is centered in one's home-based socialized orientation.

(Continued)

Academic family and educational Compadrazgo   129

Table 8.1 How academic family promotes informal learning for Latinx students (*Continued*)

Psychological	Social	Cultural
• Empowers a sense of collective strength, *ganas* (motivation) and purpose to succeed using collective goals that align education to advance Latinx communities and families. • Facilitates a collective consciousness to fulfill meaning, purpose and community responsibility in a setting that is espouses individualism and competition. • Enables one to draw from others' sense of efficacy or confidence that if others can succeed, so too can the individual. • Fosters and honors the experiences and *conocimientos* (wisdom) that academic family members have and are willing to share for educational success. • Allows a shared common knowledge of what it means, involves and is sacrificed to be successful in higher education. • Generates spaces that promote personal value and foster individual and collective educational dreams.	• Provides access to mentors and those who are willing to share their insights and perspectives about situations and experiences. • Provides a purpose beyond oneself by having role and responsibility to support and connect with others seeking a higher education. • Draws on the power and historical transmission of relationships within the learning setting. • Generates a unique connection and affiliation to the university setting that promotes contextualized integration, persistence and learning. • Offers a structure for programming and training in a nurturing and collaborative setting where specific skill sets are taught/reinforced to help students succeed in a competitive environment. • Fosters specific and culturally centered educational pipeline(s) that reinforce excellence of modeling, mentoring and networking.	• Draws on strengths of home teachings and uses it as a means to thrive. • Creates a dimensionalized cultural reflection through language, interactions and/or values, beliefs and behaviors. • Serves as a needed cultural touchstone and system of family when one's non-fictive kin cannot or is unable. • Allows access to a bilingual and multidimensional system and processes that (re) create a congruent context of academia. • Provides access to knowledge and opportunities via student narratives as example of their successes. • Broadens the essence of university for students to explore and maximize their learning opportunities (e.g. apply for professional trainings, fellowships, involvement with research).

¿Cómo se crean las familias académicas?/How are academic families created?

Latinx values play a central and salient role in Latinx college students' educational success (Arevalo et al., 2016), as does the role of family support (Gloria & Castellanos, 2012). How students create academic family as a means of success (e.g. learning, wellness, persistence decisions), however, has not yet been explored.

130 *Gloria, Castellanos, Dueñas, et al.*

The cultural processes of *compadrazgo* and choosing family are informal and processes of values socialization that vary from family to family given need and context (e.g. university setting). Creating academic family is dynamic and can be serendipitous (e.g. chance meeting) or more formalized interactions (directed by mentors). *Familismo* is a strength-based value and cultural process and subsequent educational capital that can and should be used as a form of success. For example, Latinx students may engage in an educational program with other students; however, unless they perceive the value and process of *familismo* as a viable, dynamic and powerful means to effect connections they are not tapping into their cultural and home capital. It is the educational *madrinas* and *padrinos* who need to engage and draw intentionally upon the processes of *familismo* to prime Latinx students to choose their academic family. Latinx or Latinx ally faculty/staff can translate cultural knowledge into action for Latinx students.

Creating our academic family: To elucidate how academic family can be created, we provide our narrative as one example. The structural and conceptual elements of our academic family can be traced to our beloved educational *padrino*, Dr. Joseph L. White, father of Black Psychology. As our family elder, educational godfather and trusted mentor, he had the cultural knowledge and practical wherewithal to access and integrate the Latinx value of family for us (the two lead authors). With purposeful intention, he directed us to be part of his historically rooted "freedom train" where he mobilized trusted mentoring relationships that emulated a supportive family system as key to educational advancement (Castellanos & Franco, 2018). With his simple yet poignantly culturally rooted directive—modeling and fostering sense of personal connection, community and cultural meaning (i.e. "I have a Latina I want you to mentor"), he set in motion our academic family. From this initial connection, we now serve as academic family and educational *madrinas* for Latinx students. Through creating educational opportunities and professional development activities (e.g. writing projects, research teams, traveling together for conferences, discussions about graduate school) and asking students to access their cultural strengths (i.e. intentionally implement their values and *patrónes*) and (re)imagine new possibilities of educational meaning, we provide psychological, social and cultural integration and a multi-layered platform for our far-reaching academic families.

Composite vignette—Clear about a degree, uncertain about "the education"

Although academic family is an individualized process for Latinx students, the following composite vignette synthesizes key processes of academic family and educational *compadrazgo*.

> The first time away from her family, Ruby was uncertain about how to spend her time outside of the classroom, particularly as she felt that her instructors negated her perspectives and her educational experiences differed greatly from her peers. She is close to her family and before coming to college

Academic family and educational Compadrazgo   131

she would spend every opportunity she could with them. Now at college, she experiences a sense of normlessness and feels isolated on campus. She returns home every weekend that she can afford financially and that her schedule allows. As the semester ensues, her family (mother, father, siblings, aunts, uncles and grandparents—several of whom are her *madrinas* and *padrinos*) are supportive of her attending college, yet are increasingly challenging and insistent that she return home as they feel Ruby to be progressively upset and discouraged when she calls or returns home. Ruby also feels that her family does not understand her daily school activities and unable to empathize with her stress about course assignment deadlines and anxiety about earning the needed grades to get accepted into her major.

As a first-year student, Ruby participated in a formal student diversity program where she attended cohort meetings with other first-generation college students from lower socioeconomic and diverse racial and ethnic backgrounds. While she gained useful information regarding college survival strategies, time management and utility of mental health services, Ruby's connection to her peers did not feel particularly meaningful. At one of the cohort meetings, one of the presenters took particular interest in Ruby. Her responses evidenced disconnection and uncertainty about her "space" on campus; yet, she had a strong desire to earn a degree for herself and family. The Latinx faculty member, who used an academic family approach to training, invited Ruby to the team meetings and paired Ruby with Latinx graduate students. The faculty member emailed and met monthly with Ruby over coffee to discuss the daily struggles of higher education and to help Ruby find and choose an "academic family." Being introduced to the idea and using the language of academic family was at first awkward and felt uncomfortable for Ruby given her multiple experiences and interactions that directly told her that engaging her Latinx values and cultural practices was "wrong," unwelcomed and had no merit in higher education. Ruby had never explicitly named her Latinx values or called upon her familial processes and wisdoms in the educational setting. The faculty member spoke openly about creating family and helped to reorient Ruby's Latinx values of family and community as strength-based and generationally transmitted processes and practices. Doing so allowed Ruby to (re)gain her power and knowledge to succeed by accessing and implementing her cultural and spiritual *patrón* in a culturally congruent way.

As Ruby began creating her academic family, from her connection to an already formed academic family through the Latinx faculty member, she was bought into the fold of different experiences and activities. The team flexed to incorporate Ruby into the group and held her success and wellness as part of their role and obligation and she in turn did the same for others. Several of the research team members served as a *madrina* for Ruby, inviting her to study and "writing" sessions, checking in during midterms and exams, and inviting her to attend church and Sunday dinners. As Ruby's sense of academic family grew, she engaged differently with her diversity program cohort, select

132   *Gloria, Castellanos, Dueñas, et al.*

classmates and instructors, and persons in her residence hall as different systems within her academic family. Ruby gained the language and confidence to name her lived experiences of *familismo* and *compadrazgo* and applies them as a means of survival and success. By creating and choosing an academic family, Ruby reclaimed her "voice" to meet her needs. She was increasingly confident in her abilities as a dimensionalized and whole person in higher education. Ruby actively created and owned her experience as a Latinx student in higher education who was validated and had meaningful importance.

Implications for university personnel, campus units and students

As the creation of academic families and educational *madrinas* and *padrinos* is often an informal process for Latinx students, university personnel, campus units (academic and service) and students can implement a myriad of psychosociocultural actions. First and foremost, applying the concept and language of academic family as a strength-based process to address self-perceptions, role of relationships and connections, and cultural integration of values within higher education is needed. Doing so can change the campus climate by including culturally congruent and meaningful concepts and expected interactions for Latinx students and stakeholders invested in their educational wellness and academic success (Castellanos & Gloria, 2007). By validating the Latinx students' cultural processes and values and their subsequent communities, they are provided emotional and physical spaces to perceive themselves as connected, belonging and mattering within the learning setting (Dueñas & Gloria, 2017).

Likewise, the university itself must be held accountable to recruit, hire and retain culturally competent Latinx academic faculty and staff who understand the importance and implement the practices to create academic family. More specifically, university personnel need the cultural awareness, knowledge and skills to serve as *madrinas* and *padrinos* for Latinx students who are new and first generation to higher education. Although they may not ultimately be chosen as academic family or serve as Latinx students' educational *madrinas* or *padrinos*, university personnel must nonetheless act intentionally to create the informal and formal emotional and physical spaces for proximal and distal interactions and collaborations for students to find and choose an academic family. In particular, faculty and staff can serve as relational conduits to establish connections and build collaborative interactions for success. In this same way, Latinx students need the spaces and subsequent encouragement to own their cultural community capital (Delgado Bernal, 2002; Yosso, 2005) and (re)claim their cultural and spiritual *patrónes* and subsequent wisdoms for educational success (Gloria & Castellanos, 2016). It is the investment in strength-based and culturally-rooted practices that serve as the psychosociocultural basis for Latinx informal learning in higher education and the promotion of Latinx students' efforts to create and engage academic family that facilitates educational integration and academic success.

Note

1. *Compadrazgo* (co-parenting or fictive kinship) is a cultural practice involving the expansion of family systems that encompasses the responsibility of caring and support implemented within different Latinx families and communities. The term Latinx is used in this chapter to include individuals of all gender(s) who are of Mexican, Puerto Rican, Cuban, Dominican and South and Central American heritage. This chapter uses gender-neutral language in reference to individuals (i.e. Latinx, "they") unless the original authors explicitly indicate gender pronouns.

References

Aguinaga, A., & Gloria, A. M. (2015). Effects of generational status and university environment on Latina/o undergraduates persistence decisions. *Journal of Diversity in Higher Education, 8,* 15–29. doi: 10.1037/a0038465

Anaya, G., & Cole, D. (2001). Latina/o student achievement: Exploring the influence of student-faculty interaction on college grades. *Journal of College Student Development, 42*(1), 3–14.

Arevalo, I., So, D., & McNaughton-Cassill, M. (2016). The role of collectivism among Latino American college students. *Journal of Latinos and Education, 15*(1), 3–11. doi: 10.1080/15348431.2015.1045143

Baca Zinn, M. (1994). Adaptation and continuity in Mexican-origin families. In R. L. Taylor (Ed.), *Minority families in the United States: A multicultural perspective* (pp. 64–94). Englewood Cliffs, NJ: Prentice Hall.

Baca Zinn, M., & Pok, A. Y. H. (2001). Tradition and transition in Mexican-origin families. In R. Taylor (Ed.), *Minority families in the United States: A multicultural perspective* (3rd ed., pp. 79–100). Upper Saddle River, NJ: Prentice Hall.

Castellanos, J., & Gloria, A. M. (2007). Research considerations and theoretical application for best practices in higher education: Latina/os achieving success. *Journal of Hispanic Higher Education, 6,* 378–396. doi: 10.1177/1538192707305347

Castellanos, J., & Gloria, A. M. (2016). Latina/os—Drive, community, and spirituality: The strength within (*SOMOS Latina/os—Ganas, comunidad, y el espíritu: La fuerza que llevamos por dentro*). In E. C. Chang, C. A. Downey, J. K. Hirsch, & N. J. Lin (Eds.), *Positive psychology in racial and ethnic minority groups: Theory, research, and practice* (pp. 61–82). Washington, DC: American Psychological Association.

Castellanos, J., & Gloria, A. M. (2018). Cuban Americans—From golden exiles to dusty foots: Freedom, hope, endurance, and the American dream. In P. Arredondo (Ed.), *Latinx families in the U.S.: Transcending processes of acculturation, xenophobia, through self-determination* (pp. 75–94). New York: Springer.

Castellanos, J., Gloria, A. M., Besson, D., & Clark Harvey, L. (2016). Mentoring matters: Racial and ethnic minority undergraduates' cultural fit, mentorship, and college and life satisfaction. *Journal of College Reading and Learning, 46*(2), 81–98. doi: 10.1080/10790195.2015.1121792

Castellanos, J., Gloria, A. M., Rojas Perez, O., & Fonseca, L. (2017). An etic and emic assessment of Latino male undergraduates' well-being: *Navegando los obstáculos de la universidad con mi cultura. Psychology of Men & Masculinity, 19*(2), 184–194. doi: 10.1037/men0000090

Castellanos, J. & Franco, V. (2018). Racial ethnic minority student scholarship development: A mentorship research model. American Association of Hispanics in Higher Education Annual Conference. Presentation. Costa Mesa, CA.

134 Gloria, Castellanos, Dueñas, et al.

Castillo, L. G., Conoley, C. W., & Brossart, D. F. (2004). Acculturation, white marginalization and family support as predictors of perceived distress in Mexican American female college students. *Journal of Counseling Psychology, 51*, 151–157. doi: 10.1037/00220167.51.2.151

Cauce, M. A., & Domenech-Rodriguez, M. (2002). Latino families: Myths and realities. In J. Contreras, A. Neal-Barnett, & K. Kerns (Eds.), *Latino children and families in the United States: Current research and future directions* (pp. 3–26). Westport, CT: Praeger Publishers.

Cervantes, J. M. (2010). Mestizo spirituality: Toward an integrated approach to psychotherapy for Latina/os. *Psychotherapy: Theory, Research, Practice, Training, 47*, 527–539. doi: 10.1037/a0022078

Comas-Díaz, L. (2013). Comadres: The healing power of a female bond. *Women & Therapy, 36*, 62–75. doi: 10.1080/02703149.2012.720213

Delgado Bernal, D. (2002). Critical race theory, LatCrit theory and critical raced-gendered epistemologies: Recognizing students of colour as holders and creators of knowledge. *Qualitative Inquiry, 8*(1), 105–126.

Delgado-Guerrero, M., & Gloria, A. M. (2013). *La importancia de la hermandad Latina*: Examining the psychosociocultural influences of Latina-based sororities on academic persistence decisions. *Journal of College Development, 54*(4), 361–389. doi: 10.1353/csd.2013.0067

Dueñas, M., & Gloria, A. M. (2017). *¿Pertenezco a esta universidad?* The mediating role of belonging for collective self-esteem and mattering for Latin@ undergraduates. *Journal of College Student Development, 58*(6), 891–906. doi: 10.1353/csd.2017.0070

Ebaugh, H. R., & Curry, M. (2000). Fictive kin as social capital in new immigrant communities. *Sociological Perspectives, 43*, 189–209.

Falicov, C. J. (2013). *Latino families in therapy: A guide to multicultural practice* (2nd ed.). New York City: Guilfold Press.

Gill-Hopple, K., & Brage-Hudson, D. (2012). *Compadrazgo*: A literature review. *Journal of Transcultural Nursing, 23*(2), 117–123. doi: 10.1177/1043659611433870

Gloria, A. M. (1997). Chicana academic persistence: Creating a university-based community. *Education and Urban Society, 30*, 107–121.

Gloria, A. M., & Castellanos, J. (2009). Latina/os and their communities. In Council of National Psychological Associations for the Advancement of Ethnic Minority Interests (Ed.), *Psychology education and training form culture-specific and multi-racial perspectives: Clinical issues and recommendations* (pp. 12–18). Washington, DC: American Psychological Association.

Gloria, A. M., & Castellanos, J. (2012). *Desafíos y bendiciones*: A multi-perspective examination of the educational experiences and coping responses of first-generation college Latina students. *Journal of Hispanic Higher Education, 11*(1), 81–98. doi: 10.1177/1538192711430382

Gloria, A. M., & Castellanos, J. (2013). Realidades culturales y identidades dimensionadas: The complexities of Latina diversities. In C. Enns, & E. Williams (Eds.), *Handbook of feminist multicultural counseling psychology* (pp. 169–182). New York: Oxford University Press.

Gloria, A. M., & Castellanos, J. (2016). Latinas poderosas: Shaping mjuerismo to manifest sacred spaces for healing and transformation. In. T. Bryant-Davis, & L. Comas-Díaz (Eds.), *Womanist and Mujerista psychologies: Voices of fire, acts of courage* (pp. 93–119). Washington, DC: American Psychological Association.

Academic family and educational Compadrazgo 135

Gloria, A. M., Castellanos, J., Delgado-Guerrero, M., Salazar, A. C., Gonzalez, C., Martinez, V., & Mejia, A. (2016). *El ojo en la meta*: Latino male undergraduates' coping processes. *Journal of Diversity in Higher Education, 10*(1), 11–23. doi: 10.1037/a0040216

Gloria, A. M., Castellanos, J., & Orozco, V. (2005). Perceived educational barriers, cultural fit, coping responses, and psychological well-being of Latina undergraduates. *Hispanic Journal of Behavioral Sciences, 27*(2), 161–183. doi: 10.1177/0739986305275097

Gloria, A. M., Castellanos, J., Lopez, A., & Rosales, R. (2005). A psychosociocultural examination of academic persistence of Latina/o undergraduates. *Hispanic Journal of Behavioral Sciences, 27*, 202–223.

Gloria, A. M., & Robinson-Kurpius, S. E. (1996). The validation of the cultural congruity scale and the university environment scale with Chicano/a students. *Hispanic Journal of Behavioral Sciences, 18*, 533–549.

Gloria, A. M., & Rodriguez, E. R. (2000). Counseling Latino university students: Psychosociocultural issues for consideration. *Journal of Counseling and Development, 78*, 145–154. doi: 10.1002/j.1556-6676.2000.tb02572.x

Gloria, A. M., & Segura-Herrera, T. M. (2004). Ambrocia and Omar go to college: A psychosociocultural examination of Chicana/os in higher education. In R. J. Velasquez, L. Arellano, & B. W. McNeill (Eds.), *Handbook of Chicana and Chicano psychology and mental health* (pp. 401–425). Mahwah, NJ: Erlbaum.

Hernandez, M. M., & Bamaca-Colbert, M. Y. (2016). A behavioral process of familism. *Journal of Family Theory & Review, 8*(4), 463–483. doi: 10.1111/jftr.12166

Lopez, R. A. (1999). Las comadres as a social support system. *AFFILIA, 14*(1), 24–41.

Lopez, T. (2010). Familismo. In Y. Jackson (Ed.), *Encyclopedia of multicultural psychology* (p. 211). Thousand Oaks, CA: Sage.

Mintz, S. W., & Wolf, E. R. (1950). An analysis of ritual co-parenthood (*Compadrazgo*). *Southwestern Journal of Anthropology, 6*, 341–368.

Nuñez, A. M. (2011). Counterspaces and connections in college transitions: First-generation Latino students' perspectives on Chicano studies. *Journal of College Student Development, 52*, 639–655. doi: 10.1353/csd.2011.0077

Nutini, H. G. (1984). *Ritual kinship: Ideological and structural integration of the comadrazgo system in rural Tlaxcala* (Vol. 2). Tucson: University of Arizona Press.

Ortiz, F. A. (2009). *Personalismo*. In M. A. De la Torre (Ed.), *Hispanic American religious cultures* (p. 179). Santa Barbara, CA: ABC-CLIO.

Reyes, N., & Nora, A. (2012). *Lost among the data: A review of Latino first-generation college students*. White paper prepared for the Hispanic Association of College and Universities.

Sabogal, F., Marin, G., Otero-Sabogal, R., Marin, B., & Perez-Stable, E. (1987). Hispanic familism and acculturation: What changes and what doesn't? *Hispanic Journal of Behavioral Sciences, 4*, 397–412. doi: 10.1177/07399863870094003

Santiago-Rivera, A. L., Arredondo, P., & Gallardo-Cooper, M. (2002). *Counseling Latinos and their families: A practical guide*. Thousand Oaks, CA: Sage.

Yosso, T. J. (2005). Whose culture has capital? A critical race theory discussion of community cultural wealth. *Race Ethnicity and Education, 8*(1), 69–91.

Zuniga, M. E. (1991). "Dichos" as metaphorical tools for resistant Latino clients. *Psychotherapy: Theory, Research, Practice, Training, 28*(3), 480–483. doi: 10.1037/0033-3204.28.3.480

9 Formal–informal, exclusion–inclusion: An empirical investigation of Swedish music education

Cecilia Wallerstedt

Introduction

In this chapter, a special case of informal pedagogy used in school will be in the spotlight: music education in Swedish secondary school. This case is significant to the theme of this book for two reasons. First, music is a great part of young people's everyday lives. Besides being a subject in schools, it is "out on the market" for young people—ready to be learned by anyone, anywhere (Finney, 2007). Imagine the view of a crowded bus station where many people are waiting—what are they doing? Probably almost all of them are wearing earphones and listening to music. Of course not same music, they all have their own "musical world" that they have a personal relation to. If they are interested, they can buy a cheap guitar, watch YouTube tutorials and learn how to play the songs they like to listen to. They can download softwares to their computer tablets and start creating dance music, and if they have problems, they can pose their questions on an Internet fora or Facebook group. They can communicate through Internet with people all over the world to exchange musical ideas, experiences of performances of their favorite band and samples of sound to compose with. Or can they? Is there a reason for formal music education in a world where people (at least theoretically) can educate themselves? This is an important consideration in today's digital society—irrespective of subject.

Second, music as subject in Sweden has been highly influenced by informal teaching strategies since as early as the 1970. Maybe this is related to the democratic values that are strongly interwoven in the Swedish school system. For example, it is stated in the Educational Act that the school has a two-part task: to transfer and rooting both knowledge and democratic values. In other countries, the United Kingdom for example, the interest in informal learning as model for teaching practices is a more novel idea. In the United Kingdom, this is manifested through a project called *Musical Futures* that builds on the idea that formal teaching is almost completely abandoned. The model in the project means that pupils are free to form groups, choose a song they like and then learn to play it by ear with as little interference as possible from the teacher. This is characteristic for what informal pedagogy in music means, also in other settings. The project *Musical Futures* has been illuminated through research (Green, 2017) and has been spread to other countries (Wright, 2014). As explained on this highly influential project's website: "Musical Futures is a pedagogical approach that is based on the real-world learning practices of popular and community musicians. At its heart are a set of core values and an ethos to underpin any music learning context in order to ensure an inclusive, relevant and accessible approach" (www.musicalfutures.org). The believe in informal teaching strategies as successful for building an inclusive pedagogy is strong (Burnard, Dillon, Rusinek, & Saether, 2008; Green, 2008; Lonie & Dickens, 2016; Tobias, 2015; Wright, 2013). Since Sweden has practised this kind of pedagogy in classrooms all over the country for several decades now (Georgii-Hemming & Westvall, 2010; Wallerstedt & Lindgren, 2016), the time has come for an in-depth discussion of its consequences. There are studies (Ericsson & Lindgren, 2010; Wallerstedt & Lindgren, 2016) that question if this pedagogy, that in spite of being based on democratic values and aimed at inclusion, sometimes even excludes pupils.

Johansen (2014) points out four central concepts of music education that well capture what is "at stake" in the current debate. These are the distinction between formal and informal music education practices, the expanded view of learning, the possibly expanded view of teaching and the expanded view of education. The distinction between formal and informal music education practices and "the possible transcendence of that dichotomy" (p. 76) has greatly influenced the research field. The ongoing discussion regards if informal learning constitutes "better" learning and should be implemented in schools, or if the content of informal practices (popular music) is not proper for institutional learning. One reason to consider informal learning as "better" is that it stands for something more authentic. Georgii-Hemming and Lilliedahl (2014) explain the differentiation often made, in discussions about subject matters in music, between the *ars*-dimension and the *scientia*-dimension of music. Ars counts as practical knowledge and has a slightly higher status, since it is "more natural or real" (p. 140). The scientia-dimension, on the other hand, represents the "verbal and intellectual activities" (ibid.). One scholar who has criticized the polarization between acting and verbalizing is Schön (1983), and his analytical model will be used in this chapter.

The aim of this chapter is to empirically examine a case of informal learning, especially addressing opportunities for learning that are constituted in the interaction between the teacher and the students. These opportunities will be discussed in terms of processes of exclusion and inclusion.

The chapter is structured in the following way: (i) Research on informal learning pedagogy in music as an inclusive practice is reviewed, (ii) Donald Schön's concept of reflection-in-action is presented as a tool for analyzing the teaching practice of a practice-based subject as music and (iii) the study in focus is presented. The data consists of video observations of music lessons, in two Year-9 classes for an 8-week period, where the students work with a band project. The aim of the project stated by the teacher, and that was part of the mandatory music class, was that the students should be provided the opportunity to "try how it is to make music 'for real'". An empirical case is analyzed in order to (iv) track processes of exclusion or inclusion in musical learning, and finally (v) a discussion of what has been

138 *Cecilia Wallerstedt*

revealed ends up in the conclusion that the role of the teacher is crucial in informal teaching practices.

Research on informal learning music pedagogy as an inclusive practice

A search for "inclusion" and "music education" in the research literature gives a rich span of hits. Green (2008), known for the project *Musical Futures* in the United Kingdom, explains why the method works inclusive: those students that previously were excluded in the classroom were reported as included when they were given freedom to work in groups in the classroom, without guidance from the teacher. The pupils felt that the teacher used a vocabulary that was hard to understand, and they preferred to be taught by peers instead of the teacher. "One reason for this is no doubt the relative absence of power differential existing between peers. For there was a strong feeling that teachers put on pressure" (p. 183). Green (2008) discusses that the peers were better than the teacher on meeting each other in the Zone of Proximal Development (Vygotsky, 1978). To play popular songs in what could be experienced as "real band" did also start processes of play which made the activity pleasurable and motivating for the pupils. They could imagine how they would be staging their performance in front of an audience while they rehearsed.

Wright (2013) examines the relationships between inclusion, informal learning and social justice. She turns to Freire (1970) and his concept of *liberatory education*. Freire's model of education puts the teacher in a position where he or she begins from the learner's everyday life. Wright compares features of Freire's (1970) and Green's (2017) pedagogy and finds many similarities. One is that students are empowered with control over their own learning, as they are supposed to do in informal music pedagogy where learning takes place in groups. Wright (2013) argues that informal learning as a model in music classrooms is what could empower pupils to develop, and also to enact a more socially just music education. Burnard et al. (2008) adhere to the same line of thought. They have studied classroom practices in four countries (Australia, Spain, Sweden and the United Kingdom) which are all different, but still have something in common: the teachers' works are characterized by an inclusive approach because

> [M]usic plays a crucial role in promoting 'social inclusion' (a term that refers to all children achieving and participating, despite challenges stemming from poverty, class, race, religion, linguistic and cultural heritage or gender), since it has the capacity for function as aim and means when creating an effective learning environment in multicultural schools. (p. 110)

Thus, music could be seen as a subject that has inclusive potential in it selves. In addition, there are also specific informal features of the pedagogy the teachers use that Burnard et al. (2008) identify. Since music is a practical subject, the teacher can *show* instead of talk (a so-called, and less formal, *embodied* pedagogy), they can let the students lead their own learning when working in groups, and they can create an equal relation with the students, letting them be the experts, when choosing their own music to play.

One challenge that is repeatedly stressed in the research literature is that the students bring musical experiences from outside school to inside of school, and here they face a practice where these experiences are not valued. This leads to the fact that skilled students tend to become excluded (Feichas, 2010; Tobias, 2015; Wallerstedt & Lindgren, 2016). Informal teaching strategies are often regarded as the solution for this problem. Lonie and Dickens (2016) report an interview study with young people who attended a leadership programme. They were asked about their musical learning through life. Many of the informants pointed out informal musical arenas as the places where they were included in learning processes of which they have been excluded from in schools. They "identified that most of their musical learning had taken place outside of formal spaces and curricula" and that

> they did not feel wholly excluded by their discouragement from certain formal spaces or opportunities, instead that they could navigate and negotiate 'spheres' of informal, non-formal and formal learning, most often describing situations where they would 'mix' there educational progression across diverse combinations of opportunities and styles of music. (p. 96)

What Lonie and Dickens' study shows is that learning opportunities are not exclusive to formal settings, something that we easily can recognize. What we still need to figure out then is what role the school may play. If learning is ideally self-directed, exclusively, what is the point of having music as one of the subjects in school? Is there merely a social purpose; to serve as an arena for social inclusion as discussed by Wright (2013), above? It is important to underline young people's own agency in learning music, as salient in Lonie and Dickens' (2016) study, but what could teachers do to enhance agency in students, more than avoid being an obstacle for learning?

Wright (2014) points at another interesting feature of informal pedagogy in music education, that "informal learning provides opportunities for the disruption of previously rationalized musical knowledge" (p. 32). She argues that "[i]t permits the equal/unequal relationship balance between the teacher and student to be rebalanced by allowing students to be in control of the music and the learning" (ibid.). Informal pedagogy has the potential to disrupt the social order between pupils and teachers, and this can open up for re-negotiations of what is regarded as valued knowledge in society. But this is not necessarily what happens, even in the informal classroom, as our actual case will show.

To summarize this limited literature review, two aspects of informal teaching strategies are of particular interest to focus on. The first concerns the role of language. When teachers use a vocabulary that the students do not share, the students become excluded. They simply do not understand what the teacher means. Informal learning is associated with showing rather than talking; and in a practical subject as music, it becomes inclusive to its nature, since music is

140 Cecilia Wallerstedt

regarded a universal language that people from different background share. The second aspect is about equality between teacher and students. Formal teaching is connected to a powerful teacher that limits the students' agency. When using methods where students are allowed to work in groups and choose their own music, they are said to be empowered with control over their learning and equal relationships can be built. These two aspects will be returned to in the discussion with a curiosity in what roles they play for exclusion and inclusion.

Schön's concept of reflection-in-action

To conduct the analysis of the empirical case, the theory by Schön (1983) will be used. His conceptual framework, originally developed through empirical studies of architect education, is particularly useful in order to understand what happens in the rehearsal room—an arena for learning a practical skill, in this case playing a song in a band. Schön manages to consolidate the dichotomy of the academically basic science on the one hand, and the technical skills of day-to-day practice on the other (cf. the dimensions of *ars* and *scientia*). Schön puts these together through the concept of *knowing-in-action*. Knowing is always dynamic and something that becomes visible in peoples' actions. But when we describe this knowing it turns into something more static that we can call knowledge. Schön also applies a distinction between reflect *in* action and reflect *on* action, that is, to stop and think about what has just happened. He exemplifies our capacity to *reflecting-in-action* by the way we engage in a conversation. We can both talk and at the same time think about what we are going to say next. The idea of *reflecting-in-action* has also been discussed in relation to musical contexts, both by Schön himself (on master classes in the genre of Western classical music), and in the praxial philosophy of music education. In a discussion of what musical understanding means, from a praxial approach, Gruhn (2005) explains that it "integrates so-called practical and mental skills; it brings together doing, making, feeling and thinking; and it complements action with reflection" (p. 106), and he also refers to Schön.

Being skilled at something cannot simply be equated with formulating reflections, as is typically done in formal education. Focus on the skills that play out in practical situations has also shed light on non-academic professions. The interest in these has sometimes been referred to in terms of "tacit knowledge" (Polanyi, 2009). However, Schön criticizes that in educational contexts this term simply stays with the observation that some knowledge is hard, or even meaningless, to describe in words. While Polanyi pointed to the fact that learning sometimes seems to mean to put into word something that you already can do, Schön argues that "most students do not begin with a tacit knowledge of competent designing" (1983, p. 87). Instead, this is what they are intended to develop, taking architecture education as an example. So verbalizing actions and reflections *is* important, from an educational point of view.

There is a paradox inherent when educating someone in practical skills. The student is "expected to plunge into designing, trying from the very outset to do what he does not yet know how to do, in order to get the sort of experience that

Music education in Sweden 141

will help him learn what designing means" (ibid., p. 93). There is a clear analogy to what the pupils in the rehearsal room in the music class are facing. They plunge into a practice of ensemble playing, and they are supposed to develop what Schön calls a *knowing-in-practice*, that is, a domain-specific knowing that the teacher represents. They are not skilled musicians, but still, they are supposed to manage the task of learning to play a song together with limited support from a teacher.

A practitioner's knowing is sometimes referred to as an invisible flow of talent and intuition, which Schön finds problematic. He unveils someone's talent, or "feel" for something, as a systematized bank of experiences. Those experiences enable the skilled practitioner to see situations as examples of familiar cases, and act properly on them.

> It is our capacity to see unfamiliar situations as familiar ones, and to do in the former as we have done in the latter, that enables us to bring our past experiences to bear on the unique case. It is our capacity to *see-as* and *do-as* that allows us to have a feel for problems that do not fit existing rules. (ibid., p. 68)

To educate someone to be skilled in a practice means to make someone gradually taking part in those processes (of *seeing as* and *doing as*). In this sense, Schön's philosophy harmonizes and overlaps with Lave and Wenger's (1991) sociocultural perspective on learning in communities of practice where members are described as moving from the periphery to become central participants. Also, Goodwin (1994) has described how professionals in a diversity of domains share a set of tools that enable them to see things *as* something (cf. Luria, 1976), and learning means to appropriate those domain-specific tools that form professionals' perception. What is salient in Schön's reasoning is that he adds, in difference to, for example Goodwin (1994), the *doing as*, that is, not only a professional seeing but also a professional *acting*.

Further on, Schön (1983) explains the essential process of identifying problems, and to share those in the reflective practicum:

> Through complementary acts of naming and framing, the practitioner selects things for attention and organizes them, guided by an appreciation of the situation that gives it coherence and sets a direction for action. So problem setting is an ontological process. (p. 9)

In the architect studio where the students meet their coaches, Schön identified five phases that they went through in their interaction. First, the student presented what she experienced as the problem in her work. Second, the teacher re-framed the problem in his own words and demonstrated a possible solution. Third, the student was enabled to reflect on the conversation so far. Fourth, the teacher pointed out the next step. Fifth, the student reflected on the conversation as a whole. Schön also identifies two particular problems that occur in the meetings between the students and coaches. One is what he calls *instructional gaps*. To

142   *Cecilia Wallerstedt*

demonstrate and to imitate, as well as to instruct and listen, are processes of problem solving that require *reflecting-in-action*. In those processes, gaps emerge easily, where the coach demonstrates something and the student tries to imitate, but do not discern the aspect that is the central one in the actual case. Another problem is what Schön calls *learning bindings*, which appear sometimes when the student *can* imitate, but is not *willing* to do so. The students' un-willingness can be explained by personal feelings the students have for the coach, for example, or possible, by reasons related to class and gender identity. The students, as Schön noted in his study, "feel threatened by the studio master's aura of expertise and respond to their learning predicament by becoming defensive. Under the guise of learning, they actually protect themselves against learning anything new" (p. 119).

The empirical case

The empirical case that will be analyzed is selected from a larger data set on Swedish secondary school music classes in Year 9 (students being 15–16 years old). The classes were followed during an 8-week project where they worked with pop ensemble playing. The total number of ensembles was eight and each ensemble was video-recorded for about half of their rehearsing time. The researcher used two cameras, one handheld and one stationary placed on a tripod. All video data was transcribed verbatim in full. The data generation follows the ethical guidelines of the Swedish Research Council, which means that participation is voluntary, the pupils and teachers have given their permission to take part in the study and they are informed about the purpose and their right to abort their participation at any time. The data is first analyzed through interaction analysis, meaning that every turn in the interaction is analyzed as responses to each other. Then the interactional process is explained using the conceptual framework developed by Schön (1983).

The empirical case constitutes a typical example of Swedish music education of today and thus informal learning pedagogy (Ericsson, Lindgren, & Nilsson, 2010; Erixon, Marner, Scheid, Strandberg, & Örtegren, 2012). The genre they work with is "easy-to-play pop music" (Georgii-Hemming & Westvall, 2010); the students themselves have chosen the group members, the song they practice and the instruments they play (drums, guitar, singing, etc.). They used their own mobile phones to listen to the song they tried to learn and they had lyrics and chords that they have found on the Internet (i.e. not traditional scores). The teacher has organized the teaching in line with the national curriculum and the school is a secondary school with no particular music profile. The teacher's main actions in the lessons were to go between the four rehearsal rooms and give feedback to the pupils and support them; give help with the equipment and tuning of instruments, etc. Often, the pupils saw their teacher only for a few minutes each lesson. The pupils have learned to play music mostly in this way, only a few of them do also play instruments outside school. They have had music classes once a week through primary and secondary school and now they attend ninth grade, which is the last year in compulsory school. Most students in the ensembles play on a basic level: Songs with few chords accompanied by simple rhythms on guitar, keyboard, drums and electric bass. Hence, they do not play melody lines on their instruments or improvised solos. Notably, they have not chosen to take music classes, but they were given a great deal of freedom within this mandatory school subject. At the end of the project, the students are afforded the opportunity to perform their songs at a local school concert.

Analysis of the entire data set is presented in previous articles (Wallerstedt & Hillman, 2015; Wallerstedt & Pramling, 2016). One representative case is here chosen in order to show in detail how the interaction between the pupils and the teacher turns out. In the chosen case, there are four pupils present, a girl who sings, a girl who plays the guitar and two boys who play the bass and the drums, respectively. The song they play is "Let Her Go" recorded by the artist Passenger. This is a pop song that was played occasionally on the radio at that time (2013) and it could be said to represent a singer-songwriter style. This transcription is from a video recording of one of their last rehearsals before the concert that will end the project.

Informal teaching in a formal setting—an example

This day, the teacher enters the room after the lesson has lasted for 10 minutes, and he stays for a few minutes. During this time, the five phases of coaching (Schön, 1983) are rapidly passed through. First, the students present what problem they struggle with. This is that the guitar and the bass are not well tuned. Just before the teacher entered the room, they played their song two times with a few comments on the form. Previously, they have struggled with the timing, but without being able to point out exactly what the problem is. The second phase, according to Schön's model, is that the teacher re-frames the problem in his own words and demonstrates a possible solution. In this case, the bass-player hands over his instrument to the teacher who tunes it. When the teacher is finished, he plays some "cool stuff" on the bass. He is a skilled rock musician and plays several instruments very well. In the following excerpt, the pupil's reaction on the teacher's playing reveals something about their experience of this meeting with him. The bass-player finds the teacher's level of playing unachievable (turn 54, below).

EXCERPT 1: When the teacher tunes the bass

53 GUITARIST: (points at the teacher, laughs directed towards the bassist, says with a low voice) you can do a bass solo later (laughs).
54 BASSIST: Nonono.
55 DRUMMER: I should do like that.
56 TEACHER: (finishes off by playing some more funk bass and, in almost the same movement, hands the bass over to the bassist)
57 BASSIST: Thanks.

144   *Cecilia Wallerstedt*

Three of the pupils communicate with each other while the teacher tunes the bass (turns 53–55). Their intonation indicates that they are ironic while they think of, and suggest, that they should play anything like the teacher. The guitarist even laugh at the idea that the bassist would play a solo and he answers "nonono" (turn 54).

After this, the ensemble continues presenting their "problem", now in an auditory way, that is, they perform their song so the teacher can identify what needs to be developed, or "solved". The teacher stands back and listens to the first bars. Then he starts snapping his fingers along with the pulse of the music.

EXCERPT 2: The teacher's reflection-in-action

73 TEACHER: (starts snapping his fingers, walks over and looks over the shoulder of the guitarist, quickly glances at her paper)
74 (the intro played by the guitarist ends and the singer starts to sing the first verse using the microphone, with only the guitar backing as support, out of sync; the others start after the break)
75 (during part three of the song, almost all students have stopped playing; someone carries on; after part four, all stop playing)
76 TEACHER: Okay, what you, you play it right and so, but the periods are... (takes over the guitar), if I can sit there (to the guitarist).

In this phase, the teacher identifies a problem. What the teacher recognizes seems to be something "in the book", to use Schön's terminology. He sees, or in this case *hears*, something *as* something, which immediately leads him to act in a certain way. There is a reflection going on, but we get little information on what it consists of, or how a "solution" is deliberated. When the teacher starts snapping his fingers (turn 73), he indicates that there is something wrong with the timing. In turn 76, he "reframes the problem in his own terms and proceeds to demonstrate the working out of a design solution" (Schön, 1983, p. 46). He mentions that "there is something with the periods" (turn 76). Period is a musical term not used—and perhaps not known—by the pupils. He then takes over the guitar, by physically taking the guitarist's chair and instrument, to demonstrate a solution (turn 76).

EXCERPT 3: A description of the musical demonstration

77 TEACHER: Then let's go... (plays some chords, as if to identify the chord pattern of the song without looking at the sheet) was it eh? Yes, right. (again playing the chord sequence) (starts the song with a emphasized beat, generally one beat per bar, with some elaboration in between; hums the melody in a high pitch) (looks at the guitarist; plays in a markedly different way than she does; stops). If you sing?
78 SINGER: What? Yes.
79 TEACHER: You can start, then I latch on with the guitar. (in the critical point between two periods, he plays a backing with a rhythmic figure that fills out the pause; clear beat, and the singer comes in right) Right! Oh, sorry, wrong chord by me. But you get the point (looks at the guitarist)?

Music education in Sweden 145

80 GUITARIST: Yes.

81 TEACHER: So it's the singing here that decides. And this really is a song that shouldn't be too quick.

82 GUITARIST: (laughs) That's what I have some difficulties with.

In turn 79, the teacher demonstrates on the guitar a way of playing that helps the singer to sing with timing. He finishes this demonstration by saying "you got it, right?" and the guitarist confirms, "yes" (turn 80). Later on in the observation it becomes visible that the guitarist is not able (or willing) to imitate the teacher's way of playing. The teacher adds some verbal comments to what he has showed, "So it's the song that takes the lead here" and "it's really a song that shouldn't be played too fast" (turn 81). Here, he refers to tempo, while he initially referred to the periods (cf. turn 76). The guitarist agrees that this is a problem (turn 82). She is also the one who becomes responsible for the problem that, if taking a musical perspective, is a mutual problem in the whole ensemble; that they cannot manage to play in time with each other. By using the guitarist's instrument, it could be interpreted as if the guitar(ist) is the problem—and, in a way, the key to the solution.

In the excerpt, it is an interesting interplay going on between what the teacher do (play) and what he says that reveals something about the "tacit", or in this situation rather "sounding", aspect of reflection. It is obvious that verbal language (musical terminology) is poorly used. The teacher relies on his musical demonstration. The teacher's way of playing the guitar helps the singer to find the right timing at this point (turn 79). This happens through a rhythmical playing style that clearly differs from the pupil's playing. She plays solely quarter notes, with no dynamic differentiation, and that makes it less clear where the bars begin and also where the periods (consisting of four bars) begin and end. This could analytically be what "it" refers to in turn 79. Whether the guitarist shares this understanding is far less clear.

The third phase, according to Schön (1983), is that a reflection of the conversation so far takes place. In this case, it is the teacher who reflects, while the pupils remain passive. At the same time, he points out the next step, which corresponds to the fourth phase.

EXCERPT 4: The teacher's instruction

83 TEACHER: It should go like (starts playing, adds colourings to the chords; hums the melody; plays like before with primarily one beat per bar, whole notes, and some rhythmical emphasis)

84 GUITARIST: (says something like: can't *you* play it, or: I can't play it—inaudible)

85 TEACHER: So you can play really cool, and listen to each other, and listen to her, her rhythm, 'cause the rhythm is really in the singing also *datatata-taa* (hums, in a straight pattern), so it's like that; *1-2-3-4* (sings the melody with numbers in eight time), *1-2-3-4* (sings in the same way, changes to "*nanana*" and backing after this upbeat). Get it?

86 GUITARIST: Yes. (gets the guitar back, teacher backs away towards the door)

87 TEACHER: So practice that.

146   *Cecilia Wallerstedt*

The teacher adds new modes to his explanation of the problem and its solution. He hums (turn 83) and he sings numbers; a way of counting that helps pointing out temporal aspects of the music (cf. Wallerstedt, Pramling, & Säljö, 2014). He also applies some new concepts in order to frame what it is about, "play really cool, and listen" (turn 85). In this way, he directs the attention to the mutual nature of the problem.

The fifth phase, in which the student should reflect over the conversation as a whole, is neglected. The teacher leaves the room and the pupils continue the rehearsal by playing the song from the top. The same problem remains and there is no discernible improvement.

By the end of the rehearsal, the students come back to what the teacher said, and here we can get a glimpse of what they got out of the teacher's instruction:

EXCERPT 5: Something about the rhythm

151 (short silence)
152 BASSIST: What was it he [the teacher, my comment] said now?
153 GUITARIST: I was gonna… (plays a bit on the guitar)
154 DRUMMER: Hello, you play like the whole time, make a pause like this
155 GUITARIST: What did you say?
156 DRUMMER: Yes, like you did.
157 GUITARIST: What, or?
158 DRUMMER: He meant that you should (says something softly—inadubile).
159 GUITARIST: (plays quarter notes).
160 DRUMMER: Yes, like that.

The bass-player tries to recall what the teacher said (turn 152). The guitarist applies a similar strategy to the teacher, that is, to demonstrate her understanding to the others, instead of explaining verbally (turn 153). The drummer makes a comment on this by mentioning something about the rhythm, that she should "make a pause like this" (turn 154). The guitarist seems unsure of what the drummer means (turn 157) and the drummer tries to develop his reasoning, but this is not audible (turn 158). The guitarist plays straight quarter notes, and for this the drummer comments: "Yes, like that" (turn 160), which stands in contradiction to the way the teacher actually played. The problem with the missed upbeat is still there on the concert a few weeks after this occasion, but the ensemble manage to play through the song anyway.

Discussion

Language and its role for exclusion/inclusion

The aim of this chapter has been to empirically examine a case of an informal learning pedagogy in classroom. The opportunities for learning that are constituted in the interaction between the teacher and the students have been addressed by analyzing how the students are included in processes of reflection. Informal learning is associated with being non-verbal, especially in music that is

Music education in Sweden   147

often regarded a practical subject (e.g. Burnard et al., 2008). What can be added to this line of thought given the present case? The teacher, acting as a coach, has been shown to be *reflecting-in-action* by identifying and solving a problem; by recognizing what he hears as "something about the periods" and acting on this by snapping his fingers and playing in a rhythmical style that supports the singer to sing in time. On the other hand, the pupils are given limited opportunities to share the process of *knowing-in-practice* that is going on. There seem to be too many "instructional gaps". Schön highlights that demonstration as well as imitation require problem-solving processes and *reflecting-in-action*. That the students have not managed to decode what "it" is in his musical demonstration becomes obvious in the last Excerpt (5) above. This points to a similar finding as in Pramling and Wallerstedt's (2009) study on music teaching in early childhood education: that "[v]erbal language appears to be a kind of meta-language for sense making (explaining, directing awareness, making distinctions, formulate relationships, etc.)" and this is important, "even while music education is characterised by being a non-verbal modality" (p. 149).

It should be highlighted that there is no given relatedness between informal teaching and the avoidance in use of verbal concepts. The critical point seems to be that the teacher, as the more competent partner in this case, is able to include the pupils in his area of expertise, in order to create opportunities for them to learn. There is something with the relationship between music and language that still needs to be solved, which I will discuss, follows Schön's line of thought. Schön's reasoning is built on the idea that *educating* people in a practical knowing calls for verbal language while merely practising the same knowing may not necessarily call for such language. Gruhn and Regelski (2006) argue, from a philosophical point of view, and in the context of setting a new foundation for music education, that:

> If we regard music as action, then verbal approaches and the applications of the technical terminology developed by music theory lose predominance; they are even no longer necessary to music learning since music learning is best achieved by music making, and that can be done without technical terminology. (p. 6)

In a forceful conclusion of this argumentation, they claim: "We must consider that musical interaction and musical understanding happens only within music, but without verbal or symbolic transformations" (p. 7). I would argue, based on empirical studies on musical interaction, that this conclusion is not valid. Of particular interest are empirical studies on children's music-making without guidance of teachers, that is, informal teaching situations where peers instruct each other. Such studies have shown that children are doing great efforts in *creating* a common language in order to verbally communicate about music, when making music together (Kullenberg, 2014; Wallerstedt, 2013). To communicate is fundamentally about making common, creating meaning through shared systems of signs and semiotic rules. Music is indeed an important "language", but to learn a language without a meta-language looks like going a long way around, whether it is in a formal or informal setting. In Schön's way of conceptualizing

148   *Cecilia Wallerstedt*

knowing-in-action, the contradiction between verbalizing (naming and framing, or *seeing-as*) and acting (*doing-as*) has reached a kind of peaceful settlement.

In the research literature, there are questions concerning verbalization discussed on different levels. An agreement on the need for verbalizing the subject as such can be seen. Georgii-Hemming and Lilliedahl (2014), for example, find that "the marginalization of aesthetic subjects may correlate with a difficulty and a reluctance to verbally describe the essence of music and thus specify the value of music education" (p. 142). Hence, it is pointed out that an articulation of the subject of music is welcomed. I argue that there *also* is a need of teachers introducing students to established musical terminology in order to involve pupils in processes of identifying and solving musical problems (of course not in opposition to making music). This could be an answer to the instructional gaps occurring between teachers and pupils in ensemble rehearsals illustrated here.

Teacher–students relations and their role for exclusion/inclusion

When informal learning is celebrated as being inclusive, the teacher practising formal strategies is often pointed out as the limiter (e.g. Green, 2008). Given this fact, the role of the teacher taken in the rehearsal room is important to consider. Schön's concept of *learning binding* is helpful in this respect. Learning binding is aimed to describe obstacles experienced by the students in imitating their coaches. Imitation is not an exclusively cognitive process, he claims. The relational aspect of educational experiences is something that is currently highlighted in research within the pragmatic tradition. Roth and Jornet (2014) write in the context of science education that "the emotional (affective) dimension is an integral aspect of the intellectual—it is not the result of an interpretation—because the intellectual itself is perfused with affect" (p. 122). In the first excerpt in the present study, it is shown how the teacher takes the opportunity to show his superiority when tuning the instruments. This leads to a distance shown by the pupils. To them, it seems like a joke that they should be able to play like this (turns 53–54 and 84). This incidence, followed by the teacher taking the pupil's chair, playing in an obviously more skilled and nuanced style, may have caused a learning binding, that is, a negative affective experience of being in disadvantage. How would it be possible for her to imitate his playing, inseparable from his aura of expertise? A previous study on more experienced students playing in school ensembles (Borgström Källén, 2014) shows many similar episodes. Borgström Källén addresses issues of gender and genre in her study. Interestingly, she comes to a conclusion regarding (the absence of) verbalization as well:

> From a gender perspective, the understanding of non-verbal communication as the primary communication strategy is problematic, since the results in this study indicate that the boys and the teachers primarily use the musical gestures, while girls more often use a verbal communication strategy. (p. 309)

She finds the male pupils and the teachers in her study communicating musical ideas using musical gestures, without verbalizing them. Within the genres of rock and pop, this is regarded as the ideal way of communicating, and thus an "alliance" is created between the boys and the teacher, that excludes the girls and privileges the boys, she claims. Abramo (2009) points out the same problem. In the context of American high school, Abramo discusses how it becomes an issue of power when the boys interpret the girls' verbal strategies as disturbing chats that can be neglected.

The empirical case has shown that some pupils become excluded, or bound, because of a lack of coordinated perspectives. This should not be too strongly linked to formal or informal teaching and learning. Rather, it points out a teaching competence that the teacher needs to develop: to be able to take the learners' perspective and build trustful relationships with the students. To do so is not dependent on the choice of working in groups or playing pop music, even if it can help as a stepping stone.

Conclusion

The result shows that the students struggle with musical problems they cannot manage on their own. The teacher, when attending the rehearsal room to help, avoids to meta-communicate on the problem he identifies. When giving instructions, he uses typically informal strategies (such as modelling rather than verbally explain in musically relevant terms), and this is shown not to be helpful for the student. The aim of including the students in a "real" (i.e. informal or authentic) musical setting is shown to be contra-productive. An implication drawn from this study is that the introduction of institutional (i.e. formal) concepts should not be overlooked in an informally inspired learning environment.

The empirical case scrutinized here showed that practical knowledge—the knowing of music—is shown by the teacher through his ability to identify and solve musical problems. In Schön's terminology, this could be regarded as *reflecting-in-action*, which constitutes a possible way of conceptualizing what it means to be a skilled musician. The teacher is seen, in a large extent, applying non-verbal strategies when demonstrating his solution to the musical problem as he identifies it. The pupils are not seen developing their practical skills of playing during this observation. The reasons could be summarized as follows: In the interaction between the teacher and the students the students do not become involved in the teacher's reflection work. This problem can be framed as an instructional gaps. In the interaction, there are also possible learning bindings shown. These seem to hindering the students from being able to imitate what the teacher demonstrates. An area of development in music education is argued for, and that is the use of verbal language. This is a lesson to learn for other subjects as well, when moving in a more informal direction. Speech has undeservedly been given the role as limiter of experiences, which are highly valued in an aesthetic subject such as music. But, in fact, if taking a sociocultural perspective, verbal language mediates experiences (Luria, 1976) and thus makes possible shared and enriched experiences. Giving emphasis to shared and articulated reflections in music education, regardless of genre or formal or non-formal ideals, could help realizing the democratic ambition of music for all, not only reducing it to a didactics-philosophical wish.

150　*Cecilia Wallerstedt*

References

Abramo, J. M. (2009). *Popular music and gender in the classroom (Diss)*. New York: Teachers College, Columbia University.

Borgström Källén, C. (2014). När musik gör skillnad – genus och genrepraktiker i samspel [*When music makes a difference – gender and genre practise in interplay*] (*Diss*). Gothenburg: Art Monitor.

Burnard, P., Dillon, S., Rusinek, G., & Saether, E. (2008). Inclusive pedagogies in music education: A comparative study of music teachers' perspectives from four countries. *International Journal of Music Education*, 26(2), 109–126.

Ericsson, C., & Lindgren, M. (2010). The Rockband context as discursive governance in music education in Swedish schools. *Action, Criticism, and Theory for Music Education*, 9(3), 35–54.

Ericsson, C., Lindgren, M., & Nilsson, B. (2010). The music classroom in focus: Everyday culture, identity, governance and knowledge formation. *Nordic Research in Music Education. Yearbook*, 12, 101–116. https://nmh.brage.unit.no/nmh-xmlui/bitstream/handle/11250/172293/Ericsson_Lindgren_Nilsson_2010. pdf?sequence=1&isAllowed=y

Erixon, P.-O., Marner, A., Scheid, M., Strandberg, T., & Örtegren, H. (2012). School subject paradigms and teaching practice in the screen culture: Art, music and the mother tongue (Swedish) under pressure. *European Educational Research Journal*, 11(2), 255–273.

Feichas, H. (2010). Bridging the gap: Informal learning practices as a pedagogy of integration. *British Journal of Music Education*, 27(1), 47–58.

Finney, J. (2007). Music education as identity project in a world of electronic desires. In J. Finney & P. Burnard (Eds.) *Music education with digital technology* (pp. 9–20). London: Continuum International Publishing Group.

Freire, P. (1970). *Pedagogy of the Oppressed*, trans. Myra Bergman Ramos. New York: Continuum, 65–80.

Georgii-Hemming, E., & Lilliedahl, J. (2014). Why "what" matters: On the content dimension of music didactics. *Philosophy of Music Education Review*, 22(2), 132–155.

Georgii-Hemming, E., & Westvall, M. (2010). Music education—A personal matter? Examining the current discourses of music education in Sweden. *British Journal of Music Education*, 27(1), 21–33.

Goodwin, C. (1994). Professional vision. *American Anthropologist*, 96(3), 606–633.

Green, L. (2008). Group cooperation, inclusion and disaffected pupils: Some responses to informal learning in the music classroom. Presented at the RIME conference 2007, Exeter, UK. *Music Education Research*, 10(2), 177–192.

Green, L. (2017). *Music, informal learning and the school: A new classroom pedagogy*. London: Routledge.

Gruhn, W. (2005). Understanding musical understanding. In David J. Elliott (Ed.), *Praxial music education: Reflections and dialogues* (pp. 98–111). New York: Oxford University Press.

Gruhn, W., & Regelski, T. A. (2006). Music learning in schools: Perspectives of a new foundation for music teaching and learning. *Action, Criticism, and Theory for Music Education*, 5(2), 1–27.

Johansen, G. (2014). Sociology, music education, and social change: The prospect of addressing their relations by attending to some central, expanded concepts. *Action, Criticism & Theory for Music Education*, 13(1), 70–100.

Kullenberg, T. (2014). *Signing and singing-children in teaching dialogues*. Diss. Gothenburg: Art Monitor.

Lave, J., & Wenger, E. (1991). *Situated learning: Legitimate peripheral participation*. Cambridge: Cambridge University Press.

Lonie, D., & Dickens, L. (2016). Becoming musicians: Situating young people's experiences of musical learning between formal, informal and non-formal spheres. *Cultural Geographies, 23*(1), 87–101.

Luria, A. R. (1976). *Cognitive development: Its cultural and social foundations*. Cambridge, MA & London: Harvard University press.

Polanyi, M. (2009). *The tacit dimension*. Chicago: University of Chicago Press.

Pramling, N., & Wallerstedt, C. (2009). Making musical sense: The multimodal nature of clarifying musical listening. *Music Education Research, 11*(2), 135–151.

Roth, W. M., & Jornet, A. (2014). Toward a theory of experience. *Science Education, 98*(1), 106–126.

Schön, D. A. (1983). *The reflective practitioner: How professionals think in action*. New York: Basic Books.

Tobias, E. S. (2015). Crossfading music education: Connections between secondary students' in-and out-of-school music experience. *International Journal of Music Education, 33*(1), 18–35.

Vygotsky, L. S. (1978). *Mind in society: The development of higher mental process*. In: Cambridge, MA: Harvard University Press.

Wallerstedt, C. (2013). 'Here comes the sausage': An empirical study of children's verbal communication during a collaborative music-making activity. *Music Education Research, 15*(4), 421–434.

Wallerstedt, C., & Hillman, T. (2015). 'Is it okay to use the mobile phone?' Student use of information technology in pop-band rehearsals in Swedish music education. *Journal of Music, Technology & Education, 8*(1), 71–93.

Wallerstedt, C., & Lindgren, M. (2016). Crossing the boundary from music outside to inside of school: Contemporary pedagogical challenges. *British Journal of Music Education, 33*(2), 191–203.

Wallerstedt, C., & Pramling, N. (2016). Responsive teaching, informal learning and cultural tools in year nine ensemble practice: A lost opportunity. *Instructional Science, 44*(4), 379–397.

Wallerstedt, C., Pramling, N., & Säljö, R. (2014). Learning to discern and account: The trajectory of a listening skill in an institutional setting. *Psychology of Music, 42*(3), 366–385.

Wright, R. (2013). Thinking globally, acting locally: Informal learning and social justice in music education. *Canadian Music Educator, 54*(3), 33–36.

Wright, R. (2014). The fourth sociology and music education: Towards a sociology of integration. *Action Criticism & Theory for Music Education, 13*(1), 12–39.

Part III

Informal learning as lifelong learning and its evaluation

10 Governance of informal learning as a pathway for the development of young adults' agency for sustainability

Valērijs Makerevičs and Dzintra Iliško

Introduction

The authors argue that formal and informal education are not two opposite modes of learning but complement each other organically in academia. The experience of teaching in academia of both the authors of this article has proven that formal learning alone as it is currently adopted in universities is not flexible enough due to its rigid curriculum frames. It does not meet various learning needs of students and it fails to prepare students for dealing with complex issues of life. Formal education has a large portion of rigidity determined by its well-structured and frameworks, norms and laws. Informal education allows ample variety and diversity of learning situations related to a real world issues, thus bringing a potential for enriching formal educational system. Informal learning corresponds to the arrangements of an open, dynamic and adaptable framework of knowledge building that is always in a constant process of becoming and relates to real world issues. Informal learning is serendipitous learning that takes place by meeting experts in the field, reading field-related literature, visiting museums and other different sites that enrich students' explorative capacities. Therefore, informal learning needs to be seen as a rich complementary learning resource alongside formal learning. European Union's regulations point to two main features of informal learning: social and personal. It maintains that non-formal education is a way of helping societies to be more democratic and to respect human rights. It needs to supplement formal education. The personal aspect of an informal education is to encourage developing individuals' curiosity and enthusiasm, to learn to work together and to practice democratic decision-making and negotiation, which is an important step towards active democratic citizenship. Moreover, non-formal education develops personal, social and professional skills through experimenting in a relatively safe environment.

There are no strict lines that can be drawn between formal and informal learning since visiting museums can be seen as a part of formal education or as a spontaneous desire of students to explore an issue of interest. Formal education can be rearranged as an open dynamic system as it involves flexibility and adaptability to students' needs, allowing students to participate in educational setting

156 *Valērijs Makerevičs and Dzintra Iliško*

with the objective of expanding the content on the basis of their needs and interests. Therefore, the elements of informal education should be incorporated into the framework of formal education. This goes along with the imperative set in the *Global Action Plan* (2015) towards integrating sustainability pedagogies. Sustainability pedagogies require participative student-centred approaches that include problem-solving methodologies, future's envisioning, debates and group discussions. Sustainability pedagogies will eventually lead towards reframing the learners' existing frames of references (Mezirow, 2009) and lead towards a more sustainable vision of a society. Due to its non-linear character these teaching methods can be messy, complex and unpredictable.

This kind of pedagogy requires a dedication of all staff members to revisit existing curricular structures by allowing some elements of flexibility and exploration. This requires higher transdisciplinarity in teams of like-minded educators working towards implementing new modes of learning and inquiry in academia (Jones, Selby, & Sterling, 2010). This will lead to higher students' motivation by developing a high capacity of students' autonomous learning. Sustainable pedagogies will foster students' ownership of knowledge and responsibility for a more sustainable future, and will encourage creative and critical thinking in finding new ways to react to complex everyday issues, by encouraging them to think in a system perspective and allowing them to act towards a more sustainable future (adapted from McFarlane & Ogazon, 2011; Tilbury & Wortman, 2004). The pioneers of a search for the best ways on how to integrate formal and informal education are philologists from the East and Asia. For example, the educators from Iran encouraged the use of crossword puzzles in the learning process (Amiri & Salehi, 2017).

Conceptualizing sustainability aspects of informal learning

People are learning everywhere at all times. People learn in different ways and in different situations. The learning outcomes depend on one's needs, desires and goals. However, learning that takes place outside formal system is not made visible and is not appropriately evaluated. In 1996, OSCD developed strategies for "*Lifelong learning for all.*" OESC committee made an effort to ensure that the partner countries recognize the value of informal education and validate it.

Logistics and high level of communication tools allow new forms of learning to emerge where traditional ways of learning become outdated. Higher educational establishments need to reevaluate and reform current pedagogies to more sustainable and inclusive ones, allowing more space for young adults' explorative capacities and more space for the informal learning. The UNESCO report, "Learning: *The Treasure Within*" (Delors et al., 1996) emphasizes the importance of informal learning in fostering adults' competencies to act for the well-being of oneself and the community. Informal education as a lifelong and life-wide way of learning that takes place across a wide variety of contexts—family, school, community and a daily life context. Informal learning allows more flexibility and

Sustainability aspects of informal learning   157

openness. This type of learning fits very well in an open, adaptive framework of learning. Eraut (2000) places a high value on informal learning and distinguishes between three forms of informal learning such as *incidental* (learning without any conscious attempt), *reactive* (virtually spontaneous learning) and *deliberate* (learning with an intention to acquire new knowledge) which constitute a significant part of everyday learning. Hague and Logan (2009) discuss that most of the informal learning is technology-enhanced learning that takes place at home. Web 2.0 generation finds it comfortable and most often chooses informal learning offered by the e-learning environment. Therefore, higher educations need a stronger move to transformations, innovation and connectivity to meet the needs of current new generation. Halliday-Wynes and Beddie (2009) point to informal learning as a hidden part of an iceberg that enhances numerous learning opportunities coming from social networking, blogs, wikis that can be easily accessed via smartphones. As Beer and Burrows (2007) suggest, Web 2.0 technologies have a potential for creating an opportunity for adults, for "reconfiguring their relations with objects, spaces and each other not fully explored" (para 1.2).

Educational institutions are trying their best to provide a variety of opportunities for learning—from structured to less structured, informal and student-directed by encouraging collaborative and individual inquiries and projects, leading to interdisciplinary inquiry in flexible, comfortable and appealing places for the students. Formal learning in academia is supplemental by the informal learning arrangements that take place outside formal learning institution. To meet an increasing demand for such spaces, universities create spaces by promoting both social and academic learning (O'Neill, 2013). He maintains that learning can take place anywhere, anytime, anyhow and by anyone with the goal that learning is limitless. An adaptable learning environment can be described by its flexibility, adjustability, access and expression. This means that design should foster communication and interaction. The added value to formal learning occurs through self-education and associations with external people and networks (McGiveney, 1999). Such fused spaces may facilitate context-awareness, situation-awareness and multi-scale dynamics in real time (Fused Media Lab, 2008; Hall, 2009). Informal learning modes as integrated in formal contexts allow more space for exploring real world issues, tackling them in a more sustainable way, leading towards building more sustainable communities. As Fullan and Scott (2014) assert, sustainable pedagogies have a potential to bring along transformations in higher education. Sustainability pedagogies will foster skills such as imaginative, future thinking, real world problem-solving skills (Filho, Manolas, & Pace, 2009), future mindedness (UNESCO, 2005), systems thinking (Filho et al., 2009), civic engagement (Kelly & Fetherston, 2008), transdisciplinary research (Dale & Newman, 2005) and values (cooperation, compassion, commitment, care) (Filho et al., 2009; Murray & Murray, 2007) that will support sustainable development. Sustainability pedagogies lead to students' behavioral change, encouraging them to model alternative reality and to take action. Therefore, the learning space in academia should be a model of

158 *Vaïerijs Makerevičs and Dzintra Iliško*

democracy, where the students are encouraged to take initiative in making decisions and to participate in setting objectives. Such opportunity can be offered by redesigning formal education as an open and dynamic educational space that allows integration, or even encourages the elements of informal learning to occur.

Informal learning in Latvia

Informal education becomes an issue of discussion and a focus of attention among politicians and scholars. Non-formal education takes place alongside formal education. "*Education Development Guidelines 2014–2020*" define non-formal education as the educational activity satisfying the needs of individuals, society and the labour market. The Ministry of Education has ratified the *Adult Education Governance Model* implementation plan for 2016–2020 on 3 May 2016 that sets the aim to develop internationally recognized *Adult Learning System*. This includes also a financial support for the provision of adult learning to the unemployed and jobseekers. However, the model remains rather fragmented and driven by the needs of industries and demands of labour market.

The actors engaged most in fostering diverse forms of non-formal education are non-governmental organizations and civics societal organizations in a form of different seminars, forums, workshops and creative forms. Adult non-formal educational programs are also provided by the vocational education institutions and adult education providers (education centres), as well as institutions of higher education. Adult non-formal educational programs are offered by private companies registered at the Register of Educational Institutions and accredited for a delivery of educational programs. The largest Latvian enterprises have created their own educational centres. Non-formal education in Latvia rests on basic premises of new competencies for all, more investment into human resources and prevention of exclusion. Still, non-formal education corresponds more to the needs of labour market and fulfils employee's expectations. Financial support to adult education comes from the state budget, municipality budget and other sources (grants), and projects. One of the main sources of financing lifelong learning remains investments from EU's structural funds.

The government of Latvia is working towards a validation of skills and knowledge obtained via informal education. Validation process has started in 2012 based on regulations Nr.32 of the Cabinet of Ministers "*Regulations of the recognition of the learning outcomes acquired outside formal education or achieved through professional experience*" issued on 10 January 2012 and is based on the "European guideline for validating non-formal and informal learning" (CEDEFOP, 2009) that provides a detailed description of a validation process of Bologna.

Knowledge, skills and competencies obtained during those studies can be validated and recognized. Still, there are a number of challenges that need to be raised in relation to a validation of non-formal education. Stakeholders have different notion of informal education and unwillingness to acknowledge

Sustainability aspects of informal learning   159

knowledge obtained as a result of informal education. As the director of the _Quality Evaluation Department_, Kristīne Strūberga stated, normative documents and financial regulations have been worked out that validates professional competencies obtained from the non-formal education system in one hundred professional qualifications in Latvia.

The government supports the idea of lifelong and life-wide education for the entire populations independent of age, as it is stated in EC (2000) document, that Latvia must reorient lifelong education towards economic aspect in order to cope with the changes. Latvia has ratified laws regulating adult education: _The Law of Education_ (1998), dealing with general adult education; professional education dealing with vocational and continuing educational programs, both formal and non-formal, as well as the law on higher education, dealing with formal education for adults.

The government supports various forms of informal education, such as requalification of teachers in obtaining new qualification, support of youth and adults to participate in the international projects, such as Leonardo da Vinci, Erasmus + projects.

Research methods

The authors carried out a questionnaire for the Secondary school students, University's Master and Bachelor programme students, and the teachers on diverse aspects of informal learning in their lives that allowed the authors to evaluate how informal learning complements their everyday life and addresses their professional and self-development.

The authors have also carried out two semi-structured interviews with two leading experts in the field of informal educations responsible for the young adults and youth informal education at the city level. Interview data was transcribed and the themes were identified that describe informal education in Latvia.

Research finding: Questionnaire of multiple stakeholders

The aim of this study was a deeper understanding of informal learning in the lives of young adults as well as their involvement in the setting of informal learning.

For this purpose, the authors have designed a questionnaire comprising 20 questions. The questionnaire contained five subscales, including four questions in each of the subscales. With the help of the first subscale, the authors have measured the importance of informal education and its connectedness with one's professional career. The answers to questions of the second subscale allowed a conclusion about the degree of purposefulness of choosing further education in the informal environment. The third subscale is motivational that contains the criteria of one's choice of opportunities offered by informal education, and the opportunity to engage in informal learning activities in one's region that satisfies the needs and interests of young adults. The fourth subscale shows one's attitude towards informal education available in the e-learning environment.

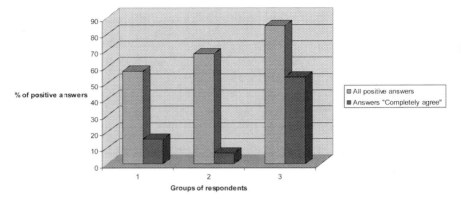

Figure 10.1 The significance of informal learning.

The first subscale includes questions on the expectations of respondents with regards to informal education. The answers were evaluated on a 5-point scale: 5—completely agree, 4—agree, 3—partly agree, 2—partly disagree, 1—fully disagree.

The participants of the research were pupils ($n = 126$), the students from the educational programs ($n = 46$) and regional teachers ($n = 33$). The questionnaire was carried out via Internet.

The results gained as a result of analyses of responses to the questions of first subscale are the following.

In Figures 10.1 to 10.5, the group of secondary pupils was labeled as group 1; the group of university students was labelled as group 2 and the group of teachers was labelled as group 3. In Figure 10.1, the research allows the researchers to conclude that the necessity of informal learning has been evaluated positively by 57.1% of pupils, 67.7% of students and 84.8% of teachers.

The number of participants who "completely agree" is quite small in the group of pupils and students. The group comprising teachers is bigger who "agree completely" with this statement and comprises 53.6% of teachers. Pupils and students are confident about the formal education that satisfy their educational needs, but educators view informal education as contributing to the education of young adults.

In Figure 10.2, the answers to the questions of the second subscale on a purposive choice of informal education reflect the following: 55.6% of pupils are confident that they make a purposeful choice to participate in the activities offered by the informal education ($n = 12.9\%$). Students' response was much higher ($n = 84\%$) (19% of whom "completely agree"). Among the respondents comprising the group of teachers ($n = 33.3\%$) of them expressed their confidence. The teachers' evaluation was higher for a purposeful choice of activities offered in informal education than by students and pupils respondents.

Sustainability aspects of informal learning 161

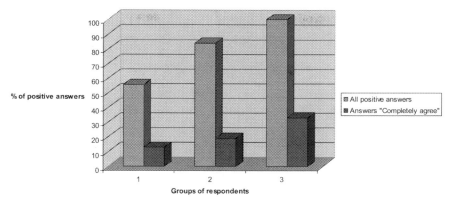

Figure 10.2 Rationality and availability of choice for informal education.

The data gained as a result of the analyses of questions comprising the third subscale regarding the motivation of students to choose informal education is reflected in Figure 10.3.

There are 63.5% of pupils who find the programmes of informal education related to their interests accessible. Pupils who "completely agree" to the availability of such programmes comprise 33.8% of participants. Among the samples of students, 57.8% participants ($n = 11.5\%$) "agree completely" and in the samples of teachers, 72.7% ($n = 10.2\%$) "completely agree."

One can evidence a low evaluation rate in all groups for "completely agreeing." This might be related to a lack of complete information about the potential and availability of informal education in regions.

The results gained in the fourth subscale are reflected in Figure 10.4.

The authors have studied the offered forms of informal learning, such as e-learning (Moodle platform). Figure 10.4 reflects the readiness of participants

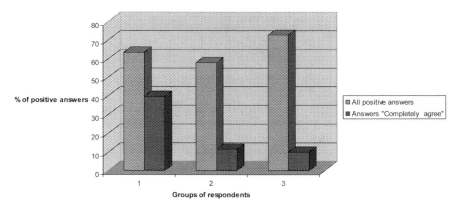

Figure 10.3 Motivation and opportunities for informal learning.

162 *Valērijs Makerevičs and Dzintra Iliško*

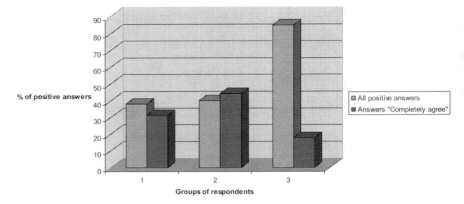

Figure 10.4 Responses of respondents towards the offered forms of informal learning.

to use opportunities offered by the e-learning environment. The students are more prepared to use opportunities provided by the e-learning environment. Majority of pupils and students gave a priority of a direct contact with the teacher and view e-learning as a complementary mode of learning to a formal learning. Teachers are ready to offer learning programmes in the e-learning environment, but are not confident if these programmes will be demanded.

Figure 10.5 shows the expectations of participants as derived from the informal learning.

In order to study the respondents' expectations, the authors posed the following question: "How can I benefit from the informal education?"

The questions were related to the success of their studies and career planning. The results were the following: pupils—85.7% provided positive answers. From them 38% provided a "completely agree" answer. Among them, 86.7% ($n = 22.2\%$) students and 87.9% ($n = 20\%$) teachers provided "completely agree" responses.

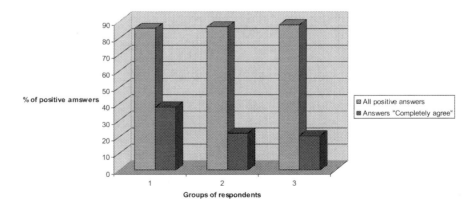

Figure 10.5 Expectation of participant of informal education.

The highest number of positive answers is in all groups. The number of participants who completely agree is not very high. This can be explained in the following way:

- The programmes of informal learning do not always relate with the needs of young people.
- Insufficient information about the available programmes of informal educational programs.
- Lack of professionals who are engaged in the field of informal education who can design the programmes that relate to the needs of young people.

The situation can be improved by

- undertaking detailed study of the needs of young people;
- designing the programmes for informal learning that relate to the needs of young adults;
- informing young adults about the opportunities of informal learning programmes;
- producing informational materials about the opportunities of informal education in the region and
- involving the administration of schools to design programmes of informal education.

Research findings: Interviews with the experts

For the purpose of the research, the authors interviewed two leading experts in the field of informal education who are responsible for the quality assurance of youth and adult informal education in the city.

Growing interest to support informal education

Both interviewed experts have recognized the growing importance of informal education for both adults and youth. Both experts emphasized that one of the factors of efficiency of informal programmes is governmental support in development of informal educational programs and the ratification of the guidelines for recognition of experience of young adults who have obtained informal education. Both experts emphasized that formal education is not sufficient enough to satisfy the needs of all students: "*Students do not obtain life skills within a framework of formal education. They are not prepared for life in a complex world where they need to solve complex problems and have an ability to develop new knowledge and, if needed, change their career.*"

Motivation to participate

The motivation of youth and adults to participate in diverse activities offered by the informal education programmes is growing. Knowledge that young adults can obtain enriches formal educational, therefore teachers are trying to motivate

164   *Valērijs Makerevičs and Dzintra Iliško*

their students to engage in diverse activities, forums and conferences organized by the NGOs and youth activists. As youth expert reported, *"the majority of learning experiences occur during interaction with real people who discuss real problems at youth forums, seminars where young adults can learn teamwork and problem solving skills."* Also, informal learning provides safe space for the otherness, heterogeneity, diversity and plurality.

Quality assurance of informal education

Quality assurance of formal education is no any longer an isolated matter. Today it intermingles with the conflicting values and demands of diverse actors and systems, such as government, markets, society, businesses and other stakeholders. Quality assurance of informal education becomes a complex mixture of ideology, governmental policy, relationships of different interest group and consideration of allowing the space for multiple stakeholders to intervene. The quality of informal education relates to a quality culture that fosters communication, exchange and dialogue with the diverse needs of young adults.

The major actors involved in the field of informal education are working towards improving the standards and quality of informal education in a variety of fields related to sport, music and crafts on a demand of young adults. The municipality is responsible for ensuring the quality of offered informal programmes by licensing those programmes. Both experts pointed to the out-of-the-box nature of informal learning that requires flexibility in the assessment methods and approaches. Both experts discuss that even if informal learning gets formalized, it should still have the essence of informal learning. But, integration of informal learning into the setting of formal learning can only expand learning opportunities and motivate young adults to increase their skills. Informal learning remains invisible since it occurs spontaneously.

The scale of informal education

The range of offered informal programmes varies from local to international scale, including participation of youth and adults in the Erasmus + and Leonardo da Vinci and other programmes aimed towards developing youth leadership and intercultural competency. The teachers who have lost their jobs can obtain the second qualification in state-financed informal programmes. As both experts have mentioned, there is an increasing shift from formal to informal learning since informal learning environment allows one to acquire new knowledge in a more flexible way. IT technologies play their role in integrating informal learning experience into a formal setting. As both experts acknowledged the role of ICT technologies, they also emphasized that students need to develop critical skills to analyze the acquired information. Their observations lead to the conclusion that students are not critical enough to evaluate the truthfulness of all the acquired information. At the same time both experts acknowledged educational use of

Sustainability aspects of informal learning 165

e-resources. The experts acknowledged the expansion of ICT technologies in all spheres of life, by emphasizing that the communication among human beings is still more efficient, both in formal and informal learning sectors.

Concerns and future perspectives

One of the concerns expressed by both experts is that NGOs tend to organize informal learning in a more structured way that destroys the essence of informal education, since informal learning occurs through diverse interaction in unstructured way. Another concern raised is that informal education currently offered by individuals not having a proper license can cause a damage to the participants. For example, as one of the experts commented: "*If the groups of sport are managed by the professionals without a proper license this may cause a damage to the health of young adults by unprofessional services.*" Therefore, municipality carries the responsibility for a close monitoring of all informal activities offered at the city level.

Complementarity of formal and informal education

Both experts acknowledged the complementarity of both formal and informal education. Formal education does not provide space for the students to develop their leadership skills enough. Therefore, informal education can serve as a means to develop such skills as self-presentation and leadership.

Conclusion

Learning involves both formal and informal learning processes that overlap and interact. The task of the educators is to facilitate diverse forms of informal learning to enrich each other in the learning process at the universities. Learning is not just about acquiring knowledge and skills; it is also about increasing self-knowledge and revision of prior knowledge, as well as it is about active knowledge construction. Learning involves socialization and internalization of values, attitudes and behaviour occurring in daily life.

Informal learning has a great potential to offer for a more desirable learning arrangements for adults and communities and it needs to be seen not as an opposite but as a complementary and integrated form of learning alongside formal learning in academia. Today we observe blurring boundaries that exist between formal, social and personal learning contexts.

Most of the informal learning forms a hidden part of the iceberg and remains unseen. Universities need to make informal learning spaces available for the students whether it is a library, a nearby park or a lobby, by allowing temporary ownership of those places. The world today is based on knowledge and experience; therefore, it offers multiple opportunities for learning. By having an instant access to information, learning is no any longer confined to a space and time. Therefore, formal arrangement of learning at the university is not

166 *Valērijs Makerevičs and Dzintra Iliško*

restricted to formal learning but is accompanied with other forms of learning. Learning of young adults is taking place via different interactions and at a variety of settings (Billett, 2010).

Implementing sustainability pedagogies can be a challenging task but also can be seen as a powerful tool for moving students towards transformational learning.

References

Amiri, B., & Salehi, H. (2017). Effects of using crossword puzzles on improving spelling among intermediate EFL learning. *Asian Journal of Education and e-Learning*, 5(5), 159–171.

Beer, D., & Burrows, R. (2007). Sociology and, of and in Web 2.0: Some initial considerations. *Sociological Research Online*, 12(5), article 17. Retrieved from http://www.socresonline.org.uk/12/5/17.html

Billett, S. (2010). Lifelong learning and self: Work, subjectivity and learning. *Studies in Continuing Education*, 32(1), 1–16.

CEDEFOR (2009). European guideline for validating non-formal and informal learning. Luxembourg: Office for Official Publications of the European Communities. Retrieved from: https://www.cedefop.europa.eu/files/4054_en.pdf

Dale, A., & Newman, L. (2005). Sustainable development, education and literacy. *International Journal of Sustainability in Higher Education*, 6(4), 351–362.

Delors, J. et al. (1996). *Learning: The treasure within. Report to UNESCO of the international commission on education for the twenty-first century*. Paris: UNESCO.

EC (2000). European Communities: A Memorandum on Lifelong Learning. Retrieved from: https://uil.unesco.org/document/european-communities-memorandum-lifelong-learning-issued-2000

Eraut, M. (2000). Non-formal learning, implicit learning and tacit knowledge in professional work. In F. Coffield (Ed.), *The necessity of informal learning*. Bristol: The Policy Press.

Faure, E. Herrera, F., Kaddoura, Abdul-Razzak, Lopes, H., Petrovsky, Arthur V., Rahnema, M., & Ward, F. C. (1972). *Learning to be: The world of education today and tomorrow*. Paris: UNESCO.

Filho, W. L., Manolas, E., & Pace, P. (2009). Education for sustainable development: Current discourses and practices and their relevance to technology education. *International Journal of Technology Design Education*, 19, 149–165.

Fullan, M., & Scott, G. (2014). *New pedagogies for deep learning whitepaper:Education PLUS*. Seattle: Collaborative Impact SPC.

Fused Media Lab (2008). *Fused-Media Lab, digital-economy innovation*. Retrieved from http://www.cse.dmu.ac.uk/~ibrahim/FML.htm

Hague, C., & Logan, A. (2009). *A review of the current landscape of adult informal learning using digital technologies*. Bristol, UK: Futurelab Retrieved July 5, 2013 from

Hall, R. (2009). Towards a fusion of formal and informal learning environments: The impact of the read/write web. *Electronic Journal of e-Learning*, 7(1), 29–40, Retrieved from www.ejel.org

Halliday-Wynes, S., & Beddie, F. (2009). *Informal learning at a glance*. Commonwealth of Australia: NCVER. Retrieved from https://ala.asn.au/public/docs/report/Informal_learning-At_a_glance.pdf

Sustainability aspects of informal learning 167

Jones, P., Selby, D., & Sterling, S. (2010). More than the sum of their parts? Interdisciplinarity and sustainability. In P. Jones, D. Selby, & S. Sterling (Eds.), *Sustainability education: Perspectives and practice across higher education.* (pp. 17–37). London: Earthscan.

Kelly, R., & Fetherston, B. (2008). Productive contradictions: Dissonance, resistance and change in an experiment with cooperative learning. *Journal of Peace Education, 5*(2), 97–111.

McFarlane, D. A., & Ogazon, A. G. (2011). The challenges of sustainability education. *Journal of Multidisciplinary Research, 3*(3), 81–107.

McGiveney, V. (1999). *Informal learning in the community. A trigger for change and development.* Leicester: NIACE.

Mezirow, J. (2009). Transformative learning theory. In J. Mezirow, & E. Taylor (Eds.), *Transformative learning in practice: Insights from community, workplace, and higher education* (pp. 18–31). San Francisco: John Wiley and Sons.

Murray, P. E., & Murray, S. A. (2007). Promoting sustainability values within career-oriented degree programmes: A case study analysis. *International Journal of Sustainability in Higher Education, 8*(3), 285–300.

O'Neill, M. (2013). Limitless learning: Creating adaptable environments to support a changing campus: By delivering adaptability in space, technology, and furnishings, old-world buildings and traditions can successfully survive amid a continual influx of new. *Planning for Higher Education, 42*(1). Retrieved from https://www.questia.com/library/journal/1G1-381056286/limitless-learning-creating-adaptable-environments

The Law of Education (1998). Riga: Saeima. Retrieved from: http://www.aic.lv/rec/Eng/leg_en/LV_lik/ed_law.htm

Tilbury, D., & Wortman, D. (2004). *Engaging people in sustainability.* Gland, Switzerland and Cambridge: IUCN Commission on Education and Communication.

UNESCO (2005). The Convention on the Protection and Promotion of the Diversity of Cultural Expressions. Retrieved from: https://en.unesco.org/creativity/convention

UNESCO (2012). *UNESCO Guidelines for the recognition, validation and accreditation of the outcomes of non-formal and informal learning.* Paris: UNESCO.

11 Integrating formal and informal learning to develop self-management skills: Challenges and opportunities for higher education in the university-to-work transition

Amelia Manuti

Introduction

The amazing progress of technology, the globalization of markets, the push to economic competition, the break of traditional career paths and consequently the development of new skills and professionalities are only some of the main transformations that have contributed to radically redesign the way people learn and develop skills, consequently influencing the meaning they attach to career and the way they plan their future in the 21th century.

While only a few decades ago, formal learning meant as the education normally acquired in a systematic intentional way within a school, higher education or university was the main and most salient element to choose and select "the right man for the right place." Nowadays the "talent war" imposes workers to compete on a different and more complex level, showing their uniqueness by accounting for several different learning experiences acquired mostly in informal and non-formal contexts.

Parallel to the cultural, economic and social revolution of the social systems, even working organizations are experiencing a time of radical change. They are called to face all the challenges described above and to keep in the market as well. That is why they are becoming more and more demanding in terms of soft skills required to workers to perform efficiently, beyond role prescriptions and technical requirements.

Therefore, an imperative for both research and professional practice in the field of higher education is to help individuals to recognize, capitalize and manage their learning, coming both from formal and informal channels, marking the difference in terms of human capital.

This evidence becomes an even more urgent theoretical and practical priority in front of another important cultural change: The advent of a new generation of learners and future workers, the Millennials. This is a generation of social and self-directed learners, whose features and expectations are completely different from those of the generations that have preceded them. Given their

Formal and informal learning for Millennials 169

personal features and the social and cultural context they live in, this generation is accustomed to learning not only in and through formal paths but also to capitalize the informal experience that answers to their needs. By this, it is evident that they learn more and better informally, thus developing skills that might help them using the knowledge they have acquired also through formal learning. Theoretically speaking, this generation could have all the features that the current labour market is looking for. However, the present formal system of education could further support the acknowledgement of this evidence by contributing to strengthen the metacognitive skills, that might help them systematizing knowledge and skills acquired in different contexts and using them when required on the job. These skills are also called self-management skills; they refer to the set of personal resources (attitudes, behaviours, motivations, skills, etc.) that could make individuals "employable" on the market, once they learn how to recontextualize what they know and what they can do with specific job demands.

In view of these premises, the aim of the chapter is to discuss how to enhance the natural interplay between formal and informal learning in higher education, to help the Millennials generation to further develop self-directed learning and self-management skills precious for an effective university-to-work transition.

Reinventing higher education: A new learning scenario for a new generation of students

Within the last decades two main phenomena have redefined the world of higher education posing challenges both to learning theory and to teaching practice. Yet, the revolution brought about by Web 2.0 and the advent of a tech-savvy generation of students—the Millennials—have shaped what McHaney (2011) calls "The New Digital Shoreline" of higher education.

This new scenario has imposed a serious rethinking about some of the most traditional teaching methodologies and practices because they reflect a world that has almost disappeared.

Accordingly, the advent of Web 2.0 or the social web has basically changed the way people live and communicate, greatly impacting on individual cognitive mindsets, and thus on the way people experience and learn (Greenhow, Robelia, & Hughes, 2009). The unfinished learning opportunities and contexts granted by technology allow people to become "ubiquitous learners" (Hwang & Tsai, 2011) supporting and encouraging informal conversation, dialogue, collaborative content generation and the sharing of knowledge, greatly influencing a vast array of representations and ideas and consequently enhancing informal learning as primary learning channel (Ebner, Lienhardt, Rohs, & Meyer, 2010; Gikas & Grant, 2013). Moreover, the opportunity to move into a variety of different, possibly unrelated fields over the course of a lifetime also allow people to shape personal learning environments (Dabbagh & Kitsantas, 2012; Siemens, 2007) and to develop wider scripts to cope and to manage complex and multidimensional tasks and situations. This leads people, who profit from the affordances

170 Amelia Manuti

given by technology, to develop faster and better soft skills useful to be flexible and employable in a very turbulent labour market. In this vein, according to some authors "know-how" and "know-what" are being supplemented with "know-where," namely with the ability to understand where to find the piece of knowledge needed (Siemens, 2005). In fact, it is evident that social media afford greater agency to the learner, allow to gain autonomy and engagement, to participate into wider often global networks and thus to actively contribute to the process of knowledge creation and sharing (Ashton & Newman, 2006; Lee, McLoughlin, & Chan, 2008). Therefore, if properly guided and managed, "the learning experiences granted by social media are active, process-based, anchored in and driven by learners' interests and therefore have the potential to cultivate self-regulated and independent learning" (McLoughlin & Lee, 2010, p. 29), a kind of learning which is very much appreciated within the current working contexts.

A second very significant factor that has contributed to redefine higher education is the evidence that the generation of students that is currently living the world we were describing earlier and thus the present learning contexts is profoundly different from the previous generation (DeBard, 2004). Empirical evidences show that Millennials, that is young people born between 1981 and 2001, learn differently, are differently engaged in learning and above all carry out different expectations and needs with respect to learning (Jonas-Dwyer & Pospisil, 2004). Some say that the Millennial students are "a mixed bag" (Papp & Matulich, 2011), in the sense that they are more academically optimistic, service-oriented and politically engaged with respect to students who were freshmen 10 years ago. In the meantime, they are more self-focussed, impatient and extremely self-confident. Millennials are ambitious, they are conscious about their knowledge and about the impact it could have on others, that is why they are continuous learners, they always seek learning opportunities that might contribute to their personal growth. On the other hand, they adapt well to new people, places and circumstances, thriving in environments featured by collaboration and teamwork. Moreover, as already stressed, Millennials are considered a digital generation (Oblinger, 2003). They possess an "information-age mindset" because they have developed a symbiotic relationship with technology and use it far more often than those of previous generations.

For all that, given the multifarious features of this generation that allow to balance the need to move into chaos as well as the need to be goal-oriented, to face challenges and to recognize opportunities, Millennial students seem to "have the numbers" to cope with both the educational and the economic context of current times dominated by great uncertainty and flexibility.

Towards a change in teaching practices: Approaching the "What's in it for me?" generation

The most evident consequence of these reflections about a rapidly changing scenario is the need to rethink the way teachers and trainers "renegotiate the learning deal" (Papp & Matulich, 2011).

Formal and informal learning for Millennials   171

It is evident that the features of this new generation of digital natives who mostly learn through social networking and through other forms of mobile communication devices require a radical change in the way knowledge is delivered and consequently in the way learners might be involved in the process of learning. Certainly, the many affordances granted by technology should be considered but not just as a simple adding to the process of knowledge creation and delivery. Rather, it is necessary to rethink what do learners seek in learning, how do they value learning, how can leaning contexts could answer to these needs through technology and accordingly how to transform the role of educators from asymmetric gatekeepers of knowledge into connected co-learners with students.

This evidence is made more complex by a further paradox: Digital natives are currently taught by a generation of teachers who are digital immigrants, who are quite unfamiliar with technology and use teaching methodologies and languages they can hardly understand because they are the same they have learnt once they were students (Prensky, 2001). As we know from the literature, Millennials are visual and kinesthetic learners, they need peer-to-peer interaction and prefer experiential learning to master concepts. Teachers who do not start from this consideration and adopt traditional methodologies to transfer knowledge risk to lose their attention and spoil a learning opportunity.

Beyond this first evidence, there are several implications about the fact that teaching to Millennials is a very peculiar task, that needs to start from a general refocusing of the process of learning in force of the very distinctive features of the addressees we are considering. Actually, if we do not examine who are the learners, where do they come from and what are their needs, how can we plan and deliver learning? Moving from this question, we will examine a few crucial points that could help reinventing higher education in relation with the profound social and generational change it is experiencing.

A first point relates to the cultural and family environment of this generation of Millennials. According to some authors, Millennials have been taught that they are "special," because relying upon their strengths they could be anything they want to be (Papp & Matulich, 2011). Therefore, they tend to feel confident about their own resources, they feel sheltered by their family and this is the attitude they show once they enter in the classroom. They feel overconfident about their resources and are profoundly convinced that they can change the world if it does not fit to their needs. In this vein, they are much motivated and goal-oriented. Nevertheless, if they do not see a benefit in what they do they tend to give up. Anyway, these optimistic and enthusiastic convincement often crash when Millennials are called to face reality, if they are not actually equipped to cope with disillusionments and with the pressure of adult life. Therefore, teachers should consider the psychosocial features of this new generation of students who could be at the same time extremely competent with technology but also very fragile from a more personal point of view.

A second evidence is that Millennials are social learners and work best in teams with one another: They prefer to learn in active, collaborative and experiential

172   *Amelia Manuti*

environments (Cao, Griffin, & Bai, 2009; Twenge, 2006). Moreover, thanks to technology they are also informal learners, who "learn any time any place" (Papp & Matulich, 2011) and mainly through multimedia tools (Cao et al., 2009; Matulich, Papp, & Haytko, 2008). This peculiar visual and interactive learning style is heavily challenged when they enter higher education where learning is mainly supposed to be a logical and linear process, where they are expected mainly to listen to oral lessons, to learn from textbooks and to manage abundant amount of written materials.

However, given these peculiarities, it should be acknowledged that many changes have recently occurred in higher education, to accommodate the Millennials' learning style and to maximize the teaching efforts. In the classroom, interactive methodologies (group discussion, role-playing, practice exercise, simulations, brainstorming, etc.) are becoming primary vehicle to help students retain material, to avoid distraction, to enhance collaboration and to engage students into the learning process. At home, independent learning is enhanced if teachers make available their learning materials into portable formats, that could be easily downloaded, listened and re-listened everywhere (Lonn & Teasley, 2009; Skipton, Matulich, Papp, & Stepro, 2006).

Learning as a new deal: New learning needs new teaching methodologies in higher education

Given the scenario drawn above, Millennials and technology have undoubtedly impacted on higher education. Nevertheless, beyond the many challenges described, many opportunities currently open to scholars and practitioners in the field.

First, these challenges give them the chance to reconsider learning as a process basically oriented to self-development and addressed to help individuals enhancing key competencies useful to cope with the several psychosocial transitions that the current labour market is demanding. Second, teachers and trainers are also given the chance to grow awareness about their role within the process of learning and to authentically perceive themselves as facilitators more than as mere transmitters of knowledge.

Yet, such reflections find a fertile ground about all the studies on self-regulated learning that conceive learning as a volitional and self-directed process and about the evidences confirming that given their features and the peculiar cultural and social context where they have grown up, Millennials are naturally born self-directed learners (Dabbagh & Kitsantas, 2012).

According to some of the main references in the field (Biggs, 1987; Schunk & Zimmerman, 1989; Simons & De Jong, 1992), self-regulated learning is a process profoundly influenced by the learner's ability to prepare to learn, to manage and evaluate the outputs of learning and to provide self feedback, while keeping high levels of motivation. Therefore, a self-regulated learner can manage learning activities by mobilizing multiple cognitive abilities and processes such as monitoring, reflection, testing, questioning and self evaluation (Stubbé & Theunissen, 2008).

Formal and informal learning for Millennials 173

Accordingly, the self-directive process allows learners "to transform their mental abilities into academic skills" (Zimmerman, 2002, p. 65). By this, learning is an activity that students do for themselves in a *proactive* way rather than as a passive event that happens to them in reaction to teaching (Zimmerman, 2000).

Into a wider perspective, self-regulated learning plays a crucial role not simply with reference to (formal and informal) education, it is a strategic ability with reference to the future process of career management and development (King, 2004; Raemdonck, Thijssen, & Valcke, 2005), being profoundly linked to other highly relevant constructs such as trainability, employability, learning orientation (Van Dam, 2004; Van der Heijde & Van der Heijden, 2006). Indeed, trainability, employability and learning orientation are core abilities to capitalize one's own learning style to adapt, to manage and to transform knowledge, thus creating a competitive advantage for organizations in terms of innovation and for individuals enhancing motivation and job satisfaction (Nauta, van Vianen, van der Heijden, van Kam, & Willemsen 2009; Van Raemdonck, Tillema, de Grip, Valcke, & Segers, 2012).

Therefore, if a learner develops self-directed learning he/she will more than likely be able to show core soft skills such as to set specific goals, to adopt strategies for attaining goals, to use time management skills, to monitor performance and to manage social and physical contexts that could be strategic in the process of future career management (Schunk, 2005).

Actually, self-directed learning is one of the modalities through which informal learning manifests itself, together with incidental/experiential learning and with socialization (Schugurensky, 2000). Differently from the last two modalities that are respectively unintentional and conscious and unintentional and unconscious, self-directed learning is intentional and conscious as it is a learning project undertaken by individuals and/or by groups in different kind of learning settings. This is the reason why self-directed learning should be exploited as a capital in higher education both for short-term as well as for long-term learning and self-development objectives.

However, although it might seem automatic to connect the positive and proactive features of the Millennial generation, with the vast opportunities provided by technology and with the development of effective learning in higher education, this process is heavily linked to the teaching style.

Yet, to really support this cultural revolution, a change in the teaching paradigm should happen: From a teacher-centred model to a learning-centred model (Monaco & Martin, 2007). This shift is necessary if the academic context would be the arena where students if properly stimulated and engaged will develop the skills useful to cope with their future career.

In fact, it is an evidence that the Millennial student enters college with a different expectation than past generations. Because of the socialization process experienced within the family, they are accustomed to feel special and to feel sheltered by their parents, that is why once in the university setting they would need assistance in developing independent thinking and decision-making skills.

174 *Amelia Manuti*

Therefore, teachers who want to capitalize these skills should provide active engagement and stimulate participation from the first day of their experience. They could exploit Millennials' preference for group activities to further develop their critical thinking, thus encouraging also the use of technology and social networks for learning purposes. Finally, they could also strategically use feedback to stimulate self-efficacy and motivation. These didactical choices could contribute to foster Millennials' natural vocation towards self-directed learning thus guiding this orientation towards formal learning objectives as well as towards a more aware development of self-management skills, crucial for their next professional future.

Enhancing informal learning in higher education: The development of self-management skills as part of graduates' attributes

The extreme autonomy that features the affirmation of the new models of "learning-on-demand" poses questions and challenges to higher education. In this vein, beside the shift in the teaching modes, to improve its effectiveness, formal higher education needs to carefully consider the potential inbuilt in informal learning, one of the main sources of learning for many young people, especially within the current scenario.

However, despite the great interest aroused around informal learning in the last decades, most research has focused primarily on three main sources of informal learning. Informal learning might come from the informal and significant network (family, friends, experts) (Collins, Brown, & Newman, 1989), it might be developed in informal environments such as leisure time spaces (e.g. Boekaert & Minnaert, 1999), and it might be produced by the interaction with mass media such as television, video or the Internet (Bransford, Sherwood, & Hasselbring, 1988). In the educational literature there are a few studies which explicitly address the benefits of creating informal learning environments, even if there are of course, even in these contexts, spaces where it can be developed and enhanced, especially during "unmanaged" moments of peer interaction.

Yet, it is evident that young people spend most of their time outside the formal learning environment of the classroom and, as argued above, use different informal channels and networks to shape personal learning environment and to develop and train the soft skills that are useful for self-directed learning.

Indeed, informal learning in all its forms contributes to developing competencies, because it is integrated in everyday activities (Barth, Godeman, Rieckmann, & Sytoltenberg, 2007). Informal learning has also a special importance for developing "self-management skills," which means the individual's perception and appraisal of themselves in terms of values, abilities, interests and goals. These competencies are closely related to the concept of career identity (Arthur, Inkson, & Pringle, 1999; Jones & deFillippi, 1996), which is the perceived congruence between aspects of the individual and their career roles, that in turn is also a crucial variable in university-to-work transition (Lent & Brown, 2013).

Formal and informal learning for Millennials 175

In this vein, self-management skills are an important part of career management skills and thus of graduates' attributes, meant as "the qualities, skills and understandings a university community agrees its students would desirably develop during their time at the institution and, consequently, shape the contribution they are able to make to their profession and as a citizen" (Bowden 2000, cited in Bridgestock, 2009, p. 32). By this, the important role played by learning environments that should be designed in a way that they might enable informal, partly unconscious learning processes and consequently the development of these crucial skills.

It is therefore essential to understand more about the processes that make up self-regulation in informal learning settings. This is true not only because of the vast influence that these settings may have on classroom learning, but also because research outcomes may provide in-depth understanding for the implementation of new learning environments in the context of life-long learning that could better consider the positive exchange between formal and informal learning spheres. Nowadays, teachers, parents and educators are convinced that to be effective, teaching methods should support the intrinsic desire to learn and should take account the characteristics of young people's experiences outside formal learning contexts. Marsick, Watkins, Callahan, and Volpe (2006) state that important arrangements for facilitating informal learning are first and foremost providing time and places for learning, examining the environment with regard to learning opportunities, directing the attention to learning processes, strengthening the capacity for reflection and creating an atmosphere of cooperation and confidence.

That is why, research should address this issue by investigating whether students use different processing and regulating modes when working in formal and informal learning contexts and how do they combine information coming from both into pieces of knowledge and competence.

This interest is particularly important if we consider that as some authors argue (Barth et al., 2007) the development of key soft skills, that is the whole of cognitive, affective and behavioural resources useful to cope with demands coming from multiple contexts, comes from the combination of formal and informal learning settings within higher education.

Conclusions

The main aim of the chapter was to discuss about the several challenges and opportunities given by the radical changes experienced in higher education, the advent of a new generation of students and the rapid advancement of technology in support of teaching and learning processes, in light with a demanding labour market pressed by global competition. In this frame, organizations bet on their human capital that becomes a strategic asset to win on the rivals and to keep in the market. Human capital however is not simply defined in terms of formal education and training: The war for talents is played into a more complex ground, where soft skills, motivation, learning abilities are the real x factor that

176　*Amelia Manuti*

could make the difference. And these features are mostly acquired and developed through informal learning.

Moving from these assumptions, the analysis of the main literature in the field has contributed to highlight the role played by higher education in preparing future workers in coping with these demands and in training to develop and acknowledge the attributes that could make them appealing to the market.

Yet, the new generation of students, the so-called Millennials, that is currently involved in higher education seem to be naturally oriented to learn differently and thus they also seem more inclined to capitalize learning that comes from informal contexts. In view of the above, our recommendation is to carefully consider the role played by higher education in the process of self-development of this generation. Teachers and trainers should enhance the interplay between formal and informal learning in college and university; they should encourage engagement, participation and self-directed learning so to support students in the process of gradual acknowledgement of the heritage of their knowledge, skills and abilities. This would make them more aware about their resources, thus strengthening their employability perception in the difficult process of university-to-work transition.

References

Arthur, M., Inkson, K., & Pringle, J. (1999). *The New Careers: Individual Action and Economic Change*. London: Sage.

Ashton, J., & Newman, L. (2006). An unfinished symphony: 21st century teacher education using knowledge creating heutagogies. *British Journal of Educational Technology*, *37*(6), 825–840.

Barth, M., Godeman, J., Rieckmann, M., & Sytoltenberg, U. (2007). Developing key competencies for sustainable development in higher education. *International Journal of Sustainability in Higher Education*, *8*(4), 416–430.

Biggs, J. B. (1987). *Student Approaches to Learning and Studying. Australian Council for Educational Research*. Hawthorn: Victoria.

Boekaert, M., & Minnaert, A. (1999). Self-regulation with respect to informal learning. *International Journal of Educational Research*, *31*(6), 533–544.

Bransford, J., Sherwood, R., & Hasselbring, T. (1988). The video revolution and its effects on development: Some initial thoughts. In G. Forman, & P. Pufall (Eds.), *Constructivism in the Computer Age*. Hillsdale, New Jersey: Lawrence Erlbaum.

Bridgestock, R. (2009). The graduate attributes we've overlooked: Enhancing graduate employability through career management skills. *Higher Education Research & Development*, *28*(1), 31–44.

Cao, Q., Griffin, T., & Bai, X. (2009). The importance of synchronous interaction for student satisfaction with course web sites. *Journal of Information Systems Education*, *20*(3) 331–338.

Collins, A., Brown, J. S., & Newman, S. E. (1989). Cognitive apprenticeship: Teaching the crafts of reading, writing and mathematics. In L. Resnick (Ed.), *Knowing, Learning and Instruction. Essays on Honor of Robert Glaser* (pp. 453–491). New Jersey: Erlbaum.

Dabbagh, N., & Kitsantas, A. (2012). Personal learning environments, social media, and self-regulated learning: A nautical formula for connectic formal and informal learning. *Internet and Higher Education*, *15*, 3–8.

DeBard, R. (2004). Millennials coming to college. *New Directions for Student Services, 106*, 33–45.

Ebner, M., Lienhardt, C., Rohs, M., & Meyer, I. (2010). Microblogs in higher education—A chance to facilitate informal and process-oriented learning? *Computers & Education, 55*, 92–100.

Gikas, J., & Grant, M. (2013). Mobile computing devices in higher education: Student perspectives on learning with cellphones, smartphones & social media. *The Internet and Higher Education, 19*, 18–26.

Greenhow, C., Robelia, B., & Hughes, J. (2009). Learning, teaching, and scholarship in a digital age web 2.0 and classroom research: What path should we take now? *Educational Researcher, 38*(4), 246–259.

Hwang, G., & Tsai, C. (2011). Research trends in mobile and ubiquitous learning: A review of publications in selected journals from 2001 to 2010. *British Journal of Educational Technology, 42*(4), 65–70.

Jonas-Dwyer, D., & Pospisil, R. (2004). The millennial effect: Implications for academic development. In Transforming Knowledge into Wisdom: Holistic Approaches to Teaching and Learning, HERDSA 2004 Conference Proceedings (pp. 4–22).

Jones, C., & deFillippi, R. (1996). Back to the future in film: Combining industry and self-knowledge to meet the career challenges of the 21st century. *Academy of Management, 1*(10), 89–103.

King, Z. (2004). Career self-management: Its nature, causes and consequences. *Journal of Vocational Behavior, 65*, 112–133.

Lee, M., McLoughlin, C., & Chan, A. (2008). Talk the talk: Learner-generated podcasts as catalysts for knowledge creation. *British Journal of Educational Technology, 39*(3), 501–521.

Lent, R., & Brown, S. (2013). Social cognitive model of career self-management: Toward a unifying view of adaptive career behavior across the life span. *Journal of Counseling Psychology, 60*(4), 557–568.

Lonn, S., & Teasley, S. (2009). Saving time or innovating practice: Investigating perceptions and uses of learning management systems. *Computers & Education, 3*(3), 686–694.

Marsick, V. J., Watkins, K. E., Callahan, M. W., & Volpe, M. (2006). Reviewing theory and research on informal and incidental learning. *Paper presented at the meeting of the Academy of Human Resource Development*, Columbus, OH.

Matulich, E., Papp, R., & Haytko, D. L. (2008). Continuous improvement through teaching innovations: A requirement for today's learners. *Marketing Education Review, 18*(1), 1–7.

McHaney, R. (2011). *The New Digital Shoreline: How Web 2.0 and Millennials are Revolutionizing Higher Education*. Sterling, VA: Stylus.

McLoughlin, C., & Lee, M. (2010). Personalised and self-regulated learning in the web 2.0 era: International exemplars of innovative pedagogy using social software. *Australasian Journal of Educational Technology, 26*(1), 28–43.

Monaco, M., & Martin, M. (2007). The millennial student: A new generation of learners. *Athletic Training Education Journal, 2*(2), 42–46.

Nauta, A., van Vianen, A., van der Heijden, B., van Kam, K., & Willemsen, M. (2009). Understanding the factors that promote employability orientation: The impact of employability culture, career satisfaction, and role breadth self-efficacy. *Journal of Occupational and Organizational Psychology, 82*(2), 233–251.

Oblinger, D. (2003). Boomers, Gen-Xers & Millennials. Understanding the new students. *Educause Review, 38*(4), 37–47.

178 Amelia Manuti

Papp, R., & Matulich, E. (2011). Negotiating the deal: Using technology to reach the millennials. *Journal of Behavioral Studies in Business, 4*, 1–12.

Prensky, M. (2001). Digital natives, digital immigrants, part II. Do they really think differently? *On the Horizon*, 9(6). Retrieved from http://www.marcprensky.com/writing/Prensky%20-%20Digital%20Natives,%20Digital%20Immigrants%20-%20Part2.pdf

Raemdonck, I., Thijssen, J., & Valcke, M. (2005). Self-directed learning and career processes. *Lifelong Learning in Europe, 10*(2), 76–81.

Schugurensky, D. (2000). The forms of informal learning: Towards a conceptualization of the field. *WALL Working Paper, 19*, 1–8.

Schunk, D. (2005). Self-regulated learning: The educational legacy of Paul R. Pintrich. *Journal of Educational Psychologist, 40*(2), 85–94.

Schunk, D., & Zimmerman, B. (1989). Social origins of self-regulatory competence. *Educational Psychologist, 32*(4), 195–208.

Siemens, G. (2005). Connectivism: A learning theory for the digital age. *International Journal of Instructional Technology and Distance Learning, 2*(1). Retrieved from http://www.itdl.org/Journal/Jan_05/article01.htm

Siemens, G. (2007). Connectivism: Creating a learning ecology in distributed environments. In T. Hugo (Ed.), *Didactics in Microlearning. Concepts, Discourses, Examples* (pp. 53–68). Munster: Waxman.

Simons, P., & De Jong, F. (1992). Self-regulation and computer-aided instruction. *Applied Psychology, 41*(4), 333–346.

Skipton, C. E., Matulich, E., Papp, R., & Stepro, J. (2006). Moving from 'Dumb' to 'Smart' classrooms. *Journal of College Teaching and Learning, 3*(6), 19–28.

Stubbé, H., & Theunissen, N. (2008). Self-directed adult learning in a ubiquitous learning environment: A meta-review. *Proceedings of Special Track on Technology Support for Self-Organised Learners*, 5–28. Retrieved April 10, 2019, from http://citeseerx.ist.psu.edu/viewdoc/summary?doi=10.1.1.140.9092

Twenge, J. (2006). *Generation Me: Why Today's Young Americans are More Confident, Assertive, Entitled and More Miserable than Ever Before.* New York: Free Press.

Van Dam, K. (2004). Antecedents and consequences of employability orientation. *The European Journal of Work and Organizational Psychology, 13*(1), 29–51.

Van der Heijde, C. M., & Van der Heijden, B. I. J. M. (2006). A competence-based and multidimensional operationalization and measurement of employability. *Human Resource Management, 45*, 449–476.

Van Raemdonck, I., Tillema, H., de Grip, A., Valcke, M., & Segers, M. (2012). Does self-directedness in learning and careers predict the employability of low-qualified employees. *Vocations and Learning, 5*(2), 137–151.

Zimmerman, B. (2000). Attaining self-regulation: A social cognitive perspective. In M. Boekaerts, P. Pintrich, & M. Zeidner (Eds.), *Handbook of Self-regulation* (13–39). Amsterdam: Elsevier.

Zimmerman, B. (2002). Becoming a self-regulated learner: An overview. *Theory into Practice, 41*(2), 64–70.

12 Informal learning assessment

Javier Calvo de Mora

Introduction

The proposed approach for building a model of assessment for learning will be based on the idea of critical thinking in social relationships among different school actors. The justification of studying each school actor is to understand the process of constructing knowledge that each student follows with the aim of counselling him/her concerning ways to improve the learning process. In this process, teachers undertake a research process focused on the ability of their students with the aim of counselling them (through teaching) to improve their learning processes by orienting them more towards critical thinking. Five actions for reflection are discussed:

1 Assessment of school work: Justification of social and cultural learning
2 Critical thinking: The formation of critical thinking in primary and secondary students
3 Critical thinking assessment: Economic and cultural references
4 Assessment of priority learning in social and cultural areas of schools
5 Conclusion: School climates of collaboration

Assessment of school work

The focus of this section is school work: Learning experiences that each student and teacher develop through an academic year. The diversity of learning experiences (problem solving, peer collaboration, decision making, writing documents, designing projects, reading and critical reasoning, experiencing and observing natural phenomena and works of art, musical production) is the focus of interest. Teachers' work is focused on interpreting these activities. It is clinical practice in the sense that teachers have to explore their learners' abilities in order to obtain more information about the qualities and strengths of each particular student. Such a commonplace is not sometimes sufficiently considered in schools: The basic assumption of school education is to improve the learning processes of each student including improvements in cognitive, emotional, social, ethical, health and physical areas.

180 *Javier Calvo de Mora*

What does it mean to improve learning? The answer depends on cultural beliefs (Kaur & Noman, 2015) about schooling practice, both in classrooms and other areas of organization. A perspective that focuses on transmitting information and reproducing knowledge focuses the improvement of learning on the adaptation of guidelines promoted by teachers with their students. By contrast, from a cultural perspective, learning improvement is focused on the individuality of each student, the diversification of their experiences and ability of each student to explain their development. That is, students can produce their own accounts expressing personal views with regards to basic topics included in different curricular subjects.

In the case of Spanish culture on school learning, a collective view prevails, as in other southern European countries such as France, Portugal or Italy. In these cultural areas any personal construction of meaning related to knowledge and learning is often marginalized because it deviates from norms and rules that are institutionally established. A problem arises in these contexts when it comes to recognizing and validating informal learning. Other cultures that are "more liberal" (in a cultural sense) face fewer problems in the recognition of informal learning. For example, the Anglo–Saxon literature on school education is more likely to acknowledge a liberal sense of learning because it acknowledges the idea of freedom and individual experience of students in the learning processes.

Irrespective of the adoption of a collectivist or individualist point of view on informal learning, there can be a practical approach to school knowledge. Lifelong learning can be viewed as primarily economic in nature (the process of permanent adaptation to the requirements of the labour market) or it can focus on liberation and personal autonomy in the context of the globalization of information and knowledge. In this book we have adopted the second approach, but without renouncing the economic discourse related to school learning. In particular we see that individual freedom can be strengthened through the improvement of critical thinking. In other words, improvement means adopting a critical stance towards the context of each subject's life, the processes and social relationships in which different groups and individuals exchange knowledge and information, the contents with which each subject interacts to differentiate between falsehoods and half-truths, and the critical view of the purposes of the different information and experiences carried out by each individual. We view this as transformative learning that allows students to develop as active citizens responsible for developing widespread social belonging.

Our view regarding the improvement of learning, therefore, means developing better conceptual tools that help students adopt critical positions in a range of areas. These include identifying a personal learning path or trajectory, recognizing critical incidents that occur in the daily life and recognizing the processes of cultural socialization in the context of the globalization of information and knowledge. With this socio-constructivist approach, the idea of improvement is focused on the construction of truthful meanings of what constitutes learning in the context of the information and knowledge in the lives of each individual (Weick & Roberts, 1993).

Informal learning assessment 181

Focussing on the meaning of what is learnt informally is the main goal of assessing different ways of acquiring information and knowledge in each individual's social and cultural environment. From this focus on the lifeworld of each subject, there are a variety of conceptual tools that make it possible to investigate what informal learning can be acquired by each individual. These include observing and inquiring students' different daily activities and experiences, understanding the cultural context and the social relationships in which each student is engaged and being aware of instruments that are available for cataloguing social relations networks (e.g. scales and measurements frequently used in social psychology).

The problem in selecting relevant informal learning is an important focus of attention in order to generate more or less comparable processes of school assessment among different student populations. Based on the literature, this chapter proposes several types of informal knowledge that can be considered (Jeong, Han, Lee, Sunalai, & Yoon, 2018):

1 Knowledge of the school organization where each student learns established rules and norms of behaviour. This learning enables access to the social and psychological keys of each organization, the most representative symbols in schools and the most significant exchanges. This can include knowledge of the rewards for obedient and submissive behaviour as well as an understanding of the dangers that may result from dissent and independent thinking in the case of authoritarian organizations. This tacit knowledge is influenced by values, attitudes, behaviours and social competences that can self-regulate the behaviour of each individual in the schooling process.

2 Student reflections on their emotional and social school experiences focussing on processes such as school bullying, marginalization, belonging to power groups or any issues characterizing the micropolitics of schools.

3 Each school actor develops personal goals and expectations about his/her role and achievements. This is largely a self-directed process based on informal learning and the influences from families, the community, peers and other social groups. At the same time individuals select informal learning strategies that will help them achieve their goals and dreams. Very often this learning is acquired through observations of what the school values and the messages that are conveyed about these to school actors.

4 The critical incidents that characterize each school will provide opportunities for informal learning. Different incidents will have more or less salience for different individuals. For example, if individuals are focussed on social relationships among groups within the school then any disruption to these will be regarded as critical. Or if the focus is on improving communications among groups then any problems with such communication will be regarded as critical. Whatever the priority for individuals, informal learning opportunities will be available when these priorities are under threat.

5 Learning can be acquired through school actors' familiarity with the social and cultural environments of which they are a part. Familiar and cultural influences

182 *Javier Calvo de Mora*

have been extensively studied in Asian contexts (Daug & Öznacar, 2015) to explain academic successes and failures of students in these geopolitical environments. Students and teachers learn the language that denotes the cognitive universe and culture in which they are immersed and that they come to view as their own. This involves individual socialization of the beliefs and expectations regarding schooling. In Asian contexts this often can include values such as perseverance, school discipline that supports dominant values, identification with school cultures, a recognition of the importance of teaching and teachers and the institutional position of each student. In other contexts there may be different value sets that equally influence school actors, sometimes positively and sometimes negatively.

6 The virtual world providing access to unlimited information is also a significant source of informal learning. This may result in learning new knowledge, but it may also be derived from the search for new and meaningful social relationships by students and adults. Unrestricted access to this kind of learning can be seen as an aspect of the democratization of knowledge but the results may not always be positive (e.g. "fake news" and online predators) and access is by no means equitable (this is as true within countries as across countries since access is very often dependent on resources that are not equally distributed). Formal learning about these issues can be important in moderating the impact of negative informal learning and highlight the necessary interaction between formal and informal learning.

Critical thinking: The formation of critical thinking in primary and secondary students

The globalization of information (whether it is substantiated scientifically or consists only of personal opinions) is present in the daily life of citizenships. Its form is largely electronic and can be found in university courses, documentaries, videogames, fake news and social media networks. The common element that characterizes the globalization of information is the dependence/passivity it creates for individuals. Power groups exercise hegemony over individuals by manipulating information and distorting truth as a means of strengthening power and social influence in society.

This relationship between power and knowledge has been extensively studied by French political philosophers such as Michael Foucault and Pierre Bourdieu. These two authors have generated a considerable literature related to practices of manipulation by educational institutions. Both authors agree that authoritarian societies legitimate their existence through processes of control over knowledge and the thought processes of individuals. The aim is the creation of a social and individual thinking based on obedience and acceptance of regime endorsed cultural, social and economic values.

There are other views concerning the relationship between knowledge and power. Neo-institutionalism, for example, while accepting that institutions can exercise significant influences in society, also highlights the agency of individuals

Informal learning assessment 183

who can resist institutional influences through evaluation of their effect. An intermediate space between authoritarian and liberal views can be seen in many Asian societies. In this geopolitical context, that includes countries such as Korea, Japan, China and Singapore, knowledge is linked to individuals and hierarchy with merit acting as process providing access to status. Thus, individual effort is seen to be important with less dependency on the alienating effect of institutions as argued by Foucault and Bourdieu.

In what cultural framework does critical thinking fit?

The answer to this question is focused on active learning methodologies that can be employed in different educational macro-cultures. The most commonly used reference to study the macro-cultural context of learning methodologies has been proposed by Geert Hofstede with a focus on constructs such as distance from power, individualism versus collectivism, masculinity versus femininity, evasion from uncertainty and long-term guidance. In particular, educational cultures that facilitate active methodologies support areas of action appropriate for each school based on inclusive and critical collective actions proposing improvements. There is an understanding in this process of the implicit risks involved in any changes to routines and habits of each school day. There is also an understanding of the need to access different sources of information, personal experiences, and analysis of social and cultural contexts close to each student. This involves recognizing the importance of informal knowledge that can be drawn on to support the development of active learning which in turn facilitates the development of learner autonomy.

Conceptual approach to critical thinking in schooling processes

A long-term goal in schooling systems is the development of critical thinking, which is focused on two organizational references: Proficiency of curriculum policy and the social influences on the behaviour of school populations.

Any organization can be categorized by two criteria: Political and cultural influences. Political influences are reflected in the hegemony of organizational rules, dictated externally or internally, in each school. For instance, educational laws can control what happens in a school on a day-to-day basis as can decisions taken by school authorities. Cultural influences are reflected in attitudes towards different organizational rules: Norms of behaviour or school discipline, norms of organizational thinking (norms focused on the cultural identity of each organization), norms of social relationships among different collectives in each organization and norms of acceptance and rejection of organizational codes and symbols related to established teaching processes, learning assessment, daily routines of behaviour in schools, procedures for school promotion of students or incentives for school improvement. All of these can contribute to the stability of a school.

One important cultural influence on schools has focused on economic views of schooling. Critical thinking has tended to create arguments against this view. It has involved the rejection of an employability narrative whereby in exchange

184 *Javier Calvo de Mora*

for accreditation and certification, schools will provide access to labour market employment. This exchange between accreditation and employment has no real correspondence: More accreditation does necessarily lead to better employment. Formal accreditation and certification requires in addition the acquisition of informal instrumental skills requested by the market labour: These include creativity, communicative capacity, innovative thinking, managing social groups, and the social capital of each student, among other personal qualities. All of these are acquired outside the institutional environment of formal education. These informal learning qualities are particularly important for success in the knowledge economy that can be characterized by the development of information technology. Given their importance in this economic context, instruments have been developed to assess the acquisition of these informal learning skills, for instance, the *California Critical Thinking Skill Test* (Knox, 2013).

Criticism of the cultural influences on schools is an additional indication of critical thinking concerning schooling processes. An issue to address from this critical view is potential inequalities among students and teachers. These may include inequality of access to sources of school information and knowledge, linguistic deficits both in the mother tongue and additional lingua franca, access to social capital and socially supportive relationships, professional development opportunities, cultural tastes, sexual orientation and lifestyles. Schools are social institutions reflecting the values of the mainstream society so that inequalities in society need to be downplayed or eliminated in schools.

Critical thinking focused on practices of cultural power in organizations

Schools are not neutral institutions. Informal learning in schools can therefore be focused on practices of organizational and institutional power. Criticisms of power related to domination or exclusion, physical and symbolic violence or group actions designed to conserve political hegemony can be made. This area of critical thinking seeks to prevent the marginalization of individuals, their freedom and autonomy. In other words, critical thinking about institutional power seeks to preserve the idea of the non-neutrality of school actions. It assumes that processes of classifying members do not validate some behaviours over others or that some specific areas of knowledge are considered legitimate and others marginal or simply ignored. This runs contrary to the usual view that learning is controlled by hegemonic groups of individuals who generate strategies of legitimation such as incentives and rewards for those who adopt behaviours related to the dominant group.

Critical thinking assessment

Political and cultural influences are complementary. Political influences seek to standardize schooling through the adoption of common rules and organizational norms across different schools. This leads to the idea of a universal

Informal learning assessment 185

model of schooling in each singular and local school reality. There are instruments to assess the compliance of schools to this model including the *California Critical Thinking Skill* questionnaire or others such as *Cornell Critical Thinking Instrument*. With these instruments, adaptations and behavioural diversions can be documented with regards to the achievement of key skills related to the needs of the knowledge economy. Cultural influences on critical thinking focus on evaluating individual actions in the cultural space of schools and the meanings held by individuals and groups regarding a sense of belonging to the school. This qualitative approach is more concerned with the assumptions and values of the different constituents in each school.

From the economic and cultural view, the formative assessment of each student (to improve her/his critical thinking) is in Figure 12.1 that draws on *Assessment for Learning. Formative Assessment* (OECD, 2008) proposed by the Organization for Economic Co-operation and Development (OECD/CERI).

Figure 12.1 shows different organizational areas where decisions are made when informal learning is considered. The main focus of attention is the establishment of a culture of assessing informal learning in each school organization. When considering new learning methods in schools, organizational and institutional changes include all organizational actions. Figure 12.1 shows some of them, for instance, decisions for change with regards to diversity of methodologies of assessing learning in each school, new micro-political processes in schools focusing on negotiation and creation of the new organizational order as well as organizational structures, participation of students in processes of school

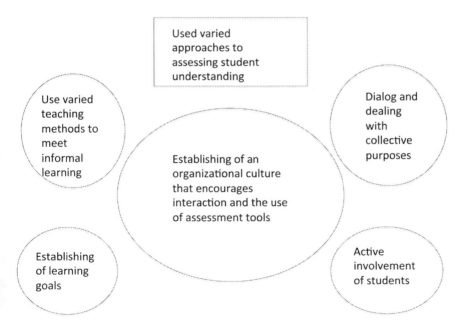

Figure 12.1 Organizational culture and assessment tools.

186 *Javier Calvo de Mora*

discussion, for instance, through actions for strengthening active responsibility in the development of the learning process, the definition of the learning goals that imply a reinforcement of the feeling of belonging of the entire school population and the practice of several learning methods that allow the interaction between diverse formal, non-formal and informal learning. Taken together, these processes can build a culture of learning.

This idea of building a culture of assessment to acknowledge the diversity of learning in schools is an academic proposal. In practice, for it to become a reality it must be seen as a priority in schools. Schools need to regard cultural issues as being important and capable of being addressed. This may mean discarding some things that do not acknowledge the diversity and plurality of schools and embracing those things that all students can celebrate. Schools must become inclusive organizations acknowledge what brings students together and neglecting those things that do not.

Assessment of priority learning in social and cultural areas of schools

Each school focuses its organizational action on relevant or significant elements for its students, where these are not constrained. For instance, there can be an issue in determining the importance of sport competition compared to the performance of music activities or vice versa. In whatever activity, the importance of informal learning can be recognized. When music is priority learning, emphasis can be placed on musical compositions, musical styles, instruments or other actions that are of interest to most students. Yet the problem can be that decisions need to be confined to the established institutional framework that can limit practical options. For example, there can be space and temporal limitations for classroom work (in the framework of a school day delimited by schedules of different subjects). This is the problem of structural segmentation, which contradicts the structural flexibility that is needed to develop processes in which several types of learning are included.

In this space, informal learning generally occupies a marginal or secondary place because the *raison d'être* of critical thinking (reflection based on facts and references of established codes and symbols) has a cross-sectional and interdisciplinary character. That is, it is not included in a specific curricular space (the classroom) nor in a specific time (a math class, for instance), but it includes wider spaces and times; for instance, several subjects or total organizational shifts of schools from one level to the next, such as different organizational levels. Thus, choosing between music or sport can be constrained by organizational barriers and informal learning can be limited.

This image of the different organizational levels that constitute a school site is represented in Figure 12.2.

This pyramid contains four organizational layers. The most visible and formal layer is the legal and regulatory framework of schools, that is, the most institutional strand of schooling processes. Another visible and easily observable aspect is the established social relationships among different school actors. Both formal and

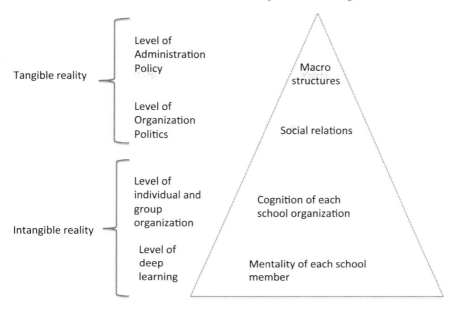

Figure 12.2 Pyramid of school levels of knowledge.

informal learning can be observed in this layer. They are observed mainly in the processes of exchanging and selecting information and knowledge that are relevant for continuing school life. For instance, agreements with regards to rules of school discipline and norms of inclusive organizational climates. The organizational layers focused on the cognition and mentality of the school population go along with the facility for informal learning: The learning acquired by experiences and reflections made by each school member. From this socio-cognitive view of schools, informal learning is used to establish a collaborative climate among several school groups.

Conclusion: Collaborative school climate

The proposal of this chapter is very simple: The improvement of student learning depends on looking beyond the social reality of the classroom to include other social spaces both within and outside the school where learning takes place. This is an acknowledgement that learning takes place on multiple sites and can be assessed along with the assessment of formal classroom learning.

At the same time there is a recognition that informal learning and its assessment will be more robust in a cooperative educational environment where everyone's voice is heard and valued. This kind of collaboration creates trust that helps to develop positive social relationships enabling decisions to be made that can support multiple forms of student learning. Thus, informal learning and collaboration are mutually supportive processes that together create a collaborative learning culture for the benefit of all students and their families.

188 *Javier Calvo de Mora*

References

Daug, G., & Öznacar, B. (2015). An evaluation of primary school according to the view of school administrators, teachers and parents. *Educational Sciences: Theory & Practice*, *15*(1), 1–16.

Jeong, S., Han, S. J., Lee, J., Sunalai, S., & Yoon, S. W. (2018). Integrative literature review on informal learning: Antecedents, conceptualizations, and future directions. *Human Resource Development Review*, *17*(2), 128–152.

Kaur, A., & Noman, M. (2015). Exploring classroom practices in collectivist cultures through the lens of Hofstede's model. *The Qualitative Report*, *20*(11), 1794–1811.

Knox, D. (2013). *The California Critical Thinking Skills Test*. Retrieved April 9, 2019, from https://www.clemson.edu/academics/programs/thinks2/documents/scholars/summer_2013/knox_cctst.pdf

OECD. (2008). *Assessment for learning—Formative assessment*. Retrieved April 9, 2019, from https://www.oecd.org/site/educeri21st/40600533.pdf

Oh, S. Y. (2016). The effect of workplace learning on organizational socialization in the youth workplace. *Asia Pacific Education Review*, *17*, 567–580.

Thys, S., & Van Haoute, M. (2016). Ethnic composition of the primary school and educational choice: Does the culture of teacher expectation matter? *Teaching and Teacher Education*, *59*, 383–391.

Van Noy, M., James, H., & Bedly, C. (2016). *Reconceptualizing learning: A review of the literature on informal learning*. New Jersey, NJ: Rutgers Education and Employment Research Centre.

Weick, K. E., & Roberts, K. H. (1993). Collective mind in organizations: Heedful interrelating on flight decks. *Administrative Science Quarterly*, *38*(3), 357–381.

13 Is an "avant-garde" assessment? The certification of competencies in the Italian higher education system

Serafina Pastore

A note to begin

Over the last 20 years, within the adult education field, the concept of learning has been consistently reviewed for its epistemological, social and policy implications (Bron & Schemmann, 2003; Feutrie, 2008; Jarvis, 2011).

Lifelong learning has been considered as a strategic lever for economic growth and social stability (Coffield, 2000; Evans, 2000). In this way, lifelong learning has been legitimated because it allows individuals to

- overcome the idea that education and learning are related only to formal contexts (e.g. school and higher education);
- respond to the social need of acquiring knowledge and competencies that are not necessarily related to the workplace but can be functional to the daily life;
- deal with economic, social and technological transformations.

In relation to European policies, the principles of dignity, autonomy, active citizenship, personal self-attainment, social inclusion and employability have influenced the concept of learning (Rogers, 2014). From this perspective, informal learning—defined as a kind of learning that is not didactic, embedded in meaningful activities, building on the learners' initiatives, interests or opportunities—has become part of the debate. This is due to the need to develop approaches, models, strategies and instruments aimed at assessment of this kind of learning.

The present chapter focuses on the assessment of informal learning, and more specifically on the certification of competencies within the Italian higher education system. To this end, in the first section, contexts and trends around informal learning, and the recognition, validation and certification of competencies are introduced. While initial attempts at validation and certification of informal learning have experimented with new approaches, models and practices of assessment, more recently several pitfalls (e.g. lack of evidence for validity) seem to undermine the power of this "avant-garde" assessment. Moving from the several meanings, and practical implications, of recognition of informal learning, the

190 *Serafina Pastore*

purpose of this section is to discuss validity in the assessment of informal learning. In the next section, the chapter tries to connect the international debate over higher education governance with models and practices of certification of competencies realized in the Italian context. The final section considers limitations and identifies areas requiring further research.

Recognition, validation and certification: One rationale, many practices

The processes of recognition, validation and certification of informal learning require us to identify and make visible the knowledge, competencies and experience acquired by a learner in different contexts. Within the lifelong and life-wide learning perspective, it is important to identify these processes and to value the learning that takes place anywhere and anytime in the life of the individual.

In European documents, recognition and validation of informal learning are considered, although from a more economic perspective, as a key aspect for the effective development of lifelong learning (Collardin & Bjørnåvold, 2005). The recognition and validation of informal learning can help individual learners to better understand the knowledge society and to better pursue their personal learning needs (CEDEFOP, 2000). All the key documents in the European area mention the equivalence of learning acquired by a learner as a fundamental principle of lifelong learning.

"Recognition", from a UNESCO perspective, is a practice that "renders visible and gives value to the hidden and unrecognized competencies that individuals have obtained in various contexts through various means in different phases of their life. Valuing and recognizing these learning outcomes may significantly improve individual's self-esteem and well-being, motivate them to further learning and strengthen their labour-market opportunities. [*Recognition, validation and accreditation practices*] may help to integrate broader sections of the population into an open and flexible education and training system and to build inclusive societies" (Rogers, 2014; p. 3).

Giving official status to competencies, or learning outcomes, is only one of the possible meanings of "recognition." There are other aspects to be considered such as acknowledgement of the value that skills and competencies have in terms of employability or academy transferability; there is the acceptance of this assessment process by different stakeholders (education, training, labour market); there are, lastly, the social value and the embedded nature of learning within a specific context (Michelson, 2006; Singh, 2015).

What exactly do we mean by "validation" and "certification"? Validation, as a form of recognition of personal and professional competencies, in line with CEDEFOP (2009), consists of external attestation of learning outcomes achieved by a learner in formal, non-formal and informal contexts. These learning outcomes are judged against defined criteria and standards: In this way, they can be used for certification and recognition of credits gaining admission and advance standing or credits in higher education (Andersson & Guo, 2009; Jarvis, 2011).

Certification is a process to formally validate knowledge, know-how and/or competencies acquired by an individual, following a standard assessment procedure (Jackson, 2011). In this process the European Qualification Framework (EQF) has an important role. This is a common framework through which to view description, comparison and contrast of qualifications, certificates and diplomas in different countries in order to facilitate work mobility.

The attention given to validation, as a means for equity and inclusion in education, as a social and professional field (Jackson, 2011), has progressively influenced not only educational research but also policy and decision-making. Different European countries, agreeing with the importance of validation and certification of informal learning, have expressed the need to make learning "beyond the classroom" visible and to value it in a more responsive and effective way. With the *European Guidelines for Validating Non Formal and Informal Learning*, the CEDEFOP (2009) provided a scheme, a model, based on three main phases:

1 *Identification:* This phase identifies competencies considering previous learning experiences and lists which competencies can be submitted for validation. This phase includes meetings to re-construct, with reference to educational and professional standards, the learner's experience.
2 *Valuation:* Competencies identified in this phase are assessed in terms of mastery and levels of conformity to the standards.
3 *Validation:* This is the end phase of the process with a decision-making result. Generally, there is a commission with experts and independent stakeholders.

Different approaches have been developed over the years (e.g. first in France and United Kingdom and then in Norway, Sweden, Denmark) with a focus on different contexts (e.g. workplace, vocational education and training, higher education) for different targets (e.g. migrants, women, students) and different aims. In 2012, the European Council issued the *Recommendations for the Validation of Non-Formal and Informal Learning*, asking all member nations to define within 2018 "necessary arrangements for validation." However, given the upsurge of methodologies and strategies designed to recognize, validate and certificate competencies, a concern has been expressed (CEDEFOP, 2009) that "solutions are looking for problems" highlighting an overproduction of methods and devices in comparison to the real needs of certification.

Different studies (Andersson, Fejes, & Sandberg, 2013; Andersson & Harris, 2006; Bjørnåvold, 2000; Castle & Attwood, 2001; Fenwick & Parsons, 2000) confirm how complex and problematic recognition of informal learning appears to be. More than this, these studies demonstrate how informal learning, even within the consistent legislative framework, has not had sufficient recognition. Pitman (2009) shows the difficulties for implementation of validation especially when this process is related to social inclusion. Some studies highlight how the power of validation in terms of liberty, social justice and equity may

192 *Serafina Pastore*

be underestimated. The comparative analysis realized by the EU Commission in 2010 confirms how weak, across the EU countries, the processes of recognition and validation may be. A latent paradox becomes evident here: Some people may be made despondent by the process of validation and, as a negative consequence, social exclusion may grow. Furthermore, what is becoming clear is the difficulty of integrating validation and certification practices into formal education systems (Council of the European Commission, 2012). In their comparative study Slowey and Schuetze (2012) address what kind of factors may constrain or facilitate access to validation practices:

- The need to differentiate between the grade awarded, in horizontal (meaning the progress through the system) and vertical (meaning consistent grades when changing from one institution to another) terms, within an education system.
- The level of autonomy and flexibility that education institutions have over assessment arrangements.
- The accessibility to lifelong learning programmes.
- The organization of learning paths.
- The financial supports.
- The identification of concrete chances of continuous learning.

Alternatively, Werquin (2010, 2014) underlines the main critical issues in validation:

- The limited opportunities for individuals to access validation practices.
- The lack of coherence between different validation approaches.
- The lack of a unique definition of validation in terms of policy.

Although the European Union has defined a common framework, there are many differences, sometimes substantial, among the European countries. In order to take account of the complex validation landscape, in 2014, the CEDEFOP with the *European Inventory on Validation of Non-Formal and Informal Learning* gave a detailed snapshot of the state of the art. The *Inventory* underlines how the gap is relevant in the development of validation and certification systems: While great attention has been reserved to the effects of validation, few efforts have been made in theoretical (what validation is and what it can accomplish) and methodological terms (approaches and practices of validation).

The scenario is not coherent and cohesive. If on the one hand, there are consistent signs of progress in the definition of achievable aims, on the other hand, there are some unresolved assessment dilemmas (e.g. who does the validation? Which criteria have to be considered in this assessment process?) Considering the impact that the results of recognition, validation and certification have, especially as expanding practices in the higher education context, these assessment processes have to be regarded more carefully. In order to methodologically frame the complex landscape of validation, the next section considers a thorny problem: The validity criteria.

Assessment dilemmas: To validate or not to validate?

Approaches and models of validation of informal learning have their rationale in the recognition of experience as a fundamental criterion for learning: Validation focuses on knowledge, abilities and competencies acquired by an individual during and through experience. If recognition is the process by which an individual's prior learning experiences are assessed as being equivalent to specific formal learning outcomes (Pitman & Vidovich, 2013), validation consists of a translation to a formal level of learning achievement. In this perspective, there is a relevant amount of research on recognition and validation of informal learning focused on the concepts of transfer and on equivalence of learning (Cooper & Harris, 2013; Harris, 2000; Trowler, 1996).

Over the years the debate on recognition and validation developed and reinforced the idea of credentialed (higher education and vocational education training) and un-credentialed (work and life experience) learning. An unresolved knot, however, remains: Is it appropriate to assess informal learning using the same criteria used for the assessment of formal learning?

Beyond the obvious observation that informal learning has its own qualities, the validation process hides the rationale of mere transposition and arrangement of informal learning to the features and criteria of formal learning. Collardin and Bjørnåvold (2005) pointed out that "there is no indication that the challenge of validate of non-formally and informally acquired competencies has led to the development and introduction of genuinely new testing and assessment methods ... [the] object (of non-formal and informal learning) to be measured is different and more complex making the requirements to reliability and validity very harder to reach" (p. 117).

Methods used in validation started to overlap with traditional methods used for the assessment of learning in formal contexts and lead to an unclear distinction of assessment aims, strategies and practices.

Previous attempts to define the *proprium* (essential characteristic) of the validation process of informal learning have generally borrowed too heavily from approaches to the assessment of formal learning. They have also determined a varied corpus of strategies rooted in theoretical approaches (narrative/biographical/diagnostic) which are different and sometimes conflicting.

Following the CEDEFOP Guidelines (2000, 2009) it is possible to distinguish several methods for the validation of informal learning:

- Debate
- Declarative methods
- Interview
- Observation
- Presentation
- Simulation and performance
- Test

194 *Serafina Pastore*

In spite of the confusing array of methods, techniques and practices, a common element remains: Gather evidence of learning in terms of what a learner knows, says, writes or is able to do in order to make visible non-formal and informal learning and get recognition from formal assessment systems. Interpretation is strictly related to the quality of inferences made about a learner's achievement, and this impacts on the validation results. In this vein, data and logic should be assembled into arguments—pro or contra—for the recognition, validation and certification of specific informal learning: All assessments require validity because without validity assessments have little or no intrinsic meaning (Newton, 2007; Nyström, 2004).

There have been considerable efforts to develop and improve structures, mechanisms and methods for recognition of all forms of learning, and to establish equivalency frameworks. However, there is a latent difficulty in comparing and contrasting different practices implemented in, across and beyond Europe due to the strong gradient of context sensitivity and the scant attention paid to validity: "As the role of assessment procedures is to provide decision-makers with correct and relevant information, it is of great importance to examine issues regarding the quality, utility and fairness in this type of assessment" (Stenlund, 2010, p. 783). Assessment and evaluation practices are not "valid or invalid" but rather the informal learning has more or less evidence to support or refute a specific interpretation (such as certifying or not a learner's competence).

Validity: A missing criterion?

In the educational assessment field the validity concept, over the years, has changed considerably. During the 1980s and 1990s validity has inspired a lively debate between a "traditional" vision and a "modern" perspective due to the increased use of assessment across scientific, social and educational settings (DeLuca, 2011; Kane, 2016). The validity is considered in terms of correspondence between detection, measurement, judgment and the assessment object. An instrument is valid when it reflects the intention of the researcher/evaluator. Traditionally, a test is valid "for anything with which it correlates" (Guilford, 1946, p. 429) or if "it measures what it purports to measure" (Shepard, 1993, p. 410). Recently DeLuca (2011) pointed out how, over the years, these synthetic definitions have become more and more complex to the point that it is possible to distinguish between the following kinds of validity:

- *Content validity:* Tests describe a performance in a specific field. This validity is about the correlation between the measure and what the instrument measures.
- *Criterion validity (predictive):* This validity is related to the accuracy of the test.
- *Construct validity:* This validity is used to make inferences on one psychological trait such as intelligence. Cronbach and Meehl (1955) introduced construct validity as an indirect method of validation to be used when dependent variables in knowledge, abilities and competencies field are not able to indicate the measure extent that the test aims to fulfil.

Avant-garde assessment 195

Table 13.1 Validity aspects

	Validity aspects	
	Test interpretation	Test use
Evidence	Construct validity	Construct validity + Relevance/utility
Consequences	Value implications	Social consequences

Source: Messick (1989, p. 20)

Cronbach, in 1971, affirmed that validity "is not a test evaluation but an interpretation of data gathered through a specific procedure" (p. 44); in this way he realized a substantive change moving from an instrumental perspective to a more social one with a strong emphasis on the interpretation of assessment inferences, evidence sources, threatened constructs and consequences. The unitary validity framework synthesized the different forms of validity (with a new emphasis on construct validity). Messick (1989) described validity in terms of an evaluative judgment integrated with the extent to which evidence and theoretical clarifications support adequacy and appropriateness of actions realized on the base of test results (Table 13.1).

Stressing the role of social consequences related to assessment, this definition has led to a deep reconceptualization of validity as a multifaceted, unified concept. However, the inclusion of these aspects determined some practical problems. In 2006, Kane suggested an argumentative approach for validity. Interpretation, coherence and plausibility are important as well as the social dimensions. Although the literature in this research field has demonstrated a great vivacity, the practice has difficulties to follow theory in a new or emerging field of education such as informal learning. Validity is a complex and crucial issue in the field of validation and certification of informal learning. Gathered data should be functional to support inferences on performances and competencies of an individual. Validity needs quality evidence as a key step in the interpretation of informal learning results, validation and assessment. However, this criterion is hard to guarantee with informal learning due to its intrinsic nature (McGivney, 2006; Nyström, 2004; Sandberg & Andersson, 2011; Stenlund, 2013).

With concern for validity, the validation of informal learning has to be accurate. In order to assure a valid and sound process of validation in the higher education field it is essential to

- define the purpose(s) of the validation process;
- explain in a transparent and clear way what kind of competencies (e.g. definition of learning outcomes) will be assessed;
- clearly explain the assessment criteria and the instruments that will be used;
- communicate and report to claimants, as well as to other stakeholders involved, the assessment results.

196 *Serafina Pastore*

Furthermore, it is important to use stable and predictive instruments: The reliability criterion allows to predetermine the interpretation of gathered evidence. Information is reliable when different measures of the same instrument are constant with different users and different conditions. Reliability for validation in higher education context refers "to the stability of the measurement, that is, the degree to which repeated measurements of the same object are consistent with each other" (Stenlund, 2013; p. 536). How can accuracy be guaranteed in the validation of informal learning? It is important to

- compare different assessments made by different stakeholders (e.g. using methods such as triangulation, reflection, collaboration, de-briefing) and;
- reduce the causes of inaccurate practices (e.g. unrealistic evaluation of individuals' competencies, neglected crucial information, underestimated impact of social environment and cultural background).

The risk of a validation process that loses its meaning and function can be reduced by considering how, and to what extent, validation outputs are credible.

Reconsidering validity (and reliability) leads us to reconsider validation instruments and to focus on criteria such as credibility, authenticity, meaningfulness and transformation. It is important that assessors reflect on all these criteria in order to assure transparency of procedures, impartiality and credibility of a learner's outcomes. Institutions will need to make significant changes if they want to guarantee the right to validation and the social recognition of what an individual has learned.

This brief review demonstrates how different efforts have been made to define and implement models of validation and certification of informal learning. However, the theoretical base seems still weak and repetitive. It is necessary to respond to the requirements of innovative, inclusive and accessible methodologies and approaches. Models and approaches of validation have to be reconsidered at the policy level taking into account the coherence and alignment within a national system. However, it is fundamental to reconsider the role, the functions and the competencies of actors who are responsible for the validation process. Moving from this last consideration the next section reports on how the validation and certification process has been designed and implemented in the Italian higher education system.

University, competencies and informal learning

Assessment of learning in higher education generally aims to

- mark and grade students' learning;
- foster students' learning progression;
- guide students' performance;
- facilitate students' orientation to future professional choices;

- identify learning difficulties and scaffold students to correct errors and misconceptions;
- give feedback to teachers in order to improve their teaching practice;
- respond to accountability requirements.

The Italian higher education system has aligned to the international trend of recognition, validation and certification of informal learning. Following the Bologna Process perspective, these forms of assessment have been perceived as a functional response to lifelong learning and social inclusion requirements and, at the same time, as an effective driver for students' employability. However, as national and international reviews confirm, in Italy the implementation of a formalized, institutionalized, coherent system of recognition, validation and certification of informal learning in higher education still requires considerable effort. While a sufficient level of advancement has been pursued during the last 10 years in the legislative field, a screening of practices of validations (Table 13.2) reveals how these actions are more frequently framed for vocational education and workplace learning rather than for higher education.

Table 13.2 Practices of validation and certification of competencies in Italy

Target	• Unemployed workers or workers who run the risk of becoming unemployed or workers with a professional re-qualification need • Workers with a need of professional certification • Immigrant workers with no formal professional and/or educational certification • Young people with high-stakes qualifications • Volunteers, apprentices
Field of application	• Training paths (since 2008) • Work experience (since 2010) • Apprenticeship (since 2013) • VET (since 2013) • Training Internship (since 2013) • Third sector
Model of reference	• VAE (Validation des acquis de l'expérience)
Instruments	• Declarative methods • Dossier and/or portfolio • Technical interviews • Observation/shadowing • Simulations • Performance assessment • Written test
Subjects responsible for Certification	• Private agencies • Associations • Local authorities • University

Source: ISFOL (2013)

198   *Serafina Pastore*

Three practices have to be considered in this framework:

- *Citizen's booklet:* Following the Law 50/2003 this instrument is finalized to register competencies acquired through education and training paths. Competencies acquired in non-formal paths that are documented and certified can be also registered in this document.
- *Vocational training paths:* Young graduate and postgraduate students, as well as unemployed people and workers, can attend these kind of courses. Validated competencies are reported and communicated in terms of credits.
- *Regional qualification and certification systems:* Some regions in Italy have designed instruments of qualification for the recognition of credits in relation to competencies acquired in formal and informal learning contexts.

All these actions, however, are not systemic.

The Law 92/2012 demonstrated a renewed interest in informal learning, considered for a long time as a neglected kind of learning. In the scenario designed by this new law two challenges emerged for the Italian higher education system:

1 The definition of prerequisites for recognition and validation of competencies in credentialed learning.
2 The alignment of learning outcomes in terms of competencies and professional standards. This implies a more effective dialogue between the university and other stakeholders (including the labour market and government agencies).

The Law 92/2012 addressed the main principles and criteria for the recognition and validation of informal learning:

- Recognition and validation of non-formal and informal learning aim to value the cultural and professional background of individuals and to translate it into credentialed learning (university credits).
- Recognition and validation of informal learning have to be evidence-based practices.
- Work experience is recognized as an essential component of the personal and professional lives of individuals.
- Institutions (education, training, labour market) involved in the recognition and validation processes have to guarantee a common service to individuals.
- Non-formal and informal learning have to be credentialed considering education, training standards as well professional qualifications.
- Recognition and validation have to follow criteria of simplicity, transparency, responsiveness to quality assurance system and valorization of the cultural and professional heritage of individuals.
- Equity has to be assured through national reference frameworks.

Avant-garde assessment 199

In this scenario, the higher education system is called to review its traditional mission introducing in each university a Centre for Lifelong Learning responsible for the following actions:

- Information and orientation of students.
- Definition of admissibility procedures.
- Support in the phase of recognition of competencies (e.g. compiling a portfolio or dossier).
- Assessment and validation of credits.
- Certification of competencies.

The alignment to the European framework is clear; however, despite the legislative design the Italian universities only very slowly moved to the practical plan. While in Europe there are remarkable and consolidated experiences of recognition and validation of informal learning in higher education contexts (e.g. VAE in France, APEL in the UK, APL in Norway), in Italy a cultural gap about lifelong learning and about the power (and the role) of recognition and validation of informal learning still persists. If on the one hand, universities recognize the rationale and the value of lifelong learning, on the other hand, there is a strong resistance to transform into credits informal learning achievements considered as a suspicious learning because they have been gained through experience and not in traditional (formal) ways. As a consequence, validation and certification practices in the Italian higher education system have never been systematically implemented until recently.

Conclusions

The process of recognition, validation and certification of competence represent a key strategy to promote and support lifelong learning, assuring flexibility, transparency, transferability and employability. This value is, without doubt, announced and assured in educational and work policy perspectives. However, despite the growing use of validation and certification in higher education, as well as in work-related contexts, in Italy, the level of implementation is really scant. Also, the traditional resistance to accept a different kind of learning and the lack of attention to validity and accuracy of validation processes still impact on this kind of assessment.

This chapter has reflected on a more systemic and robust way towards the recognition, validation and certification of competencies. Dealing with only legislative aspects, as happened in Italy, demonstrates how hard it is to translate informal learning in traditional education systems like higher education.

Further research is urgently required to gain a broader understanding and a more effective practice of validation and certification of informal learning in higher education. It is necessary to "strengthen the empirical evidence-base with respect to a broad and comprehensive view of validity" (Stenlund, 2010, p. 795) and reinforce connections between empirical research, educational practice and assessment arrangements in the higher education field. This need for new

200 Serafina Pastore

opportunities to integrate educational research into local and/or international research pathways is strictly related to validity. In this perspective, validation and certification practice should overcome the "methodological nationalism" and allow reflection on different elements such as the following:

- What are the most relevant research questions?
- How validation and certification of competencies are studied (e.g. focus on research design and methods and not only on results)?
- How to assure the quality of the assessment practices?
- How do researchers and practitioners think about issues and problems and manage responsive and effective solutions?

Like an avant-garde movement, the recognition, validation and certification processes should be, at the same time, more rigorous (assuring validity, reliability, accuracy) and transgressive highlighting new problems (in terms of methodology) and opening new scenarios for the educational assessment in the higher education field. Only in this way will these processes release the great power that assessment has in terms of change and improvement of the existing practices, models and approaches.

References

Andersson, P., & Guo, S. (2009). Governing through non/recognition: The missing 'R' in the PLAR for immigrant professionals in Canada and Sweden. *International Journal of Lifelong Education, 28*(4), 423–437.

Andersson, P., & Harris J. (Eds.). (2006). *Re-theorising the recognition of prior learning.* Leicester: NIACE.

Andersson, P., Fejes, A., & Sandberg, F. (2013). Introducing research on recognition of prior learning. *International Journal of Lifelong Learning, 32*(4), 405–411.

Bjørnåvold, J. (2000). *Identification, assessment and recognition of non-formal learning in Europe. Making learning visible.* Thessaloniki: CEDEFOP.

Bron, A., & Schemmann, M. (Ed.). (2003). Knowledge society, information society and adult education. *Bochum studies in international adult education* (Vol. IV). Munster: LIT.

Castle, J., & Attwood, G. (2001). Recognition of prior learning (RPL) for access or credit? Problematic issues in a university. *Studies in the education of Adults, 33*(1), 60–72.

CEDEFOP (2000). *Making learning visible: Identification, assessment and recognition of non-formal learning in Europe.* Thessaloniki: CEDEFOP.

CEDEFOP (2014). *Use of validation by enterprise for human resource and career development purposes.* Luxembourg: CEDEFOP.

CEDEFOP, European Commission (2009). *European guidelines for validating non-formal and informal learning,* Luxembourg: Publication Office.

Coffield, F. (2000). *The necessity of informal learning.* Bristol: The Policy Press.

Collardin, D., & Bjørnåvold, J. (2005). *The learning continuity: European inventory on validating non-formal and informal learning.* Luxembourg: Official Publications of the European Commission, CEDEFOP.

Cooper, L., & Harris, J. (2013). Recognition of prior learning: Exploring the 'knowledge question'. *International Journal of Lifelong Education, 32*(4), 447–463.

Avant-garde assessment 201

Council of the European Commission. (2012). Council recommendation of 20 December 2012 on the validation of non-formal and informal learning. *Official Journal of the European Union, C 398*, 22.12.2012.

Cronbach, L. S. (1971). Test validation. In R. L. Thorndike (Ed.), *Educational measurement* (pp. 443–507). Washington, DC: American Council on Education.

Cronbach, L. S., & Meehl, P. E. (1955). Construct validity. *Psychological Bulletin, 52*, 281–302.

DeLuca, C. (2011). Interpretive validity theory: Mapping a methodology for validating educational assessments. *Educational research, 53*(3), 303–320.

Evans, N. (Ed.). (2000). *Experiential learning around the world. Employability and the global economy*. London: Jessica Kingsley.

Fenwick, T., & Parsons, J. (2000). *The art of evaluating adult learners*. Toronto: Thompson Edition.

Feutrie, M. (2008). The recognition of individual experience in a lifelong learning perspective: Validation of non-formal and informal learning in France. *Lifelong learning in Europe, 13*(3), 164–171.

Guilford, J. P. (1946). New standards for test evaluation. *Educational and psychological measurement, 6*(5), 427–439.

Harris, J. (2000). *RPL: Power pedagogy and possibility*. Pretoria: Human Sciences Research Council (HSRC).

ISFOL, (2013). *Validazione delle competenze da esperienza: Approcci e pratiche in Italia e in Europa*. Roma: Pubblicazioni ISFOL.

Jackson, S. (Ed.). (2011). *Innovations in lifelong learning: Critical perspectives on diversity, participation, and vocational learning*. New York, NY: Routledge.

Jarvis, P. (2011). Adult education and the changing international scene: Theoretical perspectives. *PAACE Journal of Lifelong Learning, 20*, 37–50.

Kane, M. T. (2006). Validation. In R. L. Brennan (Ed.)., *Educational measurement* (4th ed., pp. 17–64). Washington, DC: American Council on Education/Praeger.

Kane, M. T. (2016). Explicating validity. *Assessment in education: Principles, policy & practice, 23*(2), 198–211.

McGivney, V. (2006). Informal learning. The challenge for research. In R., Edwards, J., Gallacher, & S., Whittaker (Eds.), *Learning outside the academy* (pp. 11–23). New York, NY: Routledge.

Messick, S. (1989). Validity. In R. L., Linn (Ed.), *Educational measurement* (3rd ed., pp. 13–103). New York, NY: American Council on Education/Macmillan.

Michelson, E. (2006). Beyond Galileo's telescope: Situated knowledge and the recognition of prior learning. In P., Andersson, & J., Harris (Eds.), *Re-theorising the recognition of prior learning* (pp. 141–162). Leicester: NIACE.

Newton, P. E. (2007). Clarifying the purposes of educational assessment. *Assessment in Education, 14*(2), 149–170.

Nyström, P. (2004). Reliability of educational assessments: The case of classification accuracy. *Scandinavian Journal of Educational Research, 48*(4), 427–440.

Pitman, T. (2009). Recognition of prior learning: The accelerated rate of change in Australian universities. *Higher Education Research & Development, 28*(2), 227–240.

Pitman, T., & Vidovich, L. (2013). Converting RPL into academic capital: Lessons from Australian universities. *International Journal of Lifelong Learning, 32*(4), 501–517.

Rogers, A. (2014). *The base of the iceberg: Informal learning and its impact on formal and non-formal learning* (Study guides in adult education). Opladen/Berlin/Toronto: Barbara Budrich Publishers.

202 *Serafina Pastore*

Sandberg, F., & Andersson, P. (2011). RPL for accreditation in higher education: As a process of mutual understanding or merely life world colonisation? *Assessment and Evaluation in Higher Education, 36*(7), 767–780.

Shepard, L. A. (1993). Evaluating test validity. *Review of Research in Education, 19*, 405–450.

Singh, M. (2015). Global perspectives on recognising non-formal and informal learning: Why recognition matters. *Technical and vocational education and training: Issues, concerns and prospects series* (Vol. 21). Hamburg: UNESCO Institute for Lifelong learning/Springer Open.

Slowey, M., & Schuetze, H. G. (Eds.) (2012). *Global perspectives on higher education and lifelong learners*. New York, NY: Routledge.

Stenlund, T. (2013). Agreement in assessment of prior learning related to higher education: An examination of interrater and intrarater reliability. *International Journal of Lifelong Learning, 32*(4), 535–547.

Stenlund, T. (2010). Assessment of prior learning in higher education: A review from a validity perspective. *Assessment & Evaluation in Higher Education, 35*(7), 783–797.

Trowler, P. (1996). Angels in marble?: Accrediting prior experiential learning in higher education. *Studies in Higher Education, 21*(1), 17–30.

Werquin, P. (2010). *Recognizing non-formal and informal learning: Outcomes, policies and practices*. Paris: OECD.

Werquin, P. (2014). RPL, labour markets and national qualifications framework: A policy perspective. In J., Harris, C., Whiak, & J., Van Kleef (Eds.), *Handbook of recognition of prior learning. Research into practice* (pp. 86–111). Leicester, UK: NIACE.

14 Conclusion

Open schools and shared responsibilities: Integrating informal and formal learning in 21st-century schools

Javier Calvo de Mora and Kerry J. Kennedy

There is ample historical research attesting to the traditional bureaucratic structure of schools and schooling (Benson, 1983; Marjoribanks, 1970; Punch, 1972). Under the influence of new institutional theory (March & Olsen, 1984; Meyer & Rowan 1977), however, education systems are now in a position to claim a more open vision for schools. In this context, bureaucratic visions of the school are no longer relevant and informal influences on student learning and students' achievement can be recognized. Informal learning is an important and everyday part of the school environment and its influence on mainstream schooling can no longer go unnoticed (Jeong, Han, Lee, Sunalai, & Yoon, 2018). Informal student learning needs to be seen as an important part of a pragmatic vision of schooling linked to the development of social and the human capital.

From a critical sociology of knowledge perspective, external influences on students' academic success have gained increasing importance (Leung & Ang, 2009; Millman, & McNamara, 2018). One example of these external influences on students' success is Bourdieu's (1967) sociocultural capital theory and the work of Mezirow (1996). They pointed to the importance of student learning outside of their respective schools as a strong influence on academic results: at home, in their cultural environment and as part of their everyday experience. In other words, informal learning can be more influential on attaining school goals than classroom teaching methodologies (Tan, 2017).

Students only spend 20% of their vital time at schools. From the cradle to the final period of the compulsory schooling, most student time is spent out of schools, for example, with family, mass media, computer games, peers, at neighbourhood experiences, and so on. In this context the key issue is a matter of the connections between different learning spaces and learning times. This is not just a local problem. It is a global problem in knowledge societies. Creating holistic spaces for learning becomes a global imperative.

This problem is magnified when there are gaps between different cultures of knowledge and behaviours between school and home. Often this "culture gap" is based on the availability of resources. "Shadow education" is a good example providing out-of-school learning experiences in order to ensure students are successful in examinations (Tsiplakides, 2018). This is a type of informal learning, but it is costly so only parents who can afford to pay are able to provide it.

204 *Javier Calvo de Mora and Kerry J. Kennedy*

The objective is to achieve school goals through informal means, but it is not available to all. Thus informal learning opportunities in this case can increase the divide between rich and poor.

An answer to this problem of inequality in schooling opportunities might be developing connections between informal, non-formal, and formal learning. This would require more proactive approaches to schooling, recognizing that not all students come to school with the same advantages. For example, active learning methodologies can provide more cohesive and integrative learning experiences to students from lower socio-economic backgrounds. Students from all the backgrounds can work together both inside and outside the classroom, learning from each other and leveraging their learning from multiple sources of cultural capital. "Levelling the playing field" in this way is a matter for system and school decision-making to ensure equity and fairness in education provision.

Schools as organizations are social actors with a specific identity easily recognizable around the world. They often represent a range of contradictions and paradoxes due to structures, authority, rules, social control, social relations, incentive structures, and social stratifications. Yet on a global scale, the main objective of schools is social and cognitive learning facilitated by social relations between different school actors and external stakeholders (Roberts, Daly, Held, & Lyle, 2016). In this sense, schools have the capacity to create innovative educational environments. Their organizational strength for innovation (Shin, 2016) is based on selection of external inputs (culture resources, social norms, services, etc.), incorporating them to improve student learning by an institutionalization process called "institutional capital" (Platje, 2008):

> A perfect institutional equilibrium, positively influencing sustainable development, is only achieved when formal and informal institutions stimulate sustainable development, and "institutional governance" is efficient in enforcing the formal rules of the game. Such rules and "institutional governance" stimulate sustainable consumption and production behaviour, and reduce opportunities for opportunistic behaviour and the transaction costs of obtaining information, while informal institutions have as a consequence that people do not show opportunistic behaviour and support the sustainable production and consumption patterns. (p. 148)

Second, the institutional capital of schools varies according to the dictates of local educational policy (Justice 2017; Lerch, Russell, & Ramírez, 2017). An important policy framework for education would include democratic decision-making. Through collective bargaining processes involving all members, democratic decision-making can create new patterns of vision, beliefs, values, and missions of schools. The full inclusion of civil society in the implementation of school policy and school democracy is an example of an open organization. This is the essence of democracy as a social, as well as collective process, building upon a growing practice of direct involvement through deliberation and decision-making process by school members. This policy process (referred to by

Open schools and shared responsibilities 205

the ancient Greeks as *Isonomia, Isegoria, and Isomeria*) refers to the creation of open institutional spaces for learning and sharing practical knowledge where all school members can express their views, values, and attitudes, and work together in a balanced and intertwined process.

Third, recognizing the importance of informal and formal institutions could be a new approach for undertaking school innovation. This is the thesis of Platje (2008) who argued for balancing of the social, political, and civil rights of students and teachers to enable schools, as formal institutions, to be an easily recognizable place and a meaningful symbol aimed at promoting autonomous learning and critical thinking.

Fourth, an underlying key concept to transform school organization beyond its traditional structures is partnership based on shared responsibilities. The partnership concept developed by Henderson (1990) rests on the belief that organizational performance can be significantly improved through joint, mutually dependent action. Unlike more transactional "arm's-length" relationships, partnership style relationships include risk sharing, exchanges without an endpoint, and mechanisms to monitor and execute the partnership.

School Councils provide an example of collaborative school governance with representatives from various stakeholders groups for which Nishimura (2017) says,

> Community participation in school management has great potentials for removing mistrust and distance between people and schools by nurturing transparency of information and a culture of mutual respect and by jointly pursuing improvement of school by sharing vision, process, and results. Individual and organizational behavioural changes are critical to increase the level of participation. In countries where the administrative structures are weak, the bottom-up approach to expanding educational opportunity and quality learning may be the only option. (p. 157)

Finally, a collaborative learning culture is needed. This occurs through the establishment of networks among different and related organizations to provide opportunities for mutual understanding of goals, values, procedures, and learning requirements. This approach shows a cycle involving creation of practical knowledge through synthesizing and reflecting information, hypothesizing some concepts, validating information and knowledge, and debating and theorizing about active experimentation and transformation of reality, these processes result in new feeling attachment to educational experiences. This process of learning permits people to communicate with each other and to establish open dialogue about education needs (Kolb, 2014; Kolb, 2005).

Argyris and Schön (1996) proposed a "double loop" of reflection in which informal learning is transformed into institutional local knowledge for school members. This approach shows that the effect of the deliberative process is the reconsideration of decisions either by the deliberation groups themselves or by critical thinking related to the real world in which people live. In other words, people's understanding is a dialogic creation from the learning experience promoted by formal, non-formal, or informal social actions. In this process of thinking, we find formal curriculum (subjects, teaching methods, testing programmes, students' promotions, etc.), along with non-formal activities as part of the social dimensions of educational institutions. These can include extracurricular activities, tutoring, and other actions that belong to the subjective and emotional realm such as inclusion into pair groups, social exclusion, leadership, and other informal learning (Thompson, Conaway, & Dolan, 2016). This is the complexity of the real world of the schools: Three words—formal, non-formal, and informal—that appear in our daily institutional life.

Everitt (2012) showed how teachers can filter institutional performance norms as they make sense of their professional experience. Similar approaches to cognitive learning highlight the importance of teachers learning through experience (Woulfin, 2016). This cycle of learning adds to the organizational cognition of school members whose effective end is to create their own cognition about schools. That is to say, actions, decisions, evaluations, resource use, participation processes, and so on are creations of the members who use their experiences to promote the collective development of schools open to the world. Yet, there is also the informal organization of schools. Learning about roles, professional hierarchies, learning skills, channels of informal communication, learning by walking around organizational sections, departments, and so on. These informal processes add to teachers' knowledge in the same way as the more formal processes described above.

These five dimensions of educational policy mentioned before (schools as social actors, institutional capital, balance between formal and formal institutions, school, transformation based on sharing responsibilities, and collaborative culture) are simply translations from neo-institutional theory based on the concept of responsibility. That is, schools are visible social realities full of meaning and social relations in which teachers and learners work together in the same place and time. This means, in the words of Hecht (2011), mutual respect and tolerance should be the basis of mainstream schooling. Inspired by this basic assumption based on responsibility, we propose four actions aimed to create new meanings of schooling based on participatory action research (PAR), an open school model, development of citizen culture in the schooling process, and curriculum in the context of information society.

Participatory action research (PAR)

Regarding schools as knowledge laboratories mean transforming the process of teaching and learning into inquiry-oriented action that can overcome the bureaucratic structure of isolated classrooms using direct instruction. Lewin (1946) proposed scientific collaboration between diverse stakeholders actively engaged in a cyclical process of planning, acting, and reflecting as the learning method. It can be utilized by students as well as adults as a way to institutionalize a natural process of critical communication (Rudman et al., 2018). The object of PAR is to promote

Open schools and shared responsibilities 207

a participatory culture involving academic subjects, informal content from the culture, and local contextual knowledge. The effect of PAR is to improve learning through the development of a critical mentality in both students and teachers joined together in peer learning and exchange of information and knowledge.

As part of this metacognitive development, teachers engage in workplace learning through dual action based on reflection and action. They can add professional knowledge whose basic quality is the experience lived during their professional biography. Most teachers participate in virtual environments where they must begin to plan how to design new learning environments that optimize learning and personal development. This process of self-regulated learning helps teachers to collaborate with students and parents and open their consciousness toward a learning focus.

For students, this practical learning has the effect of a major mental change from dependant to autonomous individuals in the context of the 70-20-10 formula for an information society: 70% of informal knowledge, 20% of non-formal knowledge, and 10% of academic/formal knowledge. In other words, this new process of children's socialization in the 21st century does not simply mean adaptation to reality, because this is not a remarkable focus. On the contrary, the new socialization for students means the right to determine their development through meaningful processes of observing, documenting, analyzing, interpreting, as well as other metacognitive learnings. These processes can facilitate the acquisition of lifelong learning focused on personal consciousness and social benefits. The effect of lifelong learning skills is a more critical citizenry: aware of the collective wealth of the culture and the importance of peace, democracy, dialogue, and other social values supporting active civil society (Deveci & Ayish, 2017).

Finally, PAR is an important methodology to facilitate learning for young people who have lost their motivation to be involved in mainstream schooling by (Ozer, Ritterman, & Wannis, 2010)

> including an emphasis on promoting youth's sense of ownership and control over the process, and promoting the social and political engagement of youth and their allies to help address problems identified in the research (p. 157).

In this sense, schools can create spaces for democratic social relations that are anchored to the wider social and cultural environment in which schools are rooted. This collective action takes place at three levels of the decision-making process: Globalization, localization, and individualization, building up new spaces for dialogue and agreement.

Open School Model

A view of schools as open, social, and cultural organization begins with certain parameters. First, the contingent character of its social and cultural identity, that is to say, its *raison d'être*, will be shaped by its large school population. Second, the identity of this organization depends on a range of factors: students' social

208 *Javier Calvo de Mora and Kerry J. Kennedy*

profile, teachers' mentality and beliefs, community involvement, stakeholders' demands, and so on. Third, the open school must adapt to population diversity mainly in aspects such as curriculum delivery, teaching method, and learning approaches since these shape the institutional structures of schools. Finally, as to the dualism and balance between excellence and equity, open schools focus on inclusion, carry out educational projects aimed to motivate its students and teachers to undertake cooperative and collaborative teams works along with other autonomous actions. As mentioned earlier, this approach requires a school model based on shared responsibilities. We call this a holistic model characterized by learning networks based on a political ethos that connects the formal and the informal: Curriculum and pedagogy together with the daily activities of the school. This can create transformative learning.

This social and economic profile of informal learning at school needs new educational institutions based on local and global networks. This involves shared responsibility, teacher workplace learning, PAR, teaching methods, as well as student participation and collaborative processes taking into account school organization as a cultural site. This can develop new educational challenges going beyond academic subjects. This means that in schools there will be different teaching practices depending on students' background and teacher experiences. A community of learners can be created to share experiences and as result to construct a local theory of teaching in a single school site where organizational actors are participants in their cognitive, social, and emotional learning. Besides the institutional visibility of the organizational process, this game of diversity among interested educational actors is conceivable through curriculum, learning, and pedagogical actions, where each individual is involved in the decision-making process connected with mainstream schooling.

This vision of schooling means a cultural change for schools. Culture is the shared beliefs and values of a school, but it is also a social record of individual learning: Lessons about the world and human nature that can guide people in the successful execution of their expectations and provide a meaning to the school work. This cultural process evolves according to natural parameters such as a need to access new educational resources, new social demands, and external demographic changes. Of particular importance is the culture of citizenship in a school as well as the curriculum.

The culture of citizenship in the schooling process

While citizenship can be viewed as a legal status related to membership of a nation state, it can also be viewed as a status within organizations like schools. The argument of this chapter so far has been that schools should be open rather than bureaucratic organizations and they should be characterized by shared responsibilities rather than the concentration of leadership in a few officials. In this context, students will be expected to participate in a school community as co-equals with teachers. Using the language of citizenship, they will have rights and responsibilities within the organization just as teachers do. What

Open schools and shared responsibilities 209

this suggests that schools should be democratic communities where learning is treasured, relationships are nurtured and participation is encouraged. This may sound radical, but it is by no means a new idea.

For John Dewey, America's foremost progressivist education philosopher of the twentieth century, a school was "a democratic community" (Dewey, 1916/1980, p. 92). He argued that "democracy is more than a form of government; it is primarily a mode of associated living, of conjoint communicated experience" (p. 93). This kind of experience, in Dewey's view, should be the basis of interactions within the school.

Schutz (2001) has shown how Dewey actively worked in the Laboratory School at the University of Chicago to put his ideas into action – so he was not just a theorist. In line with his own pragmatic philosophy he used his experience to create theory. He argued that learning should start with the experience of students and as they learn, students should be led to relate their own experience back to the needs and interests of the larger society. Thus Dewey was not an academic rationalist in any sense. He wanted to create experiences in which students could engage, learn and relate to other areas of life and living. He wanted students to solve problems. As Schutz (2001) pointed out:

> Dewey continually emphasized ...that the habits promoted in schools must enhance students ability to respond to the world *the way it is* providing them with increased control over the course of their lives and the power to contribute as effective citizens (p. 269)

In this sense, learning was a social process that did not rely on traditional academic disciplines. Experiments, excursions, the students' own experience, asking questions, interacting with others etc. were sources of learning in Dewey's democratic school environment.

Dewey's vision for schooling remains just that, a vision: something yet to be realised. His progressivism was overtaken by behaviourism, the call for social efficiency and, in recent times, by the linking of schooling to the economic needs of nations. As Merry (2018) has pointed out "the imagined schools that foster civic respect, deliberation and 'shared fate', or that encourage dissent, or that allow for a critique of power structures and modes of governance are quite remote to the experiences of most youth everywhere" (p. 11). In addition, bureaucracy has imposed an organizational structure on schools that is inimical to democracy and the creation of democratic communities: hierarchical leadership, the demands of external testing, the continued emphasis on academic and decontextualized curriculum and the constant need to appease so called 'stakeholders' (politicians, business leaders, community pressure groups) at the expense of students. Schools have become constrained organizations which is not what is needed in these current times

The challenge, then, is how do we regain Dewey's vision of schools as democratic communities? As has been shown throughout this book it is open organizations that are needed in the future. Ideas and knowledge need to be created

210 *Javier Calvo de Mora and Kerry J. Kennedy*

not from the narrow inputs of old, academic knowledge but from the fresh ideas of teachers and young people full of experience and facing a future that is uncertain but demanding. Schwab (2017) has highlighted in the context of what he calls "the fourth industrial revolution" that graduates need to be equipped with dispositions of creativity, problem solving and critical thinking. They need to be thinking individuals whose unique humanity will keep them in front of the increasing use of artificial intelligence, robots and drones. This cannot happen in today's bureaucratized schools.

What then is needed? First, there needs to be a return to Dewey's vision of schools as democratic communities. Yet this call is not new. Writing in the 1970's Kierstead and Baldwin (1976) argued that:

> Education can no longer depend on extrapolation of the future, traditional frames of reference or even predisposed plans of action. In order to solve future problems, education must produce a world of problem-solvers, responsible for their actions, tolerant of criticism, and capable of change. Dewey's "end-in-view" is still a valuable insight into our future plan (pp. 230–231).

They could have been writing about today with a view that is totally consistent with that of Schwab (2017). The consistency of arguments overtime suggests that we should no longer ignore such advice.

Second, democratic schools need to be embedded in democratic societies. The rising tide of authoritarianism in countries such as Poland and Hungry, the United States, Venezuela and Brazil along with established authoritarian countries such as China Vietnam and the Russian Federation means that democracy can no longer be taken for granted. It may be even more difficult to create democratic schools in this new toxic environment but nevertheless, the challenge is there and it is a challenge about the future, not just of school but democracy in general.

Finally, students must learn not just about citizenship but about being citizens. They must be taught the importance of participation and they must experience participation in schools as well as in the community. Being a citizen is not about standing back and watching others "do" citizenship work: being a citizen is about being actively engaged – in school, in the community and in global activities. These challenges can be confronted in democratic schools which then bear much responsibility for the future. They must develop citizens who care, who create, who act, who know, who solve problems and who think deeply about the future. This was very much part of Dewey's vision and it is even more relevant today than it was at the beginning of the twentieth century.

Curriculum in a context of the information society

The school curriculum is often seen as the means by which individuals, schools and society can achieve their objectives. This is what has attracted such keen attention from governments and the community. England has its 'National Curriculum', Australia has called its 'national' curriculum the 'Australian Curriculum' and in countries as diverse as China and the United States 'Curriculum Standards' prescribe the expected outcomes of schooling in different subject areas. This view of the curriculum comes from the original meaning of the Latin term, currēre, meaning to run. In this sense the curriculum can be framed as "the race to be run".

When the school curriculum is tightly prescribed, often by state authorities, when the same outcomes are expected of all students, when testing programmes are used to provide evidence about the attainment of these outcomes and when there is competition based on these outcomes (for example in relation to choosing who gets to go to university), then the school curriculum is indeed the 'race to be won'. At times it seems this view is so dominant that it is difficult to resist. In reality, however, the term is culturally constructed and though it has been heavily borrowed it is not hegemonic and in some spaces is heavily resisted. This resistance is importance in these times when new ways of thinking are needed to confront challenging futures.

Lee and Kennedy (2017) have highlighted the extent to which *'didactic'* traditions in Germany and a number of Nordic countries challenge the curriculum tradition associated particularly with the United States and other countries such as China, Australia and England. Indeed the term 'curriculum' is rarely used in these European contexts referred to above. The term 'didactics' is preferred. It is understood to mean 'teaching and learning' and is applied in classrooms as teachers construct learning contexts to meet the particular needs of students. Such an approach, by definition, rules out standardized curriculum. German scholars have an expression for the meaning behind this *didactic* process – they talk of *'bildung'* meaning (Schneuwly and Vollmer, 2018):

> the comprehensive education of the young ones as persons and citizens in terms of cognitive development, emotional stability, and ethical maturity which allows them to become autonomous and independent in the long run and self-responsible as individuals and social beings (p. 38)

Bildung is the motivating force of education and *didactics* is the process for getting to this end. Developing "autonomous and independent" citizens cannot be achieved with standardized curriculum. Teaching and learning activities must be tailored to the needs of students and schools and thus will vary based on multiple issues including personal, social, cultural, economic and political contexts. As Hopmann (2008, 2013) has pointed out, this is a difficult policy position to advocate in the age of international assessments, school accountability and predominantly instrumental views of schooling. Yet ironically the information society, the knowledge economy and the increasing automation of both simple and complex activities mean that more than ever we need to ensure schools move beyond standardized learning and assessment. Schools need to move towards more inclusive notions of what students should know, value and be able to do and accept that this may differ at different times, for different

212 *Javier Calvo de Mora and Kerry J. Kennedy*

groups and individuals and for different purposes. The curriculum can no longer be a straightjacket, it must become the means by which students are liberated as they move towards autonomy and independence.

A concept that is consistent with this direction towards liberation is 'personalised learning', although Gibson (2017) has shown that for some commentators the concept has its roots in neo-liberal ideology "that treats students and their families as customers that ought to have a say in the product they are consuming" (p. 17). At the same time, however, the idea that learning should start where the student is and proceed to engage her/him in a learning journey that is meaningful and relevant is consistent with the views of many European didacticians, with Dewey's progressivism and with a commitment to engage all students in learning irrespective of race, class, gender, ethnicity or sexuality. Thus personalised learning, with or without technology, may well be the best starting point for changing the culture of standardized learning and the expectation that all students learn at the same pace in the same way and achieve the same outcomes. What is more, personalised learning may take us further than *didactics* in the sense that it is less reliant on specific subject matter than *didactics*. As Meyer, Meyer and Ren (2017) have shown, subject matter experts grapple with specific kinds of subject matter so that the field of "subject matter didactics" (p. 188) can often pull teaching and learning away from student's needs to he needs of the subject matter itself. Personalised learning, on the other hand, can take informal and non-formal learning into account and through the use of social media and mobile learning acknowledge the multiple ways in which today's young people learn.

Finally, moves towards liberating learning should not result in tracking different kinds of students into different forms of learning. This was the problem in the nineteenth century when working class students were set to learnt reading, writing and arithmetic while the wealthy were more likely to sit through lessons in Greek, Latin and History. The curriculum challenge for personalised learning, therefore, is to engage students with knowledge that matters, whether it is formal or informal, and to provide the basis for members of society to see beyond their differences to commonalities and agreements that will bind them together to secure the future their society. Personalised learning will be a process, it will be multifaceted, it will be engaging and it will be relevant. Yet it will not forsake society's 'big picture' and the contributions students as the leaders in the future will make to it. Doing both these things as priorities in the education context may well be the greatest challenge facing educators in the future.

Conclusion

We do not see a 'conclusion' to this book in the traditional sense. Rather, we see the book as a conversation that, while not entirely new, has been newly argued for our globalized times. It is a conversation that needs to be ongoing. Knowledge has always been at the heart of the school curriculum and this knowledge has for the most part been confined to academic subjects. Yet in today's world knowledge can no longer be confined in this way. Students learn from their families, their peers, the media (and increasingly social media). They have access to the Internet where information (if not knowledge) abounds. They learn from all these sources as part of everyday living and these experiences should be integrated into the learning programmes of schools. This has been the argument of this book and it is the conversation that needs to continue. We hope the book has made a contribution to the conversation at an important point in our history. We look forward to the kind of open society and its schools that hopefully will characterise school learning in the future.

References

Argyris, C., & Schön, D. (1996). *Organizational learning II: Theory, method and practice.* Reading, MA: Addison Wesley.

Benson, J. (1983). The bureaucratic nature of schools and teacher job satisfaction. *Journal of Educational Administration, 21*(2), 137–148.

Bourdieu, P. (1967). Systems of education and systems of thought. *International Social Science Journal, 19*(3), 230–338. Retrieved from https://onlinelibrary.willey.com/journal

Deveci, T., & Ayish, N. (2017). Correlation between critical thinking and lifelong learning skills of freshman students. *Bertin University Journal of Faculty of Education, 6*(11), 282–303. doi: 10.14686/buefad.

Dewey, J. (1916/1980). *Democracy and Education,* in J. Boydston (Ed.). *J. Dewey - The Middle Works: 1899-1924,* [Vol. 9,1916], (1- 370). Carbondale: Southern Illinois Press.

Everitt, J. G. (2012). Teachers careers and inhabited institutions: Sense making and arsenal of teaching practice in educational institutions. *Symbolic Interaction, 35*(2), 203–220. doi: 10.1002/SYMB.16.

Gibson, B. (2017). Personalised learning: A powerful idea. *Journal of Initial Teacher Inquiry, 3,* 16-19. Accessed on 26 January 2019 from "https://ir.canterbury.ac.nz/bitstream/handle/10092/14641/Journal%20of%20Initial%20Teacher%20Inquiry_2017_PUBLISHED.pdf?sequence=3"

Hecht, Y. (2011). *Democratic education, a beginning of a story.* Israel: Alternative Education Resource Organization (AERO).

Henderson, J. (1990). Plugging into strategic partnership: The critical is connection. *Sloan Management Review, 31*(3), 391–407.

Hopmann, S. (2008). No child, no school, no state left behind: Schooling in the age of accountability. *Journal of Curriculum Studies, 40*(4), 417–456.

Hopmann, S. (2013). The end of schooling as we know it?. *Journal of Curriculum Studies, 45*(1), 1–3.

Jeong, S., Han, S. J., Lee, J., Sunalai, S., & Yoon, W. (2018). Integrative literature review on informal learning: Antecedents, conceptualizations, and future directions. *Human Resources Development Review, 17*(2), 128–152.

Justice, B. (2017). Curriculum theory and the welfare state. *Espacio, Tiempo y Educación, 4*(2), 19–42. doi: 10.14516/ete.183.

Kierstead, F. & Baldwin. D. (1976). The future of democratic education: Extrapolation or innovation? *Journal of Thought, 11*(3), 226–232.

Kolb, D. A. (2005). *Experiential learning: Experience as the source of learning and development.* Englewood Cliffs, NJ: Prentice-Hall, Inc.

214 *Javier Calvo de Mora and Kerry J. Kennedy*

Kolb, D. A. (2014). *Experiential learning: Experience as the source of learning and development.* Upper Saddle River, NJ: FT press.

Lee, J.C.K. & Kennedy K. (2017). (Eds.) *Theorizing teaching and learning in Asia and Europe – A conversation between Chinese curriculum and European didactics.* New York & London: Routledge.

Lerch, J. C., Russell, S. G., & Ramírez, F. (2017). Wither the nation. Wither the nation state? A comparative analysis of nationalism in textbooks. *Social Forces, 96*(1), 153–180. doi: 10.1093/sf/sox049.

Leung, K., & Ang, S. (2009). Culture, organization, and institution: An integrative review. In R. S. Bhagat & R. M. Steers (Eds.), *Cambridge handbook of culture, organization, and work* (pp. 23–45). Cambridge, UK: Cambridge University Press.

Lewin, K. (1946). "Action research and minority problems." In G. Lewin (Ed.), *Resolving social conflicts: Selected papers on group dynamics* (pp. 201–216). New York: Harper & Row.

March, J. G., & Olsen, J. P. (1984). The new institutionalism: Organizational factors in political life. *American Political Science Review, 78,* 734–749.

Marjoribanks, K. (1970). Bureaucratic structure in schools and its relationship to dogmatic leadership. *The Journal of Educational Research, 63*(8), 355–357.

Merry, M. (2018). Can schools teach citizenship? *Discourse: Studies in the Cultural Politics of Education.* doi: 10.1080/01596306.2018.1488242.

Meyer, M., Meyer, H. and Ren, P. (2017). The German Didactik tradition revisited. In Lee, J.C.K. & Kennedy K. (Eds.) *Theorizing teaching and learning in Asia and Europe – A conversation between Chinese curriculum and European didactics* (179–216). New York & London: Routledge.

Meyer, J. W., & Rowan, B. (1977). Institutionalized organizations: Formal structure as myth and ceremony. *American Journal of Sociology, 83,* 340–363.

Mezirow, J. (1996). Contemporary paradigms of learning. *Adult Education Quarterly, 46*(3), 158–172. doi: 10.1177/074171369604600303.

Millman, T., & McNamara, J. (2018). The long and winding road: Experiences of students entering university through transition programs. *Student Success, 9*(3), 37–49. doi: 10.5204/ssj.v9i3.465.

Nishimura, N. (2017). Community participation in school management in developing countries. *Oxford Research Encyclopedia of Education.* doi: 10.1093/acrefore/9780190264093.013.6.

Ozer, E. L., Ritterman, M. L., & Wannis, M. G. (2010). Participatory action research in middle school: Opportunities, constraints, and key process. *American Journal of Community Psychology, 46*(1–2), 152–166.

Platje, J. (2008). "Institutional capital" as a factor of sustainable development—The importance of an institutional equilibrium. *Technological and Economic Development of Economy, 14*(2), 144–150.

Punch, K. F. (1972). The study of bureaucracy in schools. *Australian Journal of Education, 16*(3), 254–261.

Roberts, C., Daly, M., Held, F., & Lyle, D. (2016). Social learning in a longitudinal clinical placement, *Advances in Health Sciences Education, 22,* 1011–1029.

Rudman, H., Bailey-Ross, C., Kendal, J., Mursic, Z., Lloyd, A., Ross, B., & Kendal, R. L. (2017). Multidisciplinary exhibit design in a science centre: A participatory action research approach. *Educational Action Research, 26*(4), 567–588.

Schneuwly, B. & Vollmer, H. (2017). Bildung and subject didactics: Exploring a classical concept for building new insights. *European Education Research Journal, 17*(1) 37–50.

Open schools and shared responsibilities   215

Schutz, A. (2001). John Dewey's conundrum: Can democratic schools empower. *Teachers College Record, 103*(2), 267–302.

Schwab, K. (2017). *The Fourth Industrial Revolution*. New York: Crown Business.

Shin, C. K. (2016). Neo institutional analysis on response of pilot schools. *Asia Pacific Education Review, 17*, 133–146. doi: 10.1007/s12564-016-9417-x.

Tan, C. Y. (2017). Do parental attitudes toward and expectations for their children's education and future jobs for their children's school achievement? *British Educational Research Journal, 43*(6), 1111–1130.

Thompson, J. J., Conaway, E., & Dolan, E. L. (2016). Undergraduate students' development of social, cultural, and human capital in a networked research experience. *Cultural Studies of Science Education, 11*(4), 959–990.

Tsiplakides, I. (2018). Shadow education and social class inequalities in secondary education in Greece: The case of teaching English as a foreign language. *International Journal of Sociology of Education, 7*(1), 71–93.

Woulfin, S. L. (2016). Duet or duel? A portrait of two logics of reading instruction in an urban school district. *American Journal of Education, 122*(3), 337–365.

Index

Note: Page numbers in **boldface** represent tables and those in *italics* represent figures.

Academic family, 119–20, 125–33
Active learning, 2, 6, 73, 183, 204
Agency, 5, 139–40, 155, 170, 182
American Association of Geographers (AAG), 109
Attitudinal familism, 122

Behavioral familism, 122

Career management skills, 175
Center for Global Geography Education (CGGE), 109–10
Certification of competencies, 189–90, 197, 199
China, 107–15, 183, 210–11
Citizenship, 4, 83–6, 88, 90–3, 155, 182, 189, 208, 210
Civic education, 83–4, 86, 95, 96
Civic learning, 83–7, 90–7
Command-and-control factory models, 52
Community of practice, 100
Computer-based education, 21
Computer-based learning, 21
Constructivist curriculum, 74
Critical thinking, 6, 7, 25, 42, 73–4, 156, 174, 179–80, 182–6, 205, 210
Cultural capital, 6, 119, 124, 203–4
Cultural *patrónes*, 121
Curriculum, 4, 8–9, 16, 23, 25, 27–8, 41–2, 71, 74, 76, 84–5, 93–5, 97, 142, 155, 183, 206, 208–12
Cybernetwork, 99–100, 102, 115

Demographic familism, 122
Digital divide, 101

Educational *compadrazgo* (co-parenting or fictive kinship), 119–20, 125, 130
Elementary school, 67, 76
Entertainment-education (E-E) model, 65
European Renaissance period, 62
Experimental data, 73

Familismo, 122, 124, 130, 132
Formal learning, 3, 7, 15–17, 20, 26, 28–30, 32, 42–3, 62–4, 69, 74, 83–5, 88, 93–6, 106, **110**, 120, 139, 155, 157, 162, 164–6, 168–9, 174–5, 182, 193, 203–4
Formalization of learning, 75
Free-choice learning, 48, 50

Geographic Information System (GIS), 99
Geographic Positioning System (GPS), 99, 115
Geography Education, 99–100, *107*–10, 113–15
Geospatial technologies (GST), 99
Global citizens, 102–4, 113, 115
Globalization, 168, 180, 182, 207
Governance, 9, 155, 158, 190, 204–5, 209

High school, 16, 112, 119, 125–7, 149
Higher Education, 47, 74, 99, 103, 105, 107, 119–22, 124, 126, 129–33, 157–9, 189–93, 195–200
Hybrid education, 64, 74

ICCS 2016, 86, 93
IEA Civic Education Study, 86

Index 217

Industrial Age, 47, 55, 62–3, 65, 74–5
Informal activity, 67, 165
Informal experiential learning, 29, 115
Informal learning, 1–9, 15, 18, 20–1,
    23–6, 28–30, 32–3, 37, 41–3, 62–5,
    67, 69, 74, 75, 76, 81, 83–7, 89–91,
    93–6, 100, **110**, 119, 125, **128–29**,
    130, 132, 136–9, 142, 146, 148,
    155–65, 168–9, 173–6, 179–82,
    184–7, 189–99, 203–6, 208
Informal pedagogy, 136, 139
Information communication technologies
    (ICT), 100
Inhomogeneities, 53
Innovation, 25, 52, 55, 57, 64–5, 75,
    103, 106, 157, 173, 204, 205
Inquiry-based learning (IBL), 108, **110**
Interaction, 2, 8–9, 17, 19, 29, 32, 36, 40,
    50–1, 66, 72, 84, 88, 90–**3**, 95, 100,
    103–5, 107–9, 111–2, 115, 120–2,
    124, 128, **129**, 131–2, 137, 141–3,
    146–7, 149, 157, 164–6, 171, 174, 182,
    186, 209

K-16 Schooling, 46
Keyboard warrior, 86
Knowledge laboratory, 6, 206

Laissez-faire approach, 52
Latinx values, 119, 121, 124, 125, **128**,
    129, 131
Learning experience, 21, 50, 62, 69, 84,
    164, 168, 170, 179, 191, 193, 203,
    204, 206
Learning framework, 5
Learning Management Systems (LMSs),
    109
Liberatory education, 138

Mathematics, 15, 16, 23, 39, 47,
    66–69, 74
Millennial, 168–74, 176
Music, 22, 39, 67–70, 88, 136–43,
    144–49, 164, 186
Music education, 136–40, 142,
    147–49

Neo-institutional perspective, 4
Net society, 101, 102
Nonlinearity, 51, 56–7
Normative familism, 122

Online collaboration, 100, 103, 113

Pedagogical practice, 76
Pedagogy, 65, 69, 70, 75–6, 124, 136–9,
    142, 146, 156, 166, 208
Political socialization, 83
Principles of individuality, 26, 38, 39, 41
Problem-based learning (PBL), 100, **110**
Public education system, 41, 46–52,
    54–60

Real learning, 15, 36
Reflection-in-action, 137, 140, 144
Remote Sensing, 99, 115
Resilient natural systems, 51
Roman model, 16

School environments, 94, 203, 209
School learning, 6, 7, 97, 180, 213
School participation, 87, 90–**1**, **93**–6
Schooling process, 181, 183, 184, 186,
    206, 208
Science, 15, 41, 46, 48, 53, 65, 70–4,
    107, 109, 140, 149
Self-determination theory, 26, 33
Self-directed learning, 55, 71, 85, 169,
    173–4, 176
Self-learning Practices, 101–3
Shanghai, 99, 107, *109*, 110–12, *113*
Social capital, 5, 54, 127, 184
Social connections, 120
Social media, 39, 83, 86, 87, **90**, **91**, 93,
    95, 96, 170, 182, 212, 213
Social networks, 2, 7, 101–3, 127, 174
Social revolution, 168
Special blended learning, 108
Sports, 22, 65, 70, 71, 87
Structural equation modelling, 88, 106
Student, 2–9, 15–23, 27–8, 36, 38–43,
    48, 62–3, 65–76, 83–99, 100–111,
    113, 115, 119–21, 124–5, 127–32,
    137–43, 145, 147–49, 155–66,
    169–73, 175–6, 179–87, 191, 196–9,
    203–12
Sustainable development, 157, 204
Sweden, 136–8, 191

Teacher, 2–9, 15–17, 19–20, 23–4, 29,
    35, 37, 39, 41, 42, 48, 54–6, 59, 63,
    67, 70–4, 83, 88, 93, 104, 106, 108,
    112–14, 136–49, 159–64, 170–6,
    179–80, 182, 184, 197, 205–8, 210
Technology, 3, 7, 22, 54, 69–70, 99, 103,
    105, 107, 114–15, 168–75, 184
The Information Age, 74, 75

218 Index

The Knowledge Age, 27, 52, 57
TRACS-Global Climate Change platform (TRACS-GCC), 111, 112

UNESCO, 156–7, 190
Universities, 16–17, 40, 48, 57, 67, 101–6, 113, 119, 121, 125, 127, **129**, 130, 132, 155, 157, 159–60, 165, 168–9, 173–6, 182, 196–9, 211

Validation, 119, 125–7, **128**, 158, 189–200
Validity, 48, 189, 190, 193–6, 199, 200

Web 2.0, 104, 157, 169

Young adults, 155–6, 159–60, 163–6